The Editors

WILLIAM L. ANDREWS is E. Maynard Adams Professor of English at the University of North Carolina at Chapel Hill. He is the author of *The Literary Career of Charles W. Chesnutt* and *To Tell a Free Story: The First Century of Afro-American Autobiography, 1760–1865.* He is the editor of *Classic Fiction of the Harlem Renaissance* and the Norton Critical Edition of Booker T. Washington's *Up From Slavery,* among others. He is an editor of *The Norton Anthology of African American Literature, The Oxford Companion to African American Literature,* and *Literature of the American South: A Norton Anthology.*

WILLIAM S. MCFEELY is Abraham Baldwin Professor of the Humanities Emeritus at the University of Georgia. He is the author of *Yankee Stepfather: General O. O. Howard and the Freedmen; Grant: A Biography,* for which he was awarded the Pulitzer Prize and the Parkman Prize; *Frederick Douglass; Sapelo's People: A Long Walk into Freedom;* and *Proximity to Death.*

A NORTON CRITICAL EDITION

Frederick Douglass

NARRATIVE OF THE LIFE OF FREDERICK DOUGLASS, AN AMERICAN SLAVE, WRITTEN BY HIMSELF

AUTHORITATIVE TEXT

CONTEXTS

CRITICISM

Edited by

William L. Andrews

UNIVERSITY OF NORTH CAROLINA AT CHAPEL HILL

and

William S. McFeely

UNIVERSITY OF GEORGIA

W • W • Norton & Company • *New York* • *London*

This title is printed on permanent paper containing 30 percent post-consumer
waste recycled fiber.

The text of this book is composed in Electra
with the display set in Bernhard Modern.
Composition and Manufacturing by
The Maple-Vail Book Manufacturing Group.
Book design by Antonina Krass.
Cover illustration: Frederick Douglass in a ca. 1850 daguerreotype, unknown
photographer. Reproduced by permission of the National Portrait Gallery,
Smithsonian Institution.

Library of Congress Cataloging-in-Publication Data
Douglass, Frederick, 1817?–1895.
Narrative of the life of Frederick Douglass : authoritative text,
contexts, criticism / edited by William L. Andrews and William S.
McFeely.
        p.   cm. — (A Norton critical edition)
Includes bibliographical references.
    1. Douglass, Frederick, 1817?–1895.   2. Afro-American
abolitionists—Biography.   3. Abolitionists—United States—
Biography.   I. Andrews, William L., 1946–
        II. McFeely,
William S.   III. Title.
E449.D75D68   1996
973.8'092   dc20 95-47594

ISBN 0-393-96966-5 (pbk.)

W. W. Norton & Company, Inc., 500 Fifth Avenue, New York, N.Y. 10110
www.wwnorton.com
W. W. Norton and Company Ltd., Castle House, 75/76 Wells Street,
London W1T 3QT

7 8 9 0

Contents

Criticism

Preface

Narrative of the Life of Frederick Douglass was published as an anti-slavery tract. It was written as a testament by a slave.

On both scores, the book was a great success. The Boston Anti-Slavery Society published the book itself from its Boston office in the spring of 1845, and it proved to be one of the most persuasive of the many publications offered in an effort to win public support for the abolition of slavery. Douglass understood that this was why the book was published and was proud that it was to be so used.

Slavery had existed around the world almost as long as there is record of human activity. It had come into particularly virulent use in the sixteenth and seventeenth centuries with the exploitation of the rich resources in the Caribbean and North and South America, where African slaves were transported to perform the labor. In the eighteenth century, challenges to slavery, particularly by Quakers, began to be heard with some force in Great Britain and the United States.

Great Britain ended slavery in its Caribbean colonies in 1833, and Emancipation Day, the first of August, was celebrated annually by American abolitionists. This small band of determined reformers had been galvanized into action by William Lloyd Garrison, who in 1831 in the first edition of his Boston antislavery newspaper, the *Liberator*, declared, "I will be heard." He called for the immediate and unconditional ending of slavery.

It was Garrison, giving a fiery abolitionist speech in New Bedford, where Douglass was living, who gave the runaway slave his great calling. As he tells in the *Narrative*, Douglass was inspired to speak out as one who had known, firsthand, what it was to be a slave. His story was a powerfully persuasive argument that slavery must end.

He had told his story from lecterns across the North for four years when he put it in print with the *Narrative*. He wanted to get his public message across, but for Douglass the book had a private importance beyond its public usage. It declared him, in print, to be a man of intellect. The book existed to rebuff the idea that an African slave was a brute without the capacity to write eloquently. The title page read *Narrative of the Life of Frederick Douglass, An American Slave, Written by Himself;* that, in the nineteenth century, was the standard device for saying my book is mine and not as-told-to or ghost written.

There was far more than such defensiveness, however, in Douglass's having written his book. It was a permanent emblem of his selfhood: its first private words, "I was born . . ."; his declaration of being; the closing sentence of his first great public act—his 1841 speech before an antislavery audience on Nantucket Island—where he wrote, "From that time until now, I have been engaged in pleading the cause of my brethren. . . ."

Along the way, the story is his, from his infancy, through his childhood and his teenage years, to, finally, his manhood—and his break for freedom. It is the tale of a young slave's life. As we, the book's readers, have made the book ours, we have learned a great deal about slavery. Indeed, with the possible exception of Harriet Beecher Stowe's *Uncle Tom's Cabin*, published in 1852, our picture of slavery has been formed more by Douglass's book than by any other source.

There are ironies in this. For example, the textbooks correctly equate slavery with the raising of the great cash crop, cotton. But there was no cotton in Douglass's Maryland. And, though Douglass was whipped on a farm, beaten in a boatyard, and humiliated along the way, he was lucky when compared with other slaves. He did, after all, escape. His story has a happy ending. He was one of a brave but small band able to get free of slavery; millions of his fellows were in places and conditions from which they could not move, but from which, involuntarily, they could be moved. They and their children after them were slaves in perpetuity. Theirs was not a happy ending.

This, Douglass knew, and so did his readers. With the *Narrative*, he implanted in our memories just how inhumane slavery was. Douglass tells of some of his experiences as a slave in his speeches as well as in his accounts of his parents and of his attempt at escape.

Although the *Narrative of the Life of Frederick Douglass* is now considered a classic American autobiography, recognition of the book as a literary monument, not just a historical document, has taken more than a century since the *Narrative*'s heyday in the late 1840s and 1850s. Widely celebrated during the antislavery movement, the *Narrative* went into eclipse later in the nineteenth century as Douglass published additional autobiographies—*My Bondage and My Freedom* (1855) and *Life and Times of Frederick Douglass* (1881, 1892)—designed to update his steadily evolving public image from that of fugitive slave to man of letters, social commentator, and race leader. The later autobiographies never sold as well or made the impact of the *Narrative*, but for at least fifty years after Douglass's death in 1895, it was the *Life and Times*, not the *Narrative*, that literary and cultural historians most often cited when referring to Douglass's signal achievement as a writer.

The heightened civil rights militancy of the 1960s, along with the rise of Black Studies in the academy, helped resurrect the *Narrative* and elevate Douglass to prominence as the key figure in the evolution of African American prose in the antebellum period. Literary historians and critics were ready to pay serious attention to Douglass as a rhetorician, a satirist, a social analyst, and a chronicler and creator of self worthy of comparison to major American writers such as Benjamin Franklin and Henry David Thoreau. In the 1970s a wealth of useful studies of the *Narrative*'s artistry helped Douglass take his place as a central figure not only in early African American literature but in the mid-nineteenth-century American literary renaissance.

In the 1980s and early 1990s, discussion of the *Narrative* has evolved from a predominately formalistic appreciation of Douglass's rhetorical art to increasingly widely ranging assessments of the relationship of the *Narrative* to historical trends and sociocultural norms and expressive traditions in the middle of the nineteenth century. In this Norton Critical Edition, four literary and cultural analyses of the *Narrative* published since 1979 have been selected to indicate some of the areas of investigation and evaluation that have engaged Douglass scholars recently. Robert B. Stepto's "Narration, Authentication, and Authorial Control in Frederick Douglass' *Narrative* of 1845" highlights some of the best work that has been done on the formal dynamics of the *Narrative* in light of what is known about the development of the slave narrative as a literary genre. The selection from William L. Andrews's *To Tell a Free Story* calls attention to the problematic relationship of the *Narrative* to the American jeremiad, a popular literary and oratorical tradition that Douglass tried to adapt in order to appeal to his middle-class northern audience. Houston A. Baker's economic reading of the *Narrative* in *Blues, Ideology, and Afro-American Literature* yields significant insights into Douglass's development from slave to freeman to abolitionist lecturer. Surveying Douglass criticism since the 1960s, Deborah E. McDowell reads the *Narrative* through a feminist lens in "In the First Place: Making Frederick Douglass and the Afro-American Narrative Tradition." The result is not only a productive dialogue with Stepto, Andrews, and Baker but also an instructive suggestion about how gender might be more thoroughly considered in interpreting the import of the *Narrative* in its own time and in ours.

The Text of
NARRATIVE OF THE LIFE OF
FREDERICK DOUGLASS,
AN AMERICAN SLAVE,
WRITTEN BY HIMSELF

Narrative of the Life of Frederick Douglass, an American Slave, Written by Himself[1]

Preface

In the month of August, 1841, I attended an anti-slavery convention in Nantucket, at which it was my happiness to become acquainted with FREDERICK DOUGLASS, the writer of the following Narrative. He was a stranger to nearly every member of that body; but, having recently made his escape from the southern prison-house of bondage, and feeling his curiosity excited to ascertain the principles and measures of the abolitionists,—of whom he had heard a somewhat vague description while he was a slave,—he was induced to give his attendance, on the occasion alluded to, though at that time a resident in New Bedford.[2]

Fortunate, most fortunate occurrence!—fortunate for the millions of his manacled brethren, yet panting for deliverance from their awful thraldom!—fortunate for the cause of negro emancipation, and of universal liberty!—fortunate for the land of his birth, which he has already done so much to save and bless!—fortunate for a large circle of friends and acquaintances, whose sympathy and affection he has strongly secured by the many sufferings he has endured, by his virtuous traits of character, by his ever-abiding remembrance of those who are in bonds, as being bound with them!—fortunate for the multitudes, in various parts of our republic, whose minds he has enlightened on the subject of slavery, and who have been melted to tears by his pathos, or roused to virtuous indignation by his stirring eloquence against the enslavers of

1. First printed in May 1845 by the Anti-Slavery Office in Boston, the source of the present text. Punctuation and hyphenation have been slightly regularized and a few typographical emendations have also been made. The spelling of names has not been altered.

When the *Narrative* was first published, the opening pages of the book were a "Preface" by William Lloyd Garrison and a "Letter from Wendell Phillips, Esq.," followed by Douglass's text as it appears in this volume.

William Lloyd Garrison (1805–1879) was the leading abolitionist at the time the *Narrative* was written. He was head of the New England Anti-Slavery Society and had founded the American Anti-Slavery Society, and he was the editor of the *Liberator*. He demanded "immediate and complete emancipation." Wendell Phillips (1811–1884), a lawyer, was scarcely less well known than Garrison as an antislavery advocate. Both were brilliant speakers who spoke often on behalf of the cause.

Garrison and Phillips were the most distinguished of the many important antislavery leaders who were present at the August 1841 antislavery meeting on Nantucket Island where Douglass gave his first great public antislavery speech. When Douglass had finished, Garrison rose to praise him warmly; immediately after the meeting, Douglass was hired as an agent of the New England Anti-Slavery Society and began his career as an orator, speaking across the North and in Great Britain in opposition to slavery.

The endorsements of Garrison and Phillips, published in the *Narrative*, served to assure white antislavery readers that the former slave's writing was to be trusted and to allay their own worries that Douglass, still technically a slave whom his master could attempt to recapture, was risking more than he should by publishing the book. Garrison and Phillips, like Douglass, were saying that having his story in print was too valuable to the cause not to have it published.

2. Douglass escaped from Hugh Auld's home in Maryland in September 1838 and settled in New Bedford, Massachusetts, where he became active among the New Bedford abolitionists.

3

men!—fortunate for himself, as it at once brought him into the field of public usefulness, "gave the world assurance of a MAN,"[3] quickened the slumbering energies of his soul, and consecrated him to the great work of breaking the rod of the oppressor, and letting the oppressed go free!

I shall never forget his first speech at the convention—the extraordinary emotion it excited in my own mind—the powerful impression it created upon a crowded auditory, completely taken by surprise—the applause which followed from the beginning to the end of his felicitous remarks. I think I never hated slavery so intensely as at that moment; certainly, my perception of the enormous outrage which is inflicted by it, on the godlike nature of its victims, was rendered far more clear than ever. There stood one, in physical proportion and stature commanding and exact—in intellect richly endowed—in natural eloquence a prodigy—in soul manifestly "created but a little lower than the angels"[4]—yet a slave, ay, a fugitive slave,—trembling for his safety, hardly daring to believe that on the American soil, a single white person could be found who would befriend him at all hazards, for the love of God and humanity! Capable of high attainments as an intellectual and moral being—needing nothing but a comparatively small amount of cultivation to make him an ornament to society and a blessing to his race—by the law of the land, by the voice of the people, by the terms of the slave code, he was only a piece of property, a beast of burden, a chattel personal, nevertheless!

A beloved friend[5] from New Bedford prevailed on Mr. DOUGLASS to address the convention. He came forward to the platform with a hesitancy and embarrassment, necessarily the attendants of a sensitive mind in such a novel position. After apologizing for his ignorance, and reminding the audience that slavery was a poor school for the human intellect and heart, he proceeded to narrate some of the facts in his own history as a slave, and in the course of his speech gave utterance to many noble thoughts and thrilling reflections. As soon as he had taken his seat, filled with hope and admiration, I rose, and declared that PATRICK HENRY,[6] of revolutionary fame, never made a speech more eloquent in the cause of liberty, than the one we had just listened to from the lips of that hunted fugitive. So I believed at that time—such is my belief now. I reminded the audience of the peril which surrounded this self-emancipated young man at the North,—even in Massachusetts, on the soil of the Pilgrim Fathers, among the descendants of revolutionary sires; and I appealed to them, whether they would ever allow him to be car-

---

3. Shakespeare, *Hamlet* 3.4.62.
4. God created people "a little lower than the angels" (Psalms 8.5) to have authority over all other living creatures. Paul calls the Hebrews to look at Christ, who was made "a little lower than the angels" (Hebrews 2.7.9).
5. William C. Coffin, New Bedford's leading abolitionist at the time.
6. U.S. patriot (1736–1799), famous for the words "I know not what course others may take, but as for me, give me liberty or give me death."

ried back into slavery,—law or no law, constitution or no constitution. The response was unanimous and in thunder-tones—"NO!" "Will you succor and protect him as a brother-man—a resident of the old Bay State."[7] "YES!" shouted the whole mass, with an energy so startling, that the ruthless tyrants south of Mason and Dixon's line[8] might almost have heard the mighty burst of feeling, and recognized it as the pledge of an invincible determination, on the part of those who gave it, never to betray him that wanders, but to hide the outcast, and firmly to abide the consequences.

It was at once deeply impressed upon my mind, that, if Mr. DOUG-LASS could be persuaded to consecrate his time and talents to the promotion of the anti-slavery enterprise, a powerful impetus would be given to it, and a stunning blow at the same time inflicted on northern prejudice against a colored complexion. I therefore endeavored to instil hope and courage into his mind, in order that he might dare to engage in a vocation so anomalous and responsible for a person in his situation; and I was seconded in this effort by warm-hearted friends, especially by the late General Agent of the Massachusetts Anti-Slavery Society, Mr. JOHN A. COLLINS, whose judgment in this instance entirely coincided with my own. At first, he could give no encouragement; with unfeigned diffidence, he expressed his conviction that he was not adequate to the performance of so great a task; the path marked out was wholly an untrodden one; he was sincerely apprehensive that he should do more harm than good. After much deliberation, however, he consented to make a trial; and ever since that period, he has acted as a lecturing agent, under the auspices either of the American or the Massachusetts Anti-Slavery Society. In labors he has been most abundant; and his success in combating prejudice, in gaining proselytes, in agitating the public mind, has far surpassed the most sanguine expectations that were raised at the commencement of his brilliant career. He has borne himself with gentleness and meekness, yet with true manliness of character. As a public speaker, he excels in pathos, wit, comparison, imitation, strength of reasoning, and fluency of language. There is in him that union of head and heart, which is indispensable to an enlightenment of the heads and a winning of the hearts of others. May his strength continue to be equal to his day! May he continue to "grow in grace, and in the knowledge of God,"[9] that he may be increasingly serviceable in the cause of bleeding humanity, whether at home or abroad!

It is certainly a very remarkable fact, that one of the most efficient advocates of the slave population, now before the public, is a fugitive slave, in the person of FREDERICK DOUGLASS; and that the free colored

7. I.e., Massachusetts.
8. The boundary between Maryland and Pennsylvania, surveyed by Charles Mason and Jeremiah Dixon between 1763 and 1767.
9. 2 Peter 3.18.

population of the United States are as ably represented by one of their own number, in the person of CHARLES LENOX REMOND,[1] whose eloquent appeals have extorted the highest applause of multitudes on both sides of the Atlantic. Let the calumniators of the colored race despise themselves for their baseness and illiberality of spirit, and henceforth cease to talk of the natural inferiority of those who require nothing but time and opportunity to attain to the highest point of human excellence.

It may, perhaps, be fairly questioned, whether any other portion of the population of the earth could have endured the privations, sufferings and horrors of slavery, without having become more degraded in the scale of humanity than the slaves of African descent. Nothing has been left undone to cripple their intellects, darken their minds, debase their moral nature, obliterate all traces of their relationship to mankind; and yet how wonderfully they have sustained the mighty load of a most frightful bondage, under which they have been groaning for centuries! To illustrate the effect of slavery on the white man,—to show that he has no powers of endurance, in such a condition, superior to those of his black brother,—DANIEL O'CONNELL,[2] the distinguished advocate of universal emancipation, and the mightiest champion of prostrate but not conquered Ireland, relates the following anecdote in a speech delivered by him in the Conciliation Hall, Dublin, before the Loyal National Repeal Association, March 31, 1845. "No matter," said Mr. O'CONNELL, "under what specious term it may disguise itself, slavery is still hideous. *It has a natural, an inevitable tendency to brutalize every noble faculty of man.* An American sailor, who was cast away on the shore of Africa, where he was kept in slavery for three years, was, at the expiration of that period, found to be imbruted and stultified—he had lost all reasoning power; and having forgotten his native language, could only utter some savage gibberish between Arabic and English, which nobody could understand, and which even he himself found difficulty in pronouncing. So much for the humanizing influence of THE DOMESTIC INSTITUTION!" Admitting this to have been an extraordinary case of mental deterioration, it proves at least that the white slave can sink as low in the scale of humanity as the black one.

Mr. DOUGLASS has very properly chosen to write his own Narrative, in his own style, and according to the best of his ability, rather than to employ some one else. It is, therefore, entirely his own production; and, considering how long and dark was the career he had to run as a slave,— how few have been his opportunities to improve his mind since he broke his iron fetters,—it is, in my judgment, highly creditable to his head

1. Black leader of the antislavery movement (1810–1873), born free in Salem, Massachusetts; he traveled widely, often with Douglass, speaking for the abolitionist cause.
2. Irish statesman (1775–1847), fighter for Catholic emancipation and Irish independence, called the "Liberator."

and heart. He who can peruse it without a tearful eye, a heaving breast, an afflicted spirit,—without being filled with an unutterable abhorrence of slavery and all its abettors, and animated with a determination to seek the immediate overthrow of that execrable system,—without trembling for the fate of this country in the hands of a righteous God, who is ever on the side of the oppressed, and whose arm is not shortened that it cannot save,—must have a flinty heart, and be qualified to act the part of a trafficker "in slaves and the souls of men."[3] I am confident that it is essentially true in all its statements; that nothing has been set down in malice, nothing exaggerated, nothing drawn from the imagination; that it comes short of the reality, rather than overstates a single fact in regard to SLAVERY AS IT IS. The experience of FREDERICK DOUGLASS, as a slave, was not a peculiar one; his lot was not especially a hard one; his case may be regarded as a very fair specimen of the treatment of slaves in Maryland, in which State it is conceded that they are better fed and less cruelly treated than in Georgia, Alabama, or Louisiana. Many have suffered incomparably more, while very few on the plantations have suffered less, than himself. Yet how deplorable was his situation! what terrible chastisements were inflicted upon his person! what still more shocking outrages were perpetrated upon his mind! with all his noble powers and sublime aspirations, how like a brute was he treated, even by those professing to have the same mind in them that was in Christ Jesus! to what dreadful liabilities was he continually subjected! how destitute of friendly counsel and aid, even in his greatest extremities! how heavy was the midnight of woe which shrouded in blackness the last ray of hope, and filled the future with terror and gloom! what longings after freedom took possession of his breast, and how his misery augmented, in proportion as he grew reflective and intelligent,—thus demonstrating that a happy slave is an extinct man! how he thought, reasoned, felt, under the lash of the driver, with the chains upon his limbs! what perils he encountered in his endeavors to escape from his horrible doom! and how signal have been his deliverance and preservation in the midst of a nation of pitiless enemies!

This Narrative contains many affecting incidents, many passages of great eloquence and power; but I think the most thrilling one of them all is the description DOUGLASS gives of his feelings, as he stood soliloquizing respecting his fate, and the chances of his one day being a freeman, on the banks of the Chesapeake Bay—viewing the receding vessels as they flew with their white wings before the breeze, and apostrophizing them as animated by the living spirit of freedom. Who can read that passage, and be insensible to its pathos and sublimity? Compressed into it is a whole Alexandrian library[4] of thought, feeling, and sentiment—

3. Revelations 18.13.
4. Alexandria, in Egypt, housed the great library center of the Greco-Roman world.

all that can, all that need be urged, in the form of expostulation, entreaty, rebuke, against that crime of crimes,—making man the property of his fellow-man! O, how accursed is that system, which entombs the godlike mind of man, defaces the divine image, reduces those who by creation were crowned with glory and honor to a level with four-footed beasts, and exalts the dealer in human flesh above all that is called God! Why should its existence be prolonged one hour? Is it not evil, only evil, and that continually? What does its presence imply but the absence of all fear of God, all regard for man, on the part of the people of the United States? Heaven speed its eternal overthrow!

So profoundly ignorant of the nature of slavery are many persons, that they are stubbornly incredulous whenever they read or listen to any recital of the cruelties which are daily inflicted on its victims. They do not deny that the slaves are held as property; but that terrible fact seems to convey to their minds no idea of injustice, exposure to outrage, or savage barbarity. Tell them of cruel scourgings, of mutilations and brandings, of scenes of pollution and blood, of the banishment of all light and knowledge, and they affect to be greatly indignant at such enormous exaggerations, such wholesale misstatements, such abominable libels on the character of the southern planters! As if all these direful outrages were not the natural results of slavery! As if it were less cruel to reduce a human being to the condition of a thing, than to give him a severe flagellation, or to deprive him of necessary food and clothing! As if whips, chains, thumb-screws, paddles, bloodhounds, overseers, drivers, patrols, were not all indispensable to keep the slaves down, and to give protection to their ruthless oppressors! As if, when the marriage institution is abolished, concubinage, adultery, and incest, must not necessarily abound; when all the rights of humanity are annihilated, any barrier remains to protect the victim from the fury of the spoiler; when absolute power is assumed over life and liberty, it will not be wielded with destructive sway! Skeptics of this character abound in society. In some few instances, their incredulity arises from a want of reflection; but, generally, it indicates a hatred of the light, a desire to shield slavery from the assaults of its foes, a contempt of the colored race, whether bond or free. Such will try to discredit the shocking tales of slaveholding cruelty which are recorded in this truthful Narrative; but they will labor in vain. Mr. DOUGLASS has frankly disclosed the place of his birth, the names of those who claimed ownership in his body and soul, and the names also of those who committed the crimes which he has alleged against them. His statements, therefore, may easily be disproved, if they are untrue.

In the course of his Narrative, he relates two instances of murderous cruelty,—in one of which a planter deliberately shot a slave belonging to a neighboring plantation, who had unintentionally gotten within his lordly domain in quest of fish; and in the other, an overseer blew out the brains of a slave who had fled to a stream of water to escape a bloody scourging. Mr. DOUGLASS states that in neither of these instances was any thing done by way of legal arrest or judicial investigation. The Baltimore American, of March 17, 1845, relates a similar case of atrocity, perpetrated with similar impunity—as follows:—"*Shooting a Slave.*— We learn, upon the authority of a letter from Charles county, Maryland, received by a gentleman of this city, that a young man, named Matthews, a nephew of General Matthews, and whose father, it is believed, holds an office at Washington, killed one of the slaves upon his father's farm by shooting him. The letter states that young Matthews had been left in charge of the farm; that he gave an order to the servant, which was disobeyed, when he proceeded to the house, *obtained a gun, and, returning, shot the servant.* He immediately, the letter continues, fled to his father's residence, where he still remains unmolested."—Let it never be forgotten, that no slaveholder or overseer can be convicted of any outrage perpetrated on the person of a slave, however diabolical it may be, on the testimony of colored witnesses, whether bond or free. By the slave code, they are adjudged to be as incompetent to testify against a white man, as though they were indeed a part of the brute creation. Hence, there is no legal protection in fact, whatever there may be in form, for the slave population; and any amount of cruelty may be inflicted on them with impunity. Is it possible for the human mind to conceive of a more horrible state of society?

The effect of a religious profession on the conduct of southern masters is vividly described in the following Narrative, and shown to be any thing but salutary. In the nature of the case, it must be in the highest degree pernicious. The testimony of Mr. DOUGLASS, on this point, is sustained by a cloud of witnesses, whose veracity is unimpeachable. "A slaveholder's profession of Christianity is a palpable imposture. He is a felon of the highest grade. He is a man-stealer. It is of no importance what you put in the other scale."

Reader! are you with the man-stealers in sympathy and purpose, or on the side of their down-trodden victims? If with the former, then are you the foe of God and man. If with the latter, what are you prepared to do and dare in their behalf? Be faithful, be vigilant, be untiring in your efforts to break every yoke, and let the oppressed go free. Come what may—cost what it may—inscribe on the banner which you unfurl to the breeze, as your religious and political motto—"NO COMPROMISE WITH SLAVERY! NO UNION WITH SLAVEHOLDERS!"

WM. LLOYD GARRISON.

BOSTON, *May* 1, 1845.

Letter from Wendell Phillips, Esq.

BOSTON, *April* 22, 1845.

My Dear Friend:

You remember the old fable of "The Man and the Lion," where the lion complained that he should not be so misrepresented "when the lions wrote history."

I am glad the time has come when the "lions write history." We have been left long enough to gather the character of slavery from the involuntary evidence of the masters. One might, indeed, rest sufficiently satisfied with what, it is evident, must be, in general, the results of such a relation, without seeking farther to find whether they have followed in every instance. Indeed, those who stare at the half-peck of corn a week, and love to count the lashes on the slave's back, are seldom the "stuff" out of which reformers and abolitionists are to be made. I remember that, in 1838, many were waiting for the results of the West India experiment,[5] before they could come into our ranks. Those "results" have come long ago; but, alas! few of that number have come with them, as converts. A man must be disposed to judge of emancipation by other tests than whether it has increased the produce of sugar,—and to hate slavery for other reasons than because it starves men and whips women,—before he is ready to lay the first stone of his anti-slavery life.

I was glad to learn, in your story, how early the most neglected of God's children waken to a sense of their rights, and of the injustice done them. Experience is a keen teacher; and long before you had mastered your A B C, or knew where the "white sails" of the Chesapeake were bound, you began, I see, to gauge the wretchedness of the slave, not by his hunger and want, not by his lashes and toil, but by the cruel and blighting death which gathers over his soul.

In connection with this, there is one circumstance which makes your recollections peculiarly valuable, and renders your early insight the more remarkable. You come from that part of the country where we are told slavery appears with its fairest features. Let us hear, then, what it is at its best estate—gaze on its bright side, if it has one; and then imagination may task her powers to add dark lines to the picture, as she travels southward to that (for the colored man) Valley of the Shadow of Death,[6] where the Mississippi sweeps along.

Again, we have known you long, and can put the most entire confi-

---

5. The British Parliament abolished slavery throughout the empire in 1833, and so in the late 1830s Britain's West Indian sugar islands were undergoing a major transition from slavery to freedom. White planters were allotted a total of twenty million pounds in compensation for their loss of "property," and a brief apprenticeship period was designed to prevent an immediate withdrawal of labor. However, many blacks left the plantations, established free villages, and became small landholders themselves. The consequent labor shortage caused bankruptcies and financial loss for many white planters in the 1840s as both sugar production and sugar prices fell, leading many white people to believe that the "experiment" had been a failure.
6. Psalms 23.4, commonly recognized by nineteenth-century readers.

dence in your truth, candor, and sincerity. Every one who has heard you speak has felt, and, I am confident, every one who reads your book will feel, persuaded that you give them a fair specimen of the whole truth. No one-sided portrait,—no wholesale complaints,—but strict justice done, whenever individual kindliness has neutralized, for a moment, the deadly system with which it was strangely allied. You have been with us, too, some years, and can fairly compare the twilight of rights, which your race enjoy at the North, with that "noon of night"[7] under which they labor south of Mason and Dixon's line. Tell us whether, after all, the half-free colored man of Massachusetts is worse off than the pampered slave of the rice swamps!

In reading your life, no one can say that we have unfairly picked out some rare specimens of cruelty. We know that the bitter drops, which even you have drained from the cup, are no incidental aggravations, no individual ills, but such as must mingle always and necessarily in the lot of every slave. They are the essential ingredients, not the occasional results, of the system.

After all, I shall read your book with trembling for you. Some years ago, when you were beginning to tell me your real name and birthplace, you may remember I stopped you, and preferred to remain ignorant of all. With the exception of a vague description, so I continued, till the other day, when you read me your memoirs. I hardly knew, at the time, whether to thank you or not for the sight of them, when I reflected that it was still dangerous, in Massachusetts, for honest men to tell their names! They say the fathers, in 1776, signed the Declaration of Independence with the halter about their necks. You, too, publish your declaration of freedom with danger compassing you around. In all the broad lands which the Constitution of the United States overshadows, there is no single spot,—however narrow or desolate,—where a fugitive slave can plant himself and say, "I am safe." The whole armory of Northern Law has no shield for you. I am free to say that, in your place, I should throw the MS. into the fire.

You, perhaps, may tell your story in safety, endeared as you are to so many warm hearts by rare gifts, and a still rarer devotion of them to the service of others. But it will be owing only to your labors, and the fearless efforts of those who, trampling the laws and Constitution of the country under their feet, are determined that they will "hide the outcast," and that their hearths shall be, spite of the law, an asylum for the oppressed, if, some time or other, the humblest may stand in our streets, and bear witness in safety against the cruelties of which he has been the victim.

Yet is is sad to think, that these very throbbing hearts which welcome

---

7. Typical abolitionist rhetoric, meaning that even the noonday sun was darkened by the moral blight of slavery.

your story, and form your best safeguard in telling it, are all beating contrary to the "statute in such case made and provided." Go on, my dear friend, till you, and those who, like you, have been saved, so as by fire, from the dark prison-house, shall stereotype these free, illegal pulses into statutes; and New England, cutting loose from a blood-stained Union, shall glory in being the house of refuge for the oppressed;—till we no longer merely "*hide* the outcast," or make a merit of standing idly by while he is hunted in our midst; but, consecrating anew the soil of the Pilgrims as an asylum for the oppressed, proclaim our *welcome* to the slave so loudly, that the tones shall reach every hut in the Carolinas, and make the broken-hearted bondman leap up at the thought of old Massachusetts.

God speed the day!

Till then, and ever,

Yours truly,

WENDELL PHILLIPS.

FREDERICK DOUGLASS.

Chapter I

I was born in Tuckahoe, near Hillsborough, and about twelve miles from Easton, in Talbot county, Maryland. I have no accurate knowledge of my age, never having seen any authentic record containing it. By far the larger part of the slaves know as little of their ages as horses know of theirs, and it is the wish of most masters within my knowledge to keep their slaves thus ignorant. I do not remember to have ever met a slave who could tell of his birthday. They seldom come nearer to it than planting-time, harvest-time, cherry-time, spring-time, or fall-time. A want of information concerning my own was a source of unhappiness to me even during childhood. The white children could tell their ages. I could not tell why I ought to be deprived of the same privilege. I was not allowed to make any inquiries of my master concerning it. He deemed all such inquiries on the part of a slave improper and imperti-nent, and evidence of a restless spirit. The nearest estimate I can give makes me now between twenty-seven and twenty-eight years of age. I come to this, from hearing my master say, some time during 1835, I was about seventeen years old.

My mother was named Harriet Bailey. She was the daughter of Isaac and Betsey Bailey, both colored, and quite dark. My mother was of a darker complexion than either my grandmother or grandfather.

My father was a white man. He was admitted to be such by all I ever heard speak of my parentage. The opinion was also whispered that my master was my father; but of the correctness of this opinion, I know nothing; the means of knowing was withheld from me. My mother and

I were separated when I was but an infant—before I knew her as my mother. It is a common custom, in the part of Maryland from which I ran away, to part children from their mothers at a very early age. Frequently, before the child has reached its twelfth month, its mother is taken from it, and hired out on some farm a considerable distance off, and the child is placed under the care of an old woman, too old for field labor. For what this separation is done, I do not know, unless it be to hinder the development of the child's affection toward its mother, and to blunt and destroy the natural affection of the mother for the child. This is the inevitable result.

I never saw my mother, to know her as such, more than four or five times in my life; and each of these times was very short in duration, and at night. She was hired by a Mr. Stewart, who lived about twelve miles from my home. She made her journeys to see me in the night, travelling the whole distance on foot, after the performance of her day's work. She was a field hand, and a whipping is the penalty of not being in the field at sunrise, unless a slave has special permission from his or her master to the contrary—a permission which they seldom get, and one that gives to him that gives it the proud name of being a kind master. I do not recollect of ever seeing my mother by the light of day. She was with me in the night. She would lie down with me, and get me to sleep, but long before I waked she was gone. Very little communication ever took place between us. Death soon ended what little we could have while she lived, and with it her hardships and suffering. She died when I was about seven years old, on one of my master's farms, near Lee's Mill. I was not allowed to be present during her illness, at her death, or burial. She was gone long before I knew any thing about it. Never having enjoyed, to any considerable extent, her soothing presence, her tender and watchful care, I received the tidings of her death with much the same emotions I should have probably felt at the death of a stranger.

Called thus suddenly away, she left me without the slightest intimation of who my father was. The whisper that my master was my father, may or may not be true; and, true or false, it is of but little consequence to my purpose whilst the fact remains, in all its glaring odiousness, that slaveholders have ordained, and by law established, that the children of slave women shall in all cases follow the condition of their mothers; and this is done too obviously to administer to their own lusts, and make a gratification of their wicked desires profitable as well as pleasurable; for by this cunning arrangement, the slaveholder, in cases not a few, sustains to his slaves the double relation of master and father.

I know of such cases; and it is worthy of remark that such slaves invariably suffer greater hardships, and have more to contend with, than others. They are, in the first place, a constant offence to their mistress. She is ever disposed to find fault with them; they can seldom do any thing to please her; she is never better pleased than when she sees them under the lash, especially when she suspects her husband of showing to his mulatto children favors which he withholds from his black slaves. The master is frequently compelled to sell this class of his slaves, out of deference to the feelings of his white wife; and, cruel as the deed may strike any one to be, for a man to sell his own children to human flesh-mongers, it is often the dictate of humanity for him to do so; for, unless he does this, he must not only whip them himself, but must stand by and see one white son tie up his brother, of but few shades darker complexion than himself, and ply the gory lash to his naked back; and if he lisp one word of disapproval, it is set down to his parental partiality, and only makes a bad matter worse, both for himself and the slave whom he would protect and defend.

Every year brings with it multitudes of this class of slaves. It was doubtless in consequence of a knowledge of this fact, that one great statesman of the south predicted the downfall of slavery by the inevitable laws of population. Whether this prophecy is ever fulfilled or not, it is nevertheless plain that a very different-looking class of people are springing up at the south, and are now held in slavery, from those originally brought to this country from Africa; and if their increase will do no other good, it will do away the force of the argument, that God cursed Ham,[8] and therefore American slavery is right. If the lineal descendants of Ham are alone to be scripturally enslaved, it is certain that slavery at the south must soon become unscriptural; for thousands are ushered into the world, annually, who, like myself, owe their existence to white fathers, and those fathers most frequently their own masters.

I have had two masters. My first master's name was Anthony. I do not remember his first name. He was generally called Captain Anthony—a title which, I presume, he acquired by sailing a craft on the Chesapeake Bay. He was not considered a rich slaveholder. He owned two or three farms, and about thirty slaves. His farms and slaves were under the care of an overseer. The overseer's name was Plummer. Mr. Plummer was a miserable drunkard, a profane swearer, and a savage monster. He always went armed with a cowskin[9] and a heavy cudgel. I have known him to cut and slash the women's heads so horribly, that even master would be enraged at his cruelty, and would threaten to whip him if he did not mind himself. Master, however, was not a humane slaveholder. It required extraordinary barbarity on the part of an overseer to affect him. He was a cruel man, hardened by a long life of slaveholding. He would at times seem to take great pleasure in whipping a slave. I have often been awakened at the dawn of day by the most heart-rending shrieks of an own aunt of mine, whom he used to tie up to a joist, and whip upon her naked back till she was literally covered with blood. No words, no tears, no prayers,

---

8. The specious argument referred to is based on an interpretation of Genesis 9.20–27, in which Noah curses his son Ham and condemns him to bondage to his brothers.
9. A whip made of raw cowhide.

from his gory victim, seemed to move his iron heart from its bloody purpose. The louder she screamed, the harder he whipped; and where the blood ran fastest, there he whipped longest. He would whip her to make her scream, and whip her to make her hush; and not until overcome by fatigue, would he cease to swing the blood-clotted cowskin. I remember the first time I ever witnessed this horrible exhibition. I was quite a child, but I well remember it. I never shall forget it whilst I remember any thing. It was the first of a long series of such outrages, of which I was doomed to be a witness and a participant. It struck me with awful force. It was the blood-stained gate, the entrance to the hell of slavery, through which I was about to pass. It was a most terrible spectacle. I wish I could commit to paper the feelings with which I beheld it.

This occurrence took place very soon after I went to live with my old master, and under the following circumstances. Aunt Hester went out one night,—where or for what I do not know,—and happened to be absent when my master desired her presence. He had ordered her not to go out evenings, and warned her that she must never let him catch her in company with a young man, who was paying attention to her, belonging to Colonel Lloyd. The young man's name was Ned Roberts, generally called Lloyd's Ned. Why master was so careful of her, may be safely left to conjecture. She was a woman of noble form, and of graceful proportions, having very few equals, and fewer superiors, in personal appearance, among the colored or white women of our neighborhood.

Aunt Hester had not only disobeyed his orders in going out, but had been found in company with Lloyd's Ned; which circumstance, I found, from what he said while whipping her, was the chief offence. Had he been a man of pure morals himself, he might have been thought interested in protecting the innocence of my aunt; but those who knew him will not suspect him of any such virtue. Before he commenced whipping Aunt Hester, he took her into the kitchen, and stripped her from neck to waist, leaving her neck, shoulders, and back, entirely naked. He then told her to cross her hands, calling her at the same time a d——d b——h. After crossing her hands, he tied them with a strong rope, and led her to a stool under a large hook in the joist, put in for the purpose. He made her get upon the stool, and tied her hands to the hook. She now stood fair for his infernal purpose. Her arms were stretched up at their full length, so that she stood upon the ends of her toes. He then said to her, "Now, you d——d b——h, I'll learn you how to disobey my orders!" and after rolling up his sleeves, he commenced to lay on the heavy cowskin, and soon the warm, red blood (amid heart-rending shrieks from her, and horrid oaths from him) came dripping to the floor. I was so terrified and horror-stricken at the sight, that I hid myself in a closet, and dared not venture out till long after the bloody transaction was over. I expected it would be my turn next. It was all new to me. I had never seen any thing like it before. I had always lived with my grandmother on the outskirts of the plantation, where she was put to raise the children of the younger women. I had therefore been, until now, out of the way of the bloody scenes that often occurred on the plantation.

Chapter II

My master's family consisted of two sons, Andrew and Richard; one daughter, Lucretia, and her husband, Captain Thomas Auld. They lived in one house, upon the home plantation of Colonel Edward Lloyd. My master was Colonel Lloyd's clerk and superintendent. He was what might be called the overseer of the overseers. I spent two years of childhood on this plantation in my old master's family. It was here that I witnessed the bloody transaction recorded in the first chapter; and as I received my first impressions of slavery on this plantation, I will give some description of it, and of slavery as it there existed. The plantation is about twelve miles north of Easton, in Talbot county, and is situated on the border of Miles River. The principal products raised upon it were tobacco, corn, and wheat. These were raised in great abundance; so that, with the products of this and the other farms belonging to him, he was able to keep in almost constant employment a large sloop, in carrying them to market at Baltimore. This sloop was named Sally Lloyd, in honor of one of the colonel's daughters. My master's son-in-law, Captain Auld, was master of the vessel; she was otherwise manned by the colonel's own slaves. Their names were Peter, Isaac, Rich, and Jake. These were esteemed very highly by the other slaves, and looked upon as the privileged ones of the plantation; for it was no small affair, in the eyes of the slaves, to be allowed to see Baltimore.

Colonel Lloyd kept from three to four hundred slaves on his home plantation, and owned a large number more on the neighboring farms belonging to him. The names of the farms nearest to the home plantation were Wye Town and New Design. "Wye Town" was under the overseership of a man named Noah Willis. New Design was under the overseership of a Mr. Townsend. The overseers of these, and all the rest of the farms, numbering over twenty, received advice and direction from the managers of the home plantation. This was the great business place. It was the seat of government for the whole twenty farms. All disputes among the overseers were settled here. If a slave was convicted of any high misdemeanor, became unmanageable, or evinced a determination to run away, he was brought immediately here, severely whipped, put on board the sloop, carried to Baltimore, and sold to Austin Woolfolk, or some other slave-trader, as a warning to the slaves remaining.

Here, too, the slaves of all the other farms received their monthly allowance of food, and their yearly clothing. The men and women slaves received, as their monthly allowance of food, eight pounds of pork, or its equivalent in fish, and one bushel of corn meal. Their yearly clothing consisted of two coarse linen shirts, one pair of linen trousers, like the shirts, one jacket, one pair of trousers for winter, made of coarse negro cloth, one pair of stockings, and one pair of shoes; the whole of which could not have cost more than seven dollars. The allowance of the slave children was given to their mothers, or the old women having the care of them. The children unable to work in the field had neither shoes, stockings, jackets, nor trousers, given to them; their clothing consisted of two coarse linen shirts per year. When these failed them, they went naked until the next allowance-day. Children from seven to ten years old, of both sexes, almost naked, might be seen at all seasons of the year.

There were no beds given the slaves, unless one coarse blanket be considered such, and none but the men and women had these. This, however, is not considered a very great privation. They find less difficulty from the want of beds, than from the want of time to sleep; for when their day's work in the field is done, the most of them having their washing, mending, and cooking to do, and having few or none of the ordinary facilities for doing either of these, very many of their sleeping hours are consumed in preparing for the field the coming day; and when this is done, old and young, male and female, married and single, drop down side by side, on one common bed,—the cold, damp floor,— each covering himself or herself with their miserable blankets; and here they sleep till they are summoned to the field by the driver's horn. At the sound of this, all must rise, and be off to the field. There must be no halting; every one must be at his or her post; and woe betides them who hear not this morning summons to the field; for if they are not awakened by the sense of hearing, they are by the sense of feeling: no age nor sex finds any favor. Mr. Severe, the overseer, used to stand by the door of the quarter, armed with a large hickory stick and heavy cowskin, ready to whip any one who was so unfortunate as not to hear, or, from any other cause, was prevented from being ready to start for the field at the sound of the horn.

Mr. Severe was rightly named: he was a cruel man. I have seen him whip a woman, causing the blood to run half an hour at the time; and this, too, in the midst of her crying children, pleading for their mother's release. He seemed to take pleasure in manifesting his fiendish barbarity. Added to his cruelty, he was a profane swearer. It was enough to chill the blood and stiffen the hair of an ordinary man to hear him talk. Scarce a sentence escaped him but that was commenced or concluded by some horrid oath. The field was the place to witness his cruelty and profanity. His presence made it both the field of blood and of blasphemy. From the rising till the going down of the sun, he was cursing, raving, cutting, and slashing among the slaves of the field, in the most frightful manner. His career was short. He died very soon after I went to

Colonel Lloyd's; and he died as he lived, uttering, with his dying groans, bitter curses and horrid oaths. His death was regarded by the slaves as the result of a merciful providence. Mr. Severe's place was filled by a Mr. Hopkins. He was a very different man. He was less cruel, less profane, and made less noise, than Mr. Severe. His course was characterized by no extraordinary demonstrations of cruelty. He whipped, but seemed to take no pleasure in it. He was called by the slaves a good overseer.

The home plantation of Colonel Lloyd wore the appearance of a country village. All the mechanical operations for all the farms were performed here. The shoemaking and mending, the blacksmithing, cartwrighting, coopering, weaving, and grain-grinding, were all performed by the slaves on the home plantation. The whole place wore a business-like aspect very unlike the neighboring farms. The number of houses, too, conspired to give it advantage over the neighboring farms. It was called by the slaves the *Great House Farm*. Few privileges were esteemed higher, by the slaves of the out-farms, than that of being selected to do errands at the Great House Farm. It was associated in their minds with greatness. A representative could not be prouder of his election to a seat in the American Congress, than a slave on one of the out-farms would be of his election to do errands at the Great House Farm. They regarded it as evidence of great confidence reposed in them by their overseers; and it was on this account, as well as a constant desire to be out of the field from under the driver's lash, that they esteemed it a high privilege, one worth careful living for. He was called the smartest and most trusty fellow, who had this honor conferred upon him the most frequently. The competitors for this office sought as diligently to please their overseers, as the office-seekers in the political parties seek to please and deceive the people. The same traits of character might be seen in Colonel Lloyd's slaves, as are seen in the slaves of the political parties.

The slaves selected to go to the Great House Farm, for the monthly allowance for themselves and their fellow-slaves, were peculiarly enthusiastic. While on their way, they would make the dense old woods, for miles around, reverberate with their wild songs, revealing at once the highest joy and the deepest sadness. They would compose and sing as they went along, consulting neither time nor tune. The thought that came up, came out—if not in the word, in the sound;—and as frequently in the one as in the other. They would sometimes sing the most pathetic sentiment in the most rapturous tone, and the most rapturous sentiment in the most pathetic tone. Into all of their songs they would manage to weave something of the Great House Farm. Especially would they do this, when leaving home. They would then sing most exultingly the following words:—

"I am going away to the Great House Farm!
O, yea! O, yea! O!"

This they would sing, as a chorus, to words which to many would seem
unmeaning jargon, but which, nevertheless, were full of meaning to
themselves. I have sometimes thought that the mere hearing of those
songs would do more to impress some minds with the horrible character
of slavery, than the reading of whole volumes of philosophy on the subject could do.

I did not, when a slave, understand the deep meaning of those rude
and apparently incoherent songs. I was myself within the circle; so that
I neither saw nor heard as those without might see and hear. They told
a tale of woe which was then altogether beyond my feeble comprehension; they were tones loud, long, and deep; they breathed the prayer and
complaint of souls boiling over with the bitterest anguish. Every tone
was a testimony against slavery, and a prayer to God for deliverance
from chains. The hearing of those wild notes always depressed my spirit,
and filled me with ineffable sadness. I have frequently found myself in
tears while hearing them. The mere recurrence to those songs, even
now, afflicts me; and while I am writing these lines, an expression of
feeling has already found its way down my cheek. To those songs I trace
my first glimmering conception of the dehumanizing character of slavery. I can never get rid of that conception. Those songs still follow me,
to deepen my hatred of slavery, and quicken my sympathies for my
brethren in bonds. If any one wishes to be impressed with the soul-
killing effects of slavery, let him go to Colonel Lloyd's plantation, and,
on allowance-day, place himself in the deep pine woods, and there let
him, in silence, analyze the sounds that shall pass through the chambers
of his soul,—and if he is not thus impressed, it will only be because
"there is no flesh in his obdurate heart." [1]

I have often been utterly astonished, since I came to the north, to
find persons who could speak of the singing, among slaves, as evidence
of their contentment and happiness. It is impossible to conceive of a
greater mistake. Slaves sing most when they are most unhappy. The
songs of the slave represent the sorrows of his heart; and he is relieved
by them, only as an aching heart is relieved by its tears. At least, such is
my experience. I have often sung to drown my sorrow, but seldom to
express my happiness. Crying for joy, and singing for joy, were alike
uncommon to me while in the jaws of slavery. The singing of a man
cast away upon a desolate island might be as appropriately considered
as evidence of contentment and happiness, as the singing of a slave; the
songs of the one and of the other are prompted by the same emotion.

1. Cf. "The Time-Piece," book 2, line 8, in William Cowper's popular poem *The Task* (1785).

Chapter III

Colonel Lloyd kept a large and finely cultivated garden, which afforded almost constant employment for four men, besides the chief gardener, (Mr. M'Durmond.) This garden was probably the greatest attraction of the place. During the summer months, people came from far and near—from Baltimore, Easton, and Annapolis—to see it. It abounded in fruits of almost every description, from the hardy apple of the north to the delicate orange of the south. This garden was not the least source of trouble on the plantation. Its excellent fruit was quite a temptation to the hungry swarms of boys, as well as the older slaves, belonging to the colonel, few of whom had the virtue or the vice to resist it. Scarcely a day passed, during the summer, but that some slave had to take the lash for stealing fruit. The colonel had to resort to all kinds of stratagems to keep his slaves out of the garden. The last and most successful one was that of tarring his fence all around, after which, if a slave was caught with any tar upon his person, it was deemed sufficient proof that he had either been into the garden, or had tried to get in. In either case, he was severely whipped by the chief gardener. This plan worked well; the slaves became as fearful of tar as of the lash. They seemed to realize the impossibility of touching *tar* without being defiled.

The colonel also kept a splendid riding equipage. His stable and carriage-house presented the appearance of some of our large city livery establishments. His horses were of the finest form and noblest blood. His carriage-house contained three splendid coaches, three or four gigs, besides dearborns and barouches[2] of the most fashionable style.

This establishment was under the care of two slaves—old Barney and young Barney—father and son. To attend to this establishment was their sole work. But it was by no means an easy employment; for in nothing was Colonel Lloyd more particular than in the management of his horses. The slightest inattention to these was unpardonable, and was visited upon those, under whose care they were placed, with the severest punishment; no excuse could shield them, if the colonel only suspected any want of attention to his horses—a supposition which he frequently indulged, and one which, of course, made the office of old and young Barney a very trying one. They never knew when they were safe from punishment. They were frequently whipped when least deserving, and escaped whipping when most deserving it. Every thing depended upon the looks of the horses, and the state of Colonel Lloyd's own mind when his horses were brought to him for use. If a horse did not move fast enough, or hold his head high enough, it was owing to some fault of his keepers. It was painful to stand near the stable-door, and hear the vari-

2. Different kinds of carriages.

ous complaints against the keepers when a horse was taken out for use. "This horse has not had proper attention. He has not been sufficiently rubbed and curried, or he has not been properly fed; his food was too wet or too dry; he got it too soon or too late; he was too hot or too cold; he had too much hay, and not enough of grain; or he had too much grain, and not enough of hay; instead of old Barney's attending to the horse, he had very improperly left it to his son." To all these complaints, no matter how unjust, the slave must answer never a word. Colonel Lloyd could not brook any contradiction from a slave. When he spoke, a slave must stand, listen, and tremble; and such was literally the case. I have seen Colonel Lloyd make old Barney, a man between fifty and sixty years of age, uncover his bald head, kneel down upon the cold, damp ground, and receive upon his naked and toil-worn shoulders more than thirty lashes at the time. Colonel Lloyd had three sons—Edward, Murray, and Daniel,—and three sons-in-law, Mr. Winder, Mr. Nicholson, and Mr. Lowndes. All of these lived at the Great House Farm, and enjoyed the luxury of whipping the servants when they pleased, from old Barney down to William Wilkes, the coach-driver. I have seen Winder make one of the house-servants stand off from him a suitable distance to be touched with the end of his whip, and at every stroke raise great ridges upon his back.

To describe the wealth of Colonel Lloyd would be almost equal to describing the riches of Job. He kept from ten to fifteen house-servants. He was said to own a thousand slaves, and I think this estimate quite within the truth. Colonel Lloyd owned so many that he did not know them when he saw them; nor did all the slaves of the out-farms know him. It is reported of him, that, while riding along the road one day, he met a colored man, and addressed him in the usual manner of speaking to colored people on the public highways of the south: "Well, boy, whom do you belong to?" "To Colonel Lloyd," replied the slave. "Well, does the colonel treat you well?" "No, sir," was the ready reply. "What, does he work you too hard?" "Yes, sir." "Well, don't he give you enough to eat?" "Yes, sir, he gives me enough, such as it is."

The colonel, after ascertaining where the slave belonged, rode on; the man also went on about his business, not dreaming that he had been conversing with his master. He thought, said, and heard nothing more of the matter, until two or three weeks afterwards. The poor man was then informed by his overseer that, for having found fault with his master, he was now to be sold to a Georgia trader. He was immediately chained and handcuffed; and thus, without a moment's warning, he was snatched away, and forever sundered, from his family and friends, by a hand more unrelenting than death. This is the penalty of telling the truth, of telling the simple truth, in answer to a series of plain questions.

It is partly in consequence of such facts, that slaves, when inquired of as to their condition and the character of their masters, almost universally say they are contented, and that their masters are kind. The slave-holders have been known to send in spies among their slaves, to ascertain their views and feelings in regard to their condition. The frequency of this has had the effect to establish among the slaves the maxim, that a still tongue makes a wise head. They suppress the truth rather than take the consequences of telling it, and in so doing prove themselves a part of the human family. If they have any thing to say of their masters, it is generally in their masters' favor, especially when speaking to an untried man. I have been frequently asked, when a slave, if I had a kind master, and do not remember ever to have given a negative answer; nor did I, in pursuing this course, consider myself as uttering what was absolutely false; for I always measured the kindness of my master by the standard of kindness set up among slaveholders around us. Moreover, slaves are like other people, and imbibe prejudices quite common to others. They think their own better than that of others. Many, under the influence of this prejudice, think their own masters are better than the masters of other slaves; and this, too, in some cases, when the very reverse is true. Indeed, it is not uncommon for slaves even to fall out and quarrel among themselves about the relative goodness of their masters, each contending for the superior goodness of his own over that of the others. At the very same time, they mutually execrate their masters when viewed separately. It was so on our plantation. When Colonel Lloyd's slaves met the slaves of Jacob Jepson, they seldom parted without a quarrel about their masters; Colonel Lloyd's slaves contending that he was the richest, and Mr. Jepson's slaves that he was the smartest, and most of a man. Colonel Lloyd's slaves would boast his ability to buy and sell Jacob Jepson. Mr. Jepson's slaves would boast his ability to whip Colonel Lloyd. These quarrels would almost always end in a fight between the parties, and those that whipped were supposed to have gained the point at issue. They seemed to think that the greatness of their masters was transferable to themselves. It was considered as being bad enough to be a slave; but to be a poor man's slave was deemed a disgrace indeed!

Chapter IV

Mr. Hopkins remained but a short time in the office of overseer. Why his career was so short, I do not know, but suppose he lacked the necessary severity to suit Colonel Lloyd. Mr. Hopkins was succeeded by Mr. Austin Gore, a man possessing, in an eminent degree, all those traits of character indispensable to what is called a first-rate overseer. Mr. Gore had served Colonel Lloyd, in the capacity of overseer, upon one of the out-farms, and had shown himself worthy of the high station of overseer upon the home or Great House Farm.

Mr. Gore was proud, ambitious, and persevering. He was artful, cruel, and obdurate. He was just the man for such a place, and it was just the place for such a man. It afforded scope for the full exercise of all his powers, and he seemed to be perfectly at home in it. He was one of those who could torture the slightest look, word, or gesture, on the part of the slave, into impudence, and would treat it accordingly. There must be no answering back to him; no explanation was allowed a slave, showing himself to have been wrongfully accused. Mr. Gore acted fully up to the maxim laid down by slaveholders,—"It is better that a dozen slaves suffer under the lash, than that the overseer should be convicted, in the presence of the slaves, of having been at fault." No matter how innocent a slave might be—it availed him nothing, when accused by Mr. Gore of any misdemeanor. To be accused was to be convicted, and to be convicted was to be punished; the one always following the other with immutable certainty. To escape punishment was to escape accusation; and few slaves had the fortune to do either, under the overseership of Mr. Gore. He was just proud enough to demand the most debasing homage of the slave, and quite servile enough to crouch, himself, at the feet of the master. He was ambitious enough to be contented with nothing short of the highest rank of overseers, and persevering enough to reach the height of his ambition. He was cruel enough to inflict the severest punishment, artful enough to descend to the lowest trickery, and obdurate enough to be insensible to the voice of a reproving conscience. He was, of all the overseers, the most dreaded by the slaves. His presence was painful; his eye flashed confusion; and seldom was his sharp, shrill voice heard, without producing horror and trembling in their ranks.

Mr. Gore was a grave man, and, though a young man, he indulged in no jokes, said no funny words, seldom smiled. His words were in perfect keeping with his looks, and his looks were in perfect keeping with his words. Overseers will sometimes indulge in a witty word, even with the slaves; not so with Mr. Gore. He spoke but to command, and commanded but to be obeyed; he dealt sparingly with his words, and bountifully with his whip, never using the former where the latter would answer as well. When he whipped, he seemed to do so from a sense of duty, and feared no consequences. He did nothing reluctantly, no matter how disagreeable; always at his post, never inconsistent. He never promised but to fulfil. He was, in a word, a man of the most inflexible firmness and stone-like coolness.

His savage barbarity was equalled only by the consummate coolness with which he committed the grossest and most savage deeds upon the slaves under his charge. Mr. Gore once undertook to whip one of Colonel Lloyd's slaves, by the name of Demby. He had given Demby but few stripes, when, to get rid of the scourging, he ran and plunged himself into a creek, and stood there at the depth of his shoulders, refusing to come out. Mr. Gore told him that he would give him three calls, and that, if he did not come out at the third call, he would shoot him. The first call was given. Demby made no response, but stood his ground. The second and third calls were given with the same result. Mr. Gore then, without consultation or deliberation with any one, not even giving Demby an additional call, raised his musket to his face, taking deadly aim at his standing victim, and in an instant poor Demby was no more. His mangled body sank out of sight, and blood and brains marked the water where he had stood.

A thrill of horror flashed through every soul upon the plantation, excepting Mr. Gore. He alone seemed cool and collected. He was asked by Colonel Lloyd and my old master, why he resorted to this extraordinary expedient. His reply was, (as well as I can remember,) that Demby had become unmanageable. He was setting a dangerous example to the other slaves,—one which, if suffered to pass without some such demonstration on his part, would finally lead to the total subversion of all rule and order upon the plantation. He argued that if one slave refused to be corrected, and escaped with his life, the other slaves would soon copy the example; the result of which would be, the freedom of the slaves, and the enslavement of the whites. Mr. Gore's defence was satisfactory. He was continued in his station as overseer upon the home plantation. His fame as an overseer went abroad. His horrid crime was not even submitted to judicial investigation. It was committed in the presence of slaves, and they of course could neither institute a suit, nor testify against him; and thus the guilty perpetrator of one of the bloodiest and most foul murders goes unwhipped of justice, and uncensured by the community in which he lives. Mr. Gore lived in St. Michael's, Talbot county, Maryland, when I left there; and if he is still alive, he very probably lives there now; and if so, he is now, as he was then, as highly esteemed and as much respected as though his guilty soul had not been stained with his brother's blood.

I speak advisedly when I say this,—that killing a slave, or any colored person, in Talbot county, Maryland, is not treated as a crime, either by the courts or the community. Mr. Thomas Lanman, of St. Michael's, killed two slaves, one of whom he killed with a hatchet, by knocking his brains out. He used to boast of the commission of the awful and bloody deed. I have heard him do so laughingly, saying, among other things, that he was the only benefactor of his country in the company, and that when others would do as much as he had done, we should be relieved of "the d——d niggers."

The wife of Mr. Giles Hick, living but a short distance from where I used to live, murdered my wife's cousin, a young girl between fifteen and sixteen years of age, mangling her person in the most horrible manner, breaking her nose and breastbone with a stick, so that the poor girl expired in a few hours afterward. She was immediately buried, but had not been in her untimely grave but a few hours before she was taken up and examined by the coroner, who decided that she had come to her death by severe beating. The offence for which this girl was thus murdered was this:—She had been set that night to mind Mrs. Hick's baby, and during the night she fell asleep, and the baby cried. She, having lost her rest for several nights previous, did not hear the crying. They were both in the room with Mrs. Hicks. Mrs. Hicks, finding the girl slow to move, jumped from her bed, seized an oak stick of wood by the fireplace, and with it broke the girl's nose and breastbone, and thus ended her life. I will not say that this most horrid murder produced no sensation in the community. It did produce sensation, but not enough to bring the murderess to punishment. There was a warrant issued for her arrest, but it was never served. Thus she escaped not only punishment, but even the pain of being arraigned before a court for her horrid crime.

Whilst I am detailing bloody deeds which took place during my stay on Colonel Lloyd's plantation, I will briefly narrate another, which occurred about the same time as the murder of Demby by Mr. Gore.

Colonel Lloyd's slaves were in the habit of spending a part of their nights and Sundays in fishing for oysters, and in this way made up the deficiency of their scanty allowance. An old man belonging to Colonel Lloyd, while thus engaged, happened to get beyond the limits of Colonel Lloyd's, and on the premises of Mr. Beal Bondly. At this trespass, Mr. Bondly took offence, and with his musket came down to the shore, and blew its deadly contents into the poor old man.

Mr. Bondly came over to see Colonel Lloyd the next day, whether to pay him for his property, or to justify himself in what he had done, I know not. At any rate, this whole fiendish transaction was soon hushed up. There was very little said about it at all, and nothing done. It was a common saying, even among little white boys, that it was worth a half-cent to kill a "nigger," and a half-cent to bury one.

Chapter V

As to my own treatment while I lived on Colonel Lloyd's plantation, it was very similar to that of the other slave children. I was not old enough to work in the field, and there being little else than field work to do, I had a great deal of leisure time. The most I had to do was to drive up the cows at evening, keep the fowls out of the garden, keep the front yard clean, and run of errands for my old master's daughter, Mrs. Lucretia Auld. The most of my leisure time I spent in helping Master Daniel Lloyd in finding his birds, after he had shot them. My connection with Master Daniel was of some advantage to me. He became quite attached to me, and was a sort of protector of me. He would not allow the older boys to impose upon me, and would divide his cakes with me. I was seldom whipped by my old master, and suffered little from any thing else than hunger and cold. I suffered much from hunger, but much more from cold. In hottest summer and coldest winter, I was kept almost naked—no shoes, no stockings, no jacket, no trousers, nothing on but a coarse tow linen shirt, reaching only to my knees. I had no bed. I must have perished with cold, but that, the coldest nights, I used to steal a bag which was used for carrying corn to the mill. I would crawl into this bag, and there sleep on the cold, damp, clay floor, with my head in and feet out. My feet have been so cracked with the frost, that the pen with which I am writing might be laid in the gashes.

We were not regularly allowanced. Our food was coarse corn meal boiled. This was called *mush*. It was put into a large wooden tray or trough, and set down upon the ground. The children were then called, like so many pigs, and like so many pigs they would come and devour the mush; some with oyster-shells, others with pieces of shingle, some with naked hands, and none with spoons. He that ate fastest got most; he that was strongest secured the best place; and few left the trough satisfied.

I was probably between seven and eight years old when I left Colonel Lloyd's plantation. I left it with joy. I shall never forget the ecstasy with which I received the intelligence that my old master (Anthony) had determined to let me go to Baltimore, to live with Mr. Hugh Auld, brother to my old master's son-in-law, Captain Thomas Auld. I received this information about three days before my departure. They were three of the happiest days I ever enjoyed. I spent the most part of all these three days in the creek, washing off the plantation scurf, and preparing myself for my departure.

The pride of appearance which this would indicate was not my own. I spent the time in washing, not so much because I wished to, but because Mrs. Lucretia had told me I must get all the dead skin off my feet and knees before I could go to Baltimore; for the people of Baltimore were very cleanly, and would laugh at me if I looked dirty. Besides, she was going to give me a pair of trousers, which I should not put on unless I got all the dirt off me. The thought of owning a pair of trousers was great indeed! It was almost a sufficient motive, not only to make me take off what would be called by pig-drovers the mange, but the skin itself. I went at it in good earnest, working for the first time with the hope of reward.

The ties that ordinarily bind children to their homes were all suspended in my case. I found no severe trial in my departure. My home was charmless; it was not home to me; on parting from it, I could not feel that I was leaving any thing which I could have enjoyed by staying. My mother was dead, my grandmother lived far off, so that I seldom saw her. I had two sisters and one brother, that lived in the same house with me; but the early separation of us from our mother had well nigh blotted the fact of our relationship from our memories. I looked for home elsewhere, and was confident of finding none which I should relish less than the one which I was leaving. If, however, I found in my new home hardship, hunger, whipping, and nakedness, I had the consolation that I should not have escaped any one of them by staying. Having already had more than a taste of them in the house of my old master, and having endured them there, I very naturally inferred my ability to endure them elsewhere, and especially at Baltimore; for I had something of the feeling about Baltimore that is expressed in the proverb, that "being hanged in England is preferable to dying a natural death in Ireland." I had the strongest desire to see Baltimore. Cousin Tom, though not fluent in speech, had inspired me with that desire by his eloquent description of the place. I could never point out any thing at the Great House, no matter how beautiful or powerful, but that he had seen something at Baltimore far exceeding, both in beauty and strength, the object which I pointed out to him. Even the Great House itself, with all its pictures, was far inferior to many buildings in Baltimore. So strong was my desire, that I thought a gratification of it would fully compensate for whatever loss of comforts I should sustain by the exchange. I left without a regret, and with the highest hopes of future happiness.

We sailed out of Miles River for Baltimore on a Saturday morning. I remember only the day of the week, for at that time I had no knowledge of the days of the month, nor the months of the year. On setting sail, I walked aft, and gave to Colonel Lloyd's plantation what I hoped would be the last look. I then placed myself in the bows of the sloop, and there spent the remainder of the day in looking ahead, interesting myself in what was in the distance rather than in things near by or behind.

In the afternoon of that day, we reached Annapolis, the capital of the State. We stopped but a few moments, so that I had no time to go on shore. It was the first large town that I had ever seen, and though it would look small compared with some of our New England factory villages, I thought it a wonderful place for its size—more imposing even than the Great House Farm!

We arrived at Baltimore early on Sunday morning, landing at Smith's Wharf, not far from Bowley's Wharf. We had on board the sloop a large flock of sheep; and after aiding in driving them to the slaughterhouse of Mr. Curtis on Louden Slater's Hill, I was conducted by Rich, one of the hands belonging on board of the sloop, to my new home in Alliciana Street, near Mr. Gardner's ship-yard, on Fells Point.

Mr. and Mrs. Auld were both at home, and met me at the door with their little son Thomas, to take care of whom I had been given. And here I saw what I had never seen before; it was a white face beaming with the most kindly emotions; it was the face of my new mistress, Sophia Auld. I wish I could describe the rapture that flashed through my soul as I beheld it. It was a new and strange sight to me, brightening up my pathway with the light of happiness. Little Thomas was told, there was his Freddy,—and I was told to take care of little Thomas; and thus I entered upon the duties of my new home with the most cheering prospect ahead.

I look upon my departure from Colonel Lloyd's plantation as one of the most interesting events of my life. It is possible, and even quite probable, that but for the mere circumstance of being removed from that plantation to Baltimore, I should have to-day, instead of being here seated by my own table, in the enjoyment of freedom and the happiness of home, writing this Narrative, been confined in the galling chains of slavery. Going to live at Baltimore laid the foundation, and opened the gateway, to all my subsequent prosperity. I have ever regarded it as the first plain manifestation of that kind providence which has ever since attended me, and marked my life with so many favors. I regarded the selection of myself as being somewhat remarkable. There were a number of slave children that might have been sent from the plantation to Baltimore. There were those younger, those older, and those of the same age. I was chosen from among them all, and was the first, last, and only choice.

I may be deemed superstitious, and even egotistical, in regarding this event as a special interposition of divine Providence in my favor. But I should be false to the earliest sentiments of my soul, if I suppressed the opinion. I prefer to be true to myself, even at the hazard of incurring the ridicule of others, rather than to be false, and incur my own abhorrence. From my earliest recollection, I date the entertainment of a deep conviction that slavery would not always be able to hold me within its foul embrace; and in the darkest hours of my career in slavery, this living word of faith and spirit of hope departed not from me, but remained like ministering angels to cheer me through the gloom. This good spirit was from God, and to him I offer thanksgiving and praise.

Chapter VI

My new mistress proved to be all she appeared when I first met her at the door,—a woman of the kindest heart and finest feelings. She had never had a slave under her control previously to myself, and prior to her marriage she had been dependent upon her own industry for a living. She was by trade a weaver; and by constant application to her business, she had been in a good degree preserved from the blighting and dehumanizing effects of slavery. I was utterly astonished at her goodness. I scarcely knew how to behave towards her. She was entirely unlike any other white woman I had ever seen. I could not approach her as I was accustomed to approach other white ladies. My early instruction was all out of place. The crouching servility, usually so acceptable a quality in a slave, did not answer when manifested toward her. Her favor was not gained by it; she seemed to be disturbed by it. She did not deem it impudent or unmannerly for a slave to look her in the face. The meanest slave was put fully at ease in her presence, and none left without feeling better for having seen her. Her face was made of heavenly smiles, and her voice of tranquil music.

But, alas! this kind heart had but a short time to remain such. The fatal poison of irresponsible power was already in her hands, and soon commenced its infernal work. That cheerful eye, under the influence of slavery, soon became red with rage; that voice, made all of sweet accord, changed to one of harsh and horrid discord; and that angelic face gave place to that of a demon.

Very soon after I went to live with Mr. and Mrs. Auld, she very kindly commenced to teach me the A, B, C. After I had learned this, she assisted me in learning to spell words of three or four letters. Just at this point of my progress, Mr. Auld found out what was going on, and at once forbade Mrs. Auld to instruct me further, telling her, among other things, that it was unlawful, as well as unsafe, to teach a slave to read. To use his own words, further, he said, "If you give a nigger an inch, he will take an ell. A nigger should know nothing but to obey his master— to do as he is told to do. Learning would *spoil* the best nigger in the world. Now," said he, "if you teach that nigger (speaking of myself) how to read, there would be no keeping him. It would forever unfit him to be a slave. He would at once become unmanageable, and of no value to his master. As to himself, it could do him no good, but a great deal of harm. It would make him discontented and unhappy." These words sank deep into my heart, stirred up sentiments within that lay slumbering, and called into existence an entirely new train of thought. It was a new and special revelation, explaining dark and mysterious things, with which my youthful understanding had struggled, but struggled in vain. I now understood what had been to me a most perplexing difficulty—to wit, the white man's power to enslave the black man. It was a grand achievement, and I prized it highly. From that moment, I understood the pathway from slavery to freedom. It was just what I wanted, and I got it at a time when I the least expected it. Whilst I was saddened by the thought of losing the aid of my kind mistress, I was gladdened by the invaluable instruction which, by the merest accident, I had gained from my master. Though conscious of the difficulty of learning without a teacher, I set out with high hope, and a fixed purpose, at whatever cost of trouble, to learn how to read. The very decided manner with which he spoke, and strove to impress his wife with the evil consequences of giving me instruction, served to convince me that he was deeply sensible of the truths he was uttering. It gave me the best assurance that I might rely with the utmost confidence on the results which, he said, would flow from teaching me to read. What he most dreaded, that I most desired. What he most loved, that I most hated. That which to him was a great evil, to be carefully shunned, was to me a great good, to be diligently sought; and the argument which he so warmly urged, against my learning to read, only served to inspire me with a desire and determination to learn. In learning to read, I owe almost as much to the bitter opposition of my master, as to the kindly aid of my mistress. I acknowledge the benefit of both.

I had resided but a short time in Baltimore before I observed a marked difference, in the treatment of slaves, from that which I had witnessed in the country. A city slave is almost a freeman, compared with a slave on the plantation. He is much better fed and clothed, and enjoys privileges altogether unknown to the slave on the plantation. There is a vestige of decency, a sense of shame, that does much to curb and check those outbreaks of atrocious cruelty so commonly enacted upon the plantation. He is a desperate slaveholder, who will shock the humanity of his non-slaveholding neighbors with the cries of his lacerated slave. Few are willing to incur the odium attaching to the reputation of being a cruel master; and above all things, they would not be known as not giving a slave enough to eat. Every city slaveholder is anxious to have it known of him, that he feeds his slaves well; and it is due to them to say, that most of them do give their slaves enough to eat. There are, however, some painful exceptions to this rule. Directly opposite to us, on Philpot Street, lived Mr. Thomas Hamilton. He owned two slaves. Their names were Henrietta and Mary. Henrietta was about twenty-two years of age, Mary was about fourteen; and of all the mangled and emaciated creatures I ever looked upon, these two were the most so. His heart must be harder than stone, that could look upon these unmoved. The head, neck, and shoulders of Mary were literally cut to pieces. I have frequently felt her head, and found it nearly covered with festering sores, caused by the lash of her cruel mistress. I do not know that her master ever whipped her, but I have been an eyewitness to the cruelty of Mrs. Hamilton. I used to be in Mr. Hamilton's house nearly every day. Mrs. Hamilton used to sit in a large chair in the middle of the room, with a heavy cowskin always by her side, and scarce an hour passed during the day but was marked by the blood of one of these slaves. The girls seldom passed her without her saying, "Move faster, you *black gip!*" at the same time giving them a blow with the cowskin over the head or shoulders, often drawing the blood. She would then say, "Take that, you *black gip!*"—continuing, "If you don't move faster, I'll move you!" Added to the cruel lashings to which these slaves were subjected, they were kept nearly half-starved. They seldom knew what it was to eat a full meal. I have seen Mary contending with the pigs for the offal thrown into the street. So much was Mary kicked and cut to pieces, that she was oftener called "*pecked*" than by her name.

Chapter VII

I lived in Master Hugh's family about seven years. During this time, I succeeded in learning to read and write. In accomplishing this, I was compelled to resort to various stratagems. I had no regular teacher. My mistress, who had kindly commenced to instruct me, had, in compliance with the advice and direction of her husband, not only ceased to instruct, but had set her face against my being instructed by any one else. It is due, however, to my mistress to say of her, that she did not adopt this course of treatment immediately. She at first lacked the depravity indispensable to shutting me up in mental darkness. It was at least necessary for her to have some training in the exercise of irresponsible power, to make her equal to the task of treating me as though I were a brute.

My mistress was, as I have said, a kind and tender-hearted woman; and in the simplicity of her soul she commenced, when I first went to live with her, to treat me as she supposed one human being ought to treat another. In entering upon the duties of a slaveholder, she did not seem to perceive that I sustained to her the relation of a mere chattel, and that for her to treat me as a human being was not only wrong, but dangerously so. Slavery proved as injurious to her as it did to me. When I went there, she was a pious, warm, and tender-hearted woman. There was no sorrow or suffering for which she had not a tear. She had bread for the hungry, clothes for the naked, and comfort for every mourner that came within her reach. Slavery soon proved its ability to divest her of these heavenly qualities. Under its influence, the tender heart became stone, and the lamblike disposition gave way to one of tiger-like fierceness. The first step in her downward course was in her ceasing to instruct me. She now commenced to practise her husband's precepts. She finally became even more violent in her opposition than her husband himself. She was not satisfied with simply doing as well as he had commanded; she seemed anxious to do better. Nothing seemed to make her more angry than to see me with a newspaper. She seemed to think that here lay the danger. I have had her rush at me with a face made all up of fury, and snatch from me a newspaper, in a manner that fully revealed her apprehension. She was an apt woman; and a little experience soon demonstrated, to her satisfaction, that education and slavery were incompatible with each other.

From this time I was most narrowly watched. If I was in a separate room any considerable length of time, I was sure to be suspected of having a book, and was at once called to give an account of myself. All this, however, was too late. The first step had been taken. Mistress, in teaching me the alphabet, had given me the *inch*, and no precaution could prevent me from taking the *ell*.

The plan which I adopted, and the one by which I was most success-ful, was that of making friends of all the little white boys whom I met in the street. As many of these as I could, I converted into teachers. With their kindly aid, obtained at different times and in different places, I finally succeeded in learning to read. When I was sent of errands, I always took my book with me, and by going one part of my errand quickly, I found time to get a lesson before my return. I used also to carry bread with me, enough of which was always in the house, and to which I was always welcome; for I was much better off in this regard than many of the poor white children in our neighborhood. This bread I used to bestow upon the hungry little urchins, who, in return, would give me that more valuable bread of knowledge. I am strongly tempted to give the names of two or three of those little boys, as a testimonial of the gratitude and affection I bear them; but prudence forbids;—not that it would injure me, but it might embarrass them; for it is almost an unpardonable offence to teach slaves to read in this Christian country. It is enough to say of the dear little fellows, that they lived on Philpot Street, very near Durgin and Bailey's ship-yard. I used to talk this matter of slavery over with them. I would sometimes say to them, I wished I could be as free as they would be when they got to be men. "You will be free as soon as you are twenty-one, *but I am a slave for life!* Have not I as good a right to be free as you have?" These words used to trouble them; they would express for me the liveliest sympathy, and console me with the hope that something would occur by which I might be free.

I was now about twelve years old, and the thought of being *a slave for life* began to bear heavily upon my heart. Just about this time, I got hold of a book entitled "The Columbian Orator." [3] Every opportunity I got, I used to read this book. Among much of other interesting matter, I found in it a dialogue between a master and his slave. The slave was repre-sented as having run away from his master three times. The dialogue represented the conversation which took place between them, when the slave was retaken the third time. In this dialogue, the whole argument in behalf of slavery was brought forward by the master, all of which was disposed of by the slave. The slave was made to say some very smart as well as impressive things in reply to his master—things which had the desired though unexpected effect; for the conversation resulted in the voluntary emancipation of the slave on the part of the master.

In the same book, I met with one of Sheridan's [4] mighty speeches on and in behalf of Catholic emancipation. These were choice documents to me. I read them over and over again with unabated interest. They gave tongue to interesting thoughts of my own soul, which had fre-

3. A popular eloquence manual compiled in 1797 by Caleb Bingham.
4. Richard Brinsley Sheridan (1751–1816), Irish dramatist and political leader. The speech in the *Columbian Orator* to which Douglass refers was actually made by the Irish patriot Arthur O'Connor.

quently flashed through my mind, and died away for want of utterance. The moral which I gained from the dialogue was the power of truth over the conscience of even a slaveholder. What I got from Sheridan was a bold denunciation of slavery, and a powerful vindication of human rights. The reading of these documents enabled me to utter my thoughts, and to meet the arguments brought forward to sustain slavery; but while they relieved me of one difficulty, they brought on another even more painful than the one of which I was relieved. The more I read, the more I was led to abhor and detest my enslavers. I could regard them in no other light than a band of successful robbers, who had left their homes, and gone to Africa, and stolen us from our homes, and in a strange land reduced us to slavery. I loathed them as being the meanest as well as the most wicked of men. As I read and contemplated the subject, behold! that very discontentment which Master Hugh had predicted would follow my learning to read had already come, to torment and sting my soul to unutterable anguish. As I writhed under it, I would at times feel that learning to read had been a curse rather than a blessing. It had given me a view of my wretched condition, without the remedy. It opened my eyes to the horrible pit, but to no ladder upon which to get out. In moments of agony, I envied my fellow-slaves for their stupidity. I have often wished myself a beast. I preferred the condition of the meanest reptile to my own. Any thing, no matter what, to get rid of thinking! It was this everlasting thinking of my condition that tormented me. There was no getting rid of it. It was pressed upon me by every object within sight or hearing, animate or inanimate. The silver trump of freedom had roused my soul to eternal wakefulness. Freedom now appeared, to disappear no more forever. It was heard in every sound, and seen in every thing. It was ever present to torment me with a sense of my wretched condition. I saw nothing without seeing it, I heard nothing without hearing it, and felt nothing without feeling it. It looked from every star, it smiled in every calm, breathed in every wind, and moved in every storm.

I often found myself regretting my own existence, and wishing myself dead; and but for the hope of being free, I have no doubt but that I should have killed myself, or done something for which I should have been killed. While in this state of mind, I was eager to hear any one speak of slavery. I was a ready listener. Every little while, I could hear something about the abolitionists. It was some time before I found what the word meant. It was always used in such connections as to make it an interesting word to me. If a slave ran away and succeeded in getting clear, or if a slave killed his master, set fire to a barn, or did any thing very wrong in the mind of a slaveholder, it was spoken of as the fruit of *abolition*. Hearing the word in this connection very often, I set about learning what it meant. The dictionary afforded me little or no help. I found it was "the act of abolishing;" but then I did not know what was to be abolished. Here I was perplexed. I did not dare to ask any one about its meaning, for I was satisfied that it was something they wanted me to know very little about. After a patient waiting, I got one of our city papers, containing an account of the number of petitions from the north, praying for the abolition of slavery in the District of Columbia, and of the slave trade between the States. From this time I understood the words *abolition* and *abolitionist*, and always drew near when that word was spoken, expecting to hear something of importance to myself and fellow-slaves. The light broke in upon me by degrees. I went one day down on the wharf of Mr. Waters; and seeing two Irishmen unloading a scow of stone, I went, unasked, and helped them. When we had finished, one of them came to me and asked me if I were a slave. I told him I was. He asked, "Are ye a slave for life?" I told him that I was. The good Irishman seemed to be deeply affected by the statement. He said to the other that it was a pity so fine a little fellow as myself should be a slave for life. He said it was a shame to hold me. They both advised me to run away to the north; that I should find friends there, and that I should be free. I pretended not to be interested in what they said, and treated them as if I did not understand them; for I feared they might be treacherous. White men have been known to encourage slaves to escape, and then, to get the reward, catch them and return them to their masters. I was afraid that these seemingly good men might use me so; but I nevertheless remembered their advice, and from that time I resolved to run away. I looked forward to a time at which it would be safe for me to escape. I was too young to think of doing so immediately; besides, I wished to learn how to write, as I might have occasion to write my own pass. I consoled myself with the hope that I should one day find a good chance. Meanwhile, I would learn to write.

The idea as to how I might learn to write was suggested to me by being in Durgin and Bailey's ship-yard, and frequently seeing the ship carpenters, after hewing, and getting a piece of timber ready for use, write on the timber the name of that part of the ship for which it was intended. When a piece of timber was intended for the larboard side, it would be marked thus—"L." When a piece was for the starboard side, it would be marked thus—"S." A piece for the larboard side forward, would be marked thus—"L. F." When a piece was for starboard side forward, it would be marked thus—"S. F." For larboard aft, it would be marked thus—"L. A." For starboard aft, it would be marked thus—"S. A." I soon learned the names of these letters, and for what they were intended when placed upon a piece of timber in the ship-yard. I immediately commenced copying them, and in a short time was able to make the four letters named. After that, when I met with any boy who I knew could write, I would tell him I could write as well as he. The next word would be, "I don't believe you. Let me see you try it." I would then make the letters which I had been so fortunate as to learn, and ask him to beat that. In this way I got a good many lessons in writing, which it is quite possible I should never have gotten in any other way. During this time, my copy-book was the board fence, brick wall, and pavement; my pen and ink was a lump of chalk. With these, I learned mainly how to write. I then commenced and continued copying the Italics in Webster's Spelling Book,[5] until I could make them all without looking on the book. By this time, my little Master Thomas had gone to school, and learned how to write, and had written over a number of copy-books. These had been brought home, and shown to some of our near neighbors, and then laid aside. My mistress used to go to class meeting at the Wilk Street meeting-house every Monday afternoon, and leave me to take care of the house. When left thus, I used to spend the time in writing in the spaces left in Master Thomas's copy-book, copying what he had written. I continued to do this until I could write a hand very similar to that of Master Thomas. Thus, after a long, tedious effort for years, I finally succeeded in learning how to write.

Chapter VIII

In a very short time after I went to live at Baltimore, my old master's youngest son Richard died; and in about three years and six months after his death, my old master, Captain Anthony, died, leaving only his son, Andrew, and daughter, Lucretia, to share his estate. He died while on a visit to see his daughter at Hillsborough. Cut off thus unexpectedly, he left no will as to the disposal of his property. It was therefore necessary to have a valuation of the property, that it might be equally divided between Mrs. Lucretia and Master Andrew. I was immediately sent for, to be valued with the other property. Here again my feelings rose up in detestation of slavery. I had now a new conception of my degraded condition. Prior to this, I had become, if not insensible to my lot, at least partly so. I left Baltimore with a young heart overborne with sadness, and a soul full of apprehension. I took passage with Captain Rowe, in the schooner Wild Cat, and, after a sail of about twenty-four hours, I found myself near the place of my birth. I had now been absent from it almost, if not quite, five years. I, however, remembered the place very well. I was only about five years old when I left it, to go and live with my old master on Colonel Lloyd's plantation; so that I was now between ten and eleven years old.

We were all ranked together at the valuation. Men and women, old and young, married and single, were ranked with horses, sheep, and swine. There were horses and men, cattle and women, pigs and children, all holding the same rank in the scale of being, and were all sub-

5. *The American Spelling Book* (1783) by Noah Webster, the leading American lexicographer of the time.

jected to the same narrow examination. Silvery-headed age and sprightly youth, maids and matrons, had to undergo the same indelicate inspection. At this moment, I saw more clearly than ever the brutalizing effects of slavery upon both slave and slaveholder.

After the valuation, then came the division. I have no language to express the high excitement and deep anxiety which were felt among us poor slaves during this time. Our fate for life was now to be decided. We had no more voice in that decision than the brutes among whom we were ranked. A single word from the white men was enough—against all our wishes, prayers, and entreaties—to sunder forever the dearest friends, dearest kindred, and strongest ties known to human beings. In addition to the pain of separation, there was the horrid dread of falling into the hands of Master Andrew. He was known to us all as being a most cruel wretch,—a common drunkard, who had, by his reckless mismanagement and profligate dissipation, already wasted a large portion of his father's property. We all felt that we might as well be sold at once to the Georgia traders, as to pass into his hands; for we knew that that would be our inevitable condition,—a condition held by us all in the utmost horror and dread.

I suffered more anxiety than most of my fellow-slaves. I had known what it was to be kindly treated; they had known nothing of the kind. They had seen little or nothing of the world. They were in very deed men and women of sorrow, and acquainted with grief. Their backs had been made familiar with the bloody lash, so that they had become callous; mine was yet tender; for while at Baltimore I got few whippings, and few slaves could boast of a kinder master and mistress than myself; and the thought of passing out of their hands into those of Master Andrew—a man who, but a few days before, to give me a sample of his bloody disposition, took my little brother by the throat, threw him on the ground, and with the heel of his boot stamped upon his head till the blood gushed from his nose and ears—was well calculated to make me anxious as to my fate. After he had committed this savage outrage upon my brother, he turned to me, and said that was the way he meant to serve me one of these days,—meaning, I suppose, when I came into his possession.

Thanks to a kind Providence, I fell to the portion of Mrs. Lucretia, and was sent immediately back to Baltimore, to live again in the family of Master Hugh. Their joy at my return equalled their sorrow at my departure. It was a glad day to me. I had escaped a [fate] worse than lion's jaws. I was absent from Baltimore, for the purpose of valuation and division, just about one month, and it seemed to have been six.

Very soon after my return to Baltimore, my mistress, Lucretia, died, leaving her husband and one child, Amanda; and in a very short time after her death, Master Andrew died. Now all the property of my old master, slaves included, was in the hands of strangers,—strangers who had had nothing to do with accumulating it. Not a slave was left free. All remained slaves, from the youngest to the oldest. If any one thing in my experience, more than another, served to deepen my conviction of the infernal character of slavery, and to fill me with unutterable loathing of slaveholders, it was their base ingratitude to my poor old grandmother. She had served my old master faithfully from youth to old age. She had been the source of all his wealth; she had peopled his plantation with slaves; she had become a great grandmother in his service. She had rocked him in infancy, attended him in childhood, served him through life, and at his death wiped from his icy brow the cold deathsweat, and closed his eyes forever. She was nevertheless left a slave—a slave for life—a slave in the hands of strangers; and in their hands she saw her children, her grandchildren, and her great-grandchildren, divided, like so many sheep, without being gratified with the small privilege of a single word, as to their or her own destiny. And, to cap the climax of their base ingratitude and fiendish barbarity, my grandmother, who was now very old, having outlived my old master and all his children, having seen the beginning and end of all of them, and her present owners finding she was of but little value, her frame already racked with the pains of old age, and complete helplessness fast stealing over her once active limbs, they took her to the woods, built her a little hut, put up a little mud-chimney, and then made her welcome to the privilege of supporting herself there in perfect loneliness; thus virtually turning her out to die! If my poor old grandmother now lives, she lives to suffer in utter loneliness; she lives to remember and mourn over the loss of children, the loss of grandchildren, and the loss of great-grandchildren. They are, in the language of the slave's poet, Whittier,[6]—

> "Gone, gone, sold and gone
> To the rice swamp dank and lone,
> Where the slave-whip ceaseless swings,
> Where the noisome insect stings,
> Where the fever-demon strews
> Poison with the falling dews,
> Where the sickly sunbeams glare
> Through the hot and misty air:—
>   Gone, gone, sold and gone
>   To the rice swamp dank and lone,
>   From Virginia hills and waters—
>   Woe is me, my stolen daughters!"

The hearth is desolate. The children, the unconscious children, who once sang and danced in her presence, are gone. She gropes her way,

6. John Greenleaf Whittier (1807–1892), American poet and abolitionist. The lines Douglass quotes below are from Whittier's antislavery poem *The Farewell of a Virginia Slave Mother to Her Daughters, Sold into Southern Bondage* (1838).

in the darkness of age, for a drink of water. Instead of the voices of her children, she hears by day the moans of the dove, and by night the screams of the hideous owl. All is gloom. The grave is at the door. And now, when weighed down by the pains and aches of old age, when the head inclines to the feet, when the beginning and ending of human existence meet, and helpless infancy and painful old age combine together—at this time, this most needful time, the time for the exercise of that tenderness and affection which children only can exercise toward a declining parent—my poor old grandmother, the devoted mother of twelve children, is left all alone, in yonder little hut, before a few dim embers. She stands—she sits—she staggers—she falls—she groans—she dies—and there are none of her children or grandchildren present, to wipe from her wrinkled brow the cold sweat of death, or to place beneath the sod her fallen remains. Will not a righteous God visit for these things?

In about two years after the death of Mrs. Lucretia, Master Thomas married his second wife. Her name was Rowena Hamilton. She was the eldest daughter of Mr. William Hamilton. Master now lived in St. Michael's. Not long after his marriage, a misunderstanding took place between himself and Master Hugh; and as a means of punishing his brother, he took me from him to live with himself at St. Michael's. Here I underwent another most painful separation. It, however, was not so severe as the one I dreaded at the division of property; for, during this interval, a great change had taken place in Master Hugh and his once kind and affectionate wife. The influence of brandy upon him, and of slavery upon her, had effected a disastrous change in the characters of both; so that, as far as they were concerned, I thought I had little to lose by the change. But it was not to them that I was attached. It was to those little Baltimore boys that I felt the strongest attachment. I had received many good lessons from them, and was still receiving them, and the thought of leaving them was painful indeed. I was leaving, too, without the hope of ever being allowed to return. Master Thomas had said he would never let me return again. The barrier betwixt himself and brother he considered impassable.

I then had to regret that I did not at least make the attempt to carry out my resolution to run away; for the chances of success are tenfold greater from the city than from the country.

I sailed from Baltimore for St. Michael's in the sloop Amanda, Captain Edward Dodson. On my passage, I paid particular attention to the direction which the steamboats took to go to Philadelphia. I found, instead of going down, on reaching North Point they went up the bay, in a north-easterly direction. I deemed this knowledge of the utmost importance. My determination to run away was again revived. I resolved to wait only so long as the offering of a favorable opportunity. When that came, I was determined to be off.

Chapter IX

I have now reached a period of my life when I can give dates. I left Baltimore, and went to live with Master Thomas Auld, at St. Michael's, in March, 1832. It was now more than seven years since I lived with him in the family of my old master, on Colonel Lloyd's plantation. We of course were now almost entire strangers to each other. He was to me a new master, and I to him a new slave. I was ignorant of his temper and disposition; he was equally so of mine. A very short time, however brought us into full acquaintance with each other. I was made acquainted with his wife not less than with himself. They were well matched, being equally mean and cruel. I was now, for the first time during a space of more than seven years, made to feel the painful gnaw-ings of hunger—a something which I had not experienced before since I left Colonel Lloyd's plantation. It went hard enough with me then, when I could look back to no period at which I had enjoyed a suffi-ciency. It was tenfold harder after living in Master Hugh's family, where I had always had enough to eat, and of that which was good. I have said Master Thomas was a mean man. He was so. Not to give a slave enough to eat, is regarded as the most aggravated development of meanness even among slaveholders. The rule is, no matter how coarse the food, only let there be enough of it. This is the theory; and in the part of Maryland from which I came, it is the general practice,—though there are many exceptions. Master Thomas gave us enough of neither coarse nor fine food. There were four slaves of us in the kitchen—my sister Eliza, my aunt Priscilla, Henny, and myself; and we were allowed less than half of a bushel of corn-meal per week, and very little else, either in the shape of meat or vegetables. It was not enough for us to subsist upon. We were therefore reduced to the wretched necessity of living at the expense of our neighbors. This we did by begging and stealing, whichever came handy in the time of need, the one being considered as legitimate as the other. A great many times have we poor creatures been nearly perishing with hunger, when food in abundance lay mould-ering in the safe[7] and smoke-house, and our pious mistress was aware of the fact; and yet that mistress and her husband would kneel every morn-ing, and pray that God would bless them in basket and store!

Bad as all slaveholders are, we seldom meet one destitute of every element of character commanding respect. My master was one of this rare sort. I do not know of one single noble act ever performed by him. The leading trait in his character was meanness; and if there were any other element in his nature, it was made subject to this. He was mean; and, like most other mean men, he lacked the ability to conceal his meanness. Captain Auld was not born a slaveholder. He had been a

---

7. A meat safe is a structure for preserving food.

poor man, master only of a Bay craft. He came into possession of all his slaves by marriage; and of all men, adopted slaveholders are the worst. He was cruel, but cowardly. He commanded without firmness. In the enforcement of his rules he was at times rigid, and at times lax. At times, he spoke to his slaves with the firmness of Napoleon and the fury of a demon; at other times, he might well be mistaken for an inquirer who had lost his way. He did nothing of himself. He might have passed for a lion, but for his ears. In all things noble which he attempted, his own meanness shone most conspicuous. His airs, words, and actions, were the airs, words, and actions of born slaveholders, and, being assumed, were awkward enough. He was not even a good imitator. He possessed all the disposition to deceive, but wanted the power. Having no resources within himself, he was compelled to be the copyist of many, and being such, he was forever the victim of inconsistency; and of consequence he was an object of contempt, and was held as such even by his slaves. The luxury of having slaves of his own to wait upon him was something new and unprepared for. He was a slaveholder without the ability to hold slaves. He found himself incapable of managing his slaves either by force, fear, or fraud. We seldom called him "master;" we generally called him "Captain Auld," and were hardly disposed to title him at all. I doubt not that our conduct had much to do with making him appear awkward, and of consequence fretful. Our want of reverence for him must have perplexed him greatly. He wished to have us call him master, but lacked the firmness necessary to command us to do so. His wife used to insist upon our calling him so, but to no purpose. In August, 1832, my master attended a Methodist camp-meeting[8] held in the Bay-side, Talbot county, and there experienced religion. I indulged a faint hope that his conversion would lead him to emancipate his slaves, and that, if he did not do this, it would, at any rate, make him more kind and humane. I was disappointed in both these respects. It neither made him to be humane to his slaves, nor to emancipate them. If it had any effect on his character, it made him more cruel and hateful in all his ways; for I believe him to have been a much worse man after his conversion than before. Prior to his conversion, he relied upon his own depravity to shield and sustain him in his savage barbarity; but after his conversion, he found religious sanction and support for his slaveholding cruelty. He made the greatest pretensions to piety. His house was the house of prayer. He prayed morning, noon, and night. He very soon distinguished himself among his brethren, and was soon made a class-leader and exhorter. His activity in revivals was great, and he proved himself an instrument in the hands of the church in converting many souls. His house was the preachers' home. They used to take great pleasure in coming there to put up; for while he starved us,

8. A popular form of nineteenth-century evangelical religious gathering.

he stuffed them. We have had three or four preachers there at a time. The names of those who used to come most frequently while I lived there, were Mr. Storks, Mr. Ewery, Mr. Humphry, and Mr. Hickey. I have also seen Mr. George Cookman[9] at our house. We slaves loved Mr. Cookman. We believed him to be a good man. We thought him instrumental in getting Mr. Samuel Harrison, a very rich slaveholder, to emancipate his slaves; and by some means got the impression that he was laboring to effect the emancipation of all the slaves. When he was at our house, we were sure to be called in to prayers. When the others were there, we were sometimes called in and sometimes not. Mr. Cookman took more notice of us than either of the other ministers. He could not come among us without betraying his sympathy for us, and, stupid as we were, we had the sagacity to see it.

While I lived with my master in St. Michael's, there was a white young man, a Mr. Wilson, who proposed to keep a Sabbath school for the instruction of such slaves as might be disposed to learn to read the New Testament. We met but three times, when Mr. West and Mr. Fairbanks, both class-leaders, with many others, came upon with us with sticks and other missiles, drove us off, and forbade us to meet again. Thus ended our little Sabbath school in the pious town of St. Michael's.

I have said my master found religious sanction for his cruelty. As an example, I will state one of many facts going to prove the charge. I have seen him tie up a lame young woman, and whip her with a heavy cowskin upon her naked shoulders, causing the warm red blood to drip; and, in justification of the bloody deed, he would quote this passage of Scripture—"He that knoweth his master's will, and doeth it not, shall be beaten with many stripes."[1]

Master would keep this lacerated young woman tied up in this horrid situation four or five hours at a time. I have known him to tie her up early in the morning, and whip her before breakfast; leave her, go to his store, return at dinner, and whip her again, cutting her in the places already made raw with his cruel lash. The secret of master's cruelty toward "Henny" is found in the fact of her being almost helpless. When quite a child, she fell into the fire, and burned herself horribly. Her hands were so burnt that she never got the use of them. She could do very little but bear heavy burdens. She was to master a bill of expense; and as he was a mean man, she was a constant offence to him. He seemed desirous of getting the poor girl out of existence. He gave her away once to his sister; but, being a poor gift, she was not disposed to keep her. Finally, my benevolent master, to use his own words, "set her adrift to take care of herself." Here was a recently-converted man, holding on upon the mother, and at the same time turning out her helpless

9. A prominent English Methodist minister (1800–1841).
1. Luke 12.47.

child, to starve and die! Master Thomas was one of the many pious
slaveholders who hold slaves for the very charitable purpose of taking
care of them.

My master and myself had quite a number of differences. He found
me unsuitable to his purpose. My city life, he said, had had a very
pernicious effect upon me. It had almost ruined me for every good purpose, and fitted me for every thing which was bad. One of my greatest
faults was that of letting his horse run away, and go down to his father-
in-law's farm, which was about five miles from St. Michael's. I would
then have to go after it. My reason for this kind of carelessness, or care-
fulness, was, that I could always get something to eat when I went there.
Master William Hamilton, my master's father-in-law, always gave his
slaves enough to eat. I never left there hungry, no matter how great the
need of my speedy return. Master Thomas at length said he would stand
it no longer. I had lived with him nine months, during which time he
had given me a number of severe whippings, all to no good purpose. He
resolved to put me out, as he said, to be broken; and, for this purpose,
he let me for one year to a man named Edward Covey. Mr. Covey was
a poor man, a farm-renter. He rented the place upon which he lived, as
also the hands with which he tilled it. Mr. Covey had acquired a very
high reputation for breaking young slaves, and this reputation was of
immense value to him. It enabled him to get his farm tilled with much
less expense to himself than he could have had it done without such a
reputation. Some slaveholders thought it not much loss to allow Mr.
Covey to have their slaves one year, for the sake of training to which
they were subjected, without any other compensation. He could hire
young help with great ease, in consequence of this reputation. Added to
the natural good qualities of Mr. Covey, he was a professor of religion—
a pious soul—a member and a class-leader in the Methodist church. All
of this added weight to his reputation as a "nigger-breaker." I was aware
of all the facts, having been made acquainted with them by a young
man who had lived there. I nevertheless made the change gladly; for I
was sure of getting enough to eat, which is not the smallest consider-
ation to a hungry man.

Chapter X

I left Master Thomas's house, and went to live with Mr. Covey, on
the 1st of January, 1833. I was now, for the first time in my life, a field
hand. In my new employment, I found myself even more awkward than
a country boy appeared to be in a large city. I had been at my new home
but one week before Mr. Covey gave me a very severe whipping, cutting
my back, causing the blood to run, and raising ridges on my flesh as
large as my little finger. The details of this affair are as follows: Mr.
Covey sent me, very early in the morning of one of our coldest days in

the month of January, to the woods, to get a load of wood. He gave me a team of unbroken oxen. He told me which was the in-hand ox, and which the off-hand one.[2] He then tied the end of a large rope around the horns of the in-hand-ox, and gave me the other end of it, and told me, if the oxen started to run, that I must hold on upon the rope. I had never driven oxen before, and of course I was very awkward. I, however, succeeded in getting to the edge of the woods with little difficulty; but I had got a very few rods into the woods, when the oxen took fright, and started full tilt, carrying the cart against trees, and over stumps, in the most frightful manner. I expected every moment that my brains would be dashed out against the trees. After running thus for a considerable distance, they finally upset the cart, dashing it with great force against a tree, and threw themselves into a dense thicket. How I escaped death, I do not know. There I was, entirely alone, in a thick wood, in a place new to me. My cart was upset and shattered, my oxen were entangled among the young trees, and there was none to help me. After a long spell of effort, I succeeded in getting my cart righted, my oxen disentangled, and again yoked to the cart. I now proceeded with my team to the place where I had, the day before, been chopping wood, and loaded my cart pretty heavily, thinking in this way to tame my oxen. I then proceeded on my way home. I had now consumed one half of the day. I got out of the woods safely, and now felt out of danger. I stopped my oxen to open the woods gate; and just as I did so, before I could get hold of my ox-rope, the oxen again started, rushed through the gate, catching it between the wheel and the body of the cart, tearing it to pieces, and coming within a few inches of crushing me against the gate-post. Thus twice, in one short day, I escaped death by the merest chance. On my return, I told Mr. Covey what had happened, and how it happened. He ordered me to return to the woods again immediately. I did so, and he followed on after me. Just as I got into the woods, he came up and told me to stop my cart, and that he would teach me how to trifle away my time, and break gates. He then went to a large gum-tree, and with his axe cut three large switches, and, after trimming them up neatly with his pocket-knife, he ordered me to take off my clothes. I made him no answer, but stood with my clothes on. He repeated his order. I still made him no answer, nor did I move to strip myself. Upon this he rushed at me with the fierceness of a tiger, tore off my clothes, and lashed me till he had worn out his switches, cutting me so savagely as to leave the marks visible for a long time after. This whipping was the first of a number just like it, and for similar offences.

I lived with Mr. Covey one year. During the first six months, of that year, scarce a week passed without his whipping me. I was seldom free from a sore back. My awkwardness was almost always his excuse for

2. The one on the right of a pair hitched to a wagon. "In-hand ox": the one to the left.

whipping me. We were worked fully up to the point of endurance. Long before day we were up, our horses fed, and by the first approach of day we were off to the field with our hoes and ploughing teams. Mr. Covey gave us enough to eat, but scarce time to eat it. We were often less than five minutes taking our meals. We were often in the field from the first approach of day till its last lingering ray had left us; and at saving-fodder time, midnight often caught us in the field binding blades.[3]

Covey would be out with us. The way he used to stand it, was this. He would spend the most of his afternoons in bed. He would then come out fresh in the evening, ready to urge us on with his words, example, and frequently with the whip. Mr. Covey was one of the few slaveholders who could and did work with his hands. He was a hard-working man. He knew by himself just what a man or a boy could do. There was no deceiving him. His work went on in his absence almost as well as in his presence; and he had the faculty of making us feel that he was ever present with us. This he did by surprising us. He seldom approached the spot where we were at work openly, if he could do it secretly. He always aimed at taking us by surprise. Such was his cunning, that we used to call him, among ourselves, "the snake." When we were at work in the cornfield, he would sometimes crawl on his hands and knees to avoid detection, and all at once he would rise nearly in our midst, and scream out, "Ha, ha! Come, come! Dash on, dash on!" This being his mode of attack, it was never safe to stop a single minute. His comings were like a thief in the night. He appeared to us as being ever at hand. He was under every tree, behind every stump, in every bush, and at every window, on the plantation. He would sometimes mount his horse, as if bound to St. Michael's, a distance of seven miles, and in half an hour afterwards you would see him coiled up in the corner of the wood-fence, watching every motion of the slaves. He would, for this purpose, leave his horse tied up in the woods. Again, he would sometimes walk up to us, and give us orders as though he was upon the point of starting on a long journey, turn his back upon us, and make as though he was going to the house to get ready; and, before he would get half way thither, he would turn short and crawl into a fence-corner, or behind some tree, and there watch us till the going down of the sun.

Mr. Covey's *forte* consisted in his power to deceive. His life was devoted to planning and perpetrating the grossest deceptions. Every thing he possessed in the shape of learning or religion, he made conform to his disposition to deceive. He seemed to think himself equal to deceiving the Almighty. He would make a short prayer in the morning, and a long prayer at night; and, strange as it may seem, few men would at times appear more devotional than he. The exercises of his family devotions were always commenced with singing; and, as he was a very

---

3. I.e., of wheat or other plants. "Saving-fodder time": harvest time.

poor singer himself, the duty of raising the hymn generally came upon me. He would read his hymn, and nod at me to commence. I would at times do so; at others, I would not. My non-compliance would almost always produce much confusion. To show himself independent of me, he would start and stagger through with his hymn in the most discordant manner. In this state of mind, he prayed with more than ordinary spirit. Poor man! such was his disposition, and success at deceiving, I do verily believe that he sometimes deceived himself into the solemn belief, that he was a sincere worshiper of the most high God; and this, too, at a time when he may be said to have been guilty of compelling his woman slave to commit the sin of adultery. The facts in the case are these: Mr. Covey was a poor man; he was just commencing in life; he was only able to buy one slave; and, shocking as is the fact, he bought her, as he said, for *a breeder.* This woman was named Caroline. Mr. Covey bought her from Mr. Thomas Lowe, about six miles from St. Michael's. She was a large, able-bodied woman, about twenty years old. She had already given birth to one child, which proved her to be just what he wanted. After buying her, he hired a married man of Mr. Samuel Harrison, to live with him one year; and him he used to fasten up with her every night! The result was, that, at the end of the year, the miserable woman gave birth to twins. At this result Mr. Covey seemed to be highly pleased, both with the man and the wretched woman. Such was his joy, and that of his wife, that nothing they could do for Caroline during her confinement was too good, or too hard, to be done. The children were regarded as being quite an addition to his wealth.

If at any one time of my life more than another, I was made to drink the bitterest dregs of slavery, that time was during the first six months of my stay with Mr. Covey. We were worked in all weathers. It was never too hot or too cold; it could never rain, blow, hail, or snow, too hard for us to work in the field. Work, work, work, was scarcely more the order of the day than of the night. The longest days were too short for him, and the shortest nights too long for him. I was somewhat unmanageable when I first went there, but a few months of this discipline tamed me. Mr. Covey succeeded in breaking me. I was broken in body, soul, and spirit. My natural elasticity was crushed, my intellect languished, the disposition to read departed, the cheerful spark that lingered about my eye died; the dark night of slavery closed in upon me; and behold a man transformed into a brute!

Sunday was my only leisure time. I spent this in a sort of beast-like stupor, between sleep and wake, under some large tree. At times I would rise up, a flash of energetic freedom would dart through my soul, accompanied with a faint beam of hope, that flickered for a moment, and then vanished. I sank down again, mourning over my wretched condition. I was sometimes prompted to take my life, and that of Covey, but was prevented by a combination of hope and fear. My sufferings on this plantation seem now like a dream rather than a stern reality.

Our house stood within a few rods of the Chesapeake Bay, whose broad bosom was ever white with sails from every quarter of the habitable globe. Those beautiful vessels, robed in purest white, so delightful to the eye of freemen, were to me so many shrouded ghosts, to terrify and torment me with thoughts of my wretched condition. I have often, in the deep stillness of a summer's Sabbath, stood all alone upon the lofty banks of that noble bay, and traced, with saddened heart and tearful eye, the countless number of sails moving off to the mighty ocean. The sight of these always affected me powerfully. My thoughts would compel utterance; and there, with no audience but the Almighty, I would pour out my soul's complaint, in my rude way, with an apostrophe to the moving multitude of ships:—

"You are loosed from your moorings, and are free; I am fast in my chains, and am a slave! You move merrily before the gentle gale, and I sadly before the bloody whip! You are freedom's swift-winged angels, that fly round the world; I am confined in bands of iron! O that I were free! Oh, that I were on one of your gallant decks, and under your protecting wing! Alas! betwixt me and you, the turbid waters roll. Go on, go on. O that I could also go! Could I but swim! If I could fly! O, why was I born a man, of whom to make a brute! The glad ship is gone; she hides in the dim distance. I am left in the hottest hell of unending slavery. O God, save me! God, deliver me! Let me be free! Is there any God? Why am I a slave? I will run away. I will not stand it. Get caught, or get clear, I'll try it. I had as well die with ague as the fever. I have only one life to lose. I had as well be killed running as die standing. Only think of it; one hundred miles straight north, and I am free! Try it? Yes! God helping me, I will. It cannot be that I shall live and die a slave. I will take to the water. This very bay shall yet bear me into freedom. The steamboats steered in a north-east course from North Point. I will do the same; and when I get to the head of the bay, I will turn my canoe adrift, and walk straight through Delaware into Pennsylvania. When I get there, I shall not be required to have a pass; I can travel without being disturbed. Let but the first opportunity offer, and, come what will, I am off. Meanwhile, I will try to bear up under the yoke. I am not the only slave in the world. Why should I fret? I can bear as much as any of them. Besides, I am but a boy, and all boys are bound to some one. It may be that my misery in slavery will only increase my happiness when I get free. There is a better day coming."

Thus I used to think, and thus I used to speak to myself; goaded almost to madness at one moment, and at the next reconciling myself to my wretched lot.

I have already intimated that my condition was much worse, during the first six months of my stay at Mr. Covey's, than in the last six. The circumstances leading to the change in Mr. Covey's course toward me form an epoch in my humble history. You have seen how a man was made a slave; you shall see how a slave was made a man. On one of the hottest days of the month of August, 1833, Bill Smith, William Hughes, a slave named Eli, and myself, were engaged in fanning wheat.[4] Hughes was clearing the fanned wheat from before the fan, Eli was turning, Smith was feeding, and I was carrying wheat to the fan. The work was simple, requiring strength rather than intellect; yet, to one entirely unused to such work, it came very hard. About three o'clock of that day, I broke down; my strength failed me; I was seized with a violent aching of the head, attended with extreme dizziness; I trembled in every limb. Finding what was coming, I nerved myself up, feeling it would never do to stop work. I stood as long as I could stagger to the hopper with grain. When I could stand no longer, I fell, and felt as if held down by an immense weight. The fan of course stopped; every one had his own work to do; and no one could do the work of the other, and have his own go on at the same time.

Mr. Covey was at the house, about one hundred yards from the tread-ing-yard where we were fanning. On hearing the fan stop, he left imme-diately, and came to the spot where we were. He hastily inquired what the matter was. Bill answered that I was sick, and there was no one to bring wheat to the fan. I had by this time crawled away under the side of the post and rail-fence by which the yard was enclosed, hoping to find relief by getting out of the sun. He then asked where I was. He was told by one of the hands. He came to the spot, and, after looking at me awhile, asked me what was the matter. I told him as well as I could, for I scarce had strength to speak. He then gave me a savage kick in the side, and told me to get up. I tried to do so, but fell back in the attempt. He gave me another kick, and again told me to rise. I again tried, and succeeded in gaining my feet; but, stooping to get the tub with which I was feeding the fan, I again staggered and fell. While down in this situa-tion, Mr. Covey took up the hickory slat with which Hughes had been striking off the half-bushel measure, and with it gave me a heavy blow upon the head, making a large wound, and the blood ran freely; and with this again told me to get up. I made no effort to comply, having now made up my mind to let him do his worst. In a short time after receiving this blow, my head grew better. Mr. Covey had now left me to my fate. At this moment I resolved, for the first time, to go to my master, enter a complaint, and ask his protection. In order to do this, I must that afternoon walk seven miles; and this, under the circumstances, was truly a severe undertaking. I was exceedingly feeble; made so as much by the kicks and blows which I received, as by the severe fit of sickness to which I had been subjected. I, however, watched my chance, while Covey was looking in an opposite direction, and started for St. Michael's. I suc-

---

4. I.e., separating the wheat from the chaff.

ceeded in getting a considerable distance on my way to the woods, when Covey discovered me, and called after me to come back, threatening what he would do if I did not come. I disregarded both his calls and his threats, and made my way to the woods as fast as my feeble state would allow; and thinking I might be overhauled by him if I kept the road, I walked through the woods, keeping far enough from the road to avoid detection, and near enough to prevent losing my way. I had not gone far before my little strength again failed me. I could go no farther. I fell down, and lay for a considerable time. The blood was yet oozing from the wound on my head. For a time I thought I should bleed to death; and think now that I should have done so, but that the blood so matted my hair as to stop the wound. After lying there about three quarters of an hour, I nerved myself up again, and started on my way, through bogs and briers, barefooted and bareheaded, tearing my feet sometimes at nearly every step; and after a journey of about seven miles, occupying some five hours to perform it, I arrived at master's store. I then presented an appearance enough to affect any but a heart of iron. From the crown of my head to my feet, I was covered with blood. My hair was all clotted with dust and blood; my shirt was stiff with blood. My legs and feet were torn in sundry places with briers and thorns, and were also covered with blood. I suppose I looked like a man who had escaped a den of wild beasts, and barely escaped them. In this state I appeared before my master, humbly entreating him to interpose his authority for my protection. I told him all the circumstances as well as I could, and it seemed, as I spoke, at times to affect him. He would then walk the floor, and seek to justify Covey by saying he expected I deserved it. He asked me what I wanted. I told him, to let me get a new home; that as sure as I lived with Mr. Covey again, I should live with but to die with him; that Covey would surely kill me; he was in a fair way for it. Master Thomas ridiculed the idea that there was any danger of Mr. Covey's killing me, and said that he knew Mr. Covey; that he was a good man, and that he could not think of taking me from him; that, should he do so, he would lose the whole year's wages; that I belonged to Mr. Covey for one year, and that I must go back to him, come what might; and that I must not trouble him with any more stories, or that he would himself *get hold of me.* After threatening me thus, he gave me a very large dose of salts, telling me that I might remain in St. Michael's that night, (it being quite late,) but that I must be off back to Mr. Covey's early in the morning; and that if I did not, he would *get hold of me,* which meant that he would whip me. I remained all night, and, according to his orders, I started off to Covey's in the morning, (Saturday morning), wearied in body and broken in spirit. I got no supper that night, or breakfast that morning. I reached Covey's about nine o'clock; and just as I was getting over the fence that divided Mrs. Kemp's fields from ours, out ran Covey with his cowskin, to give me another whipping. Before he could reach me, I succeeded in getting to the cornfield; and as the corn was very high, it afforded me the means of hiding. He seemed very angry, and searched for me a long time. My behavior was altogether unaccountable. He finally gave up the chase, thinking, I suppose, that I must come home for something to eat; he would give himself no further trouble in looking for me. I spent that day mostly in the woods, having the alternative before me,—to go home and be whipped to death, or stay in the woods and be starved to death. That night, I fell in with Sandy Jenkins, a slave with whom I was somewhat acquainted. Sandy had a free wife[5] who lived about four miles from Mr. Covey's; and it being Saturday, he was on his way to see her. I told him my circumstances, and he very kindly invited me to go home with him. I went home with him, and talked this whole matter over, and got his advice as to what course it was best for me to pursue. I found Sandy an old adviser. He told me, with great solemnity, I must go back to Covey; but that before I went, I must go with him into another part of the woods, where there was a certain *root*, which, if I would take some of it with me, carrying it *always on my right side*, would render it impossible for Mr. Covey, or any other white man, to whip me. He said he had carried it for years; and since he had done so, he had never received a blow, and never expected to while he carried it. I at first rejected the idea, that the simple carrying of a root in my pocket would have any such effect as he had said, and was not disposed to take it; but Sandy impressed the necessity with much earnestness, telling me it could do no harm, if it did no good. To please him, I at length took the root, and, according to his direction, carried it upon my right side. This was Sunday morning. I immediately started for home; and upon entering the yard gate, out came Mr. Covey on his way to meeting. He spoke to me very kindly, bade me drive the pigs from a lot near by, and passed on towards the church. Now, this singular conduct of Mr. Covey really made me begin to think that there was something in the *root* which Sandy had given me; and had it been on any other day than Sunday, I could have attributed the conduct to no other cause then the influence of that root; and as it was, I was half inclined to think the *root* to be something more than I at first had taken it to be. All went well till Monday morning. On this morning, the virtue of the *root* was fully tested. Long before daylight, I was called to go and rub, curry, and feed, the horses. I obeyed, and was glad to obey. But whilst thus engaged, whilst in the act of throwing down some blades from the loft, Mr. Covey entered the stable with a long rope; and just as I was half out of the loft, he caught hold of my legs, and was about tying me. As soon as I found what he was up to, I gave a sudden spring, and as I did so, he holding to my legs, I was brought sprawling on the stable floor. Mr. Covey seemed now to think he had me, and could do what

---

5. I.e., his wife had been either born free or set free and was not legally a slave.

he pleased; but at this moment—from whence came the spirit I don't know—I resolved to fight; and, suiting my action to the resolution, I seized Covey hard by the throat; and as I did so, I rose. He held on to me, and I to him. My resistance was so entirely unexpected, that Covey seemed taken all aback. He trembled like a leaf. This gave me assurance, and I held him uneasy, causing the blood to run where I touched him with the ends of my fingers. Mr. Covey soon called out to Hughes for help. Hughes came, and, while Covey held me, attempted to tie my right hand. While he was in the act of doing so, I watched my chance, and gave him a heavy kick close under the ribs. This kick fairly sickened Hughes, so that he left me in the hands of Mr. Covey. This kick had the effect of not only weakening Hughes, but Covey also. When he saw Hughes bending over with pain, his courage quailed. He asked me if I meant to persist in my resistance. I told him I did, come what might; that he had used me like a brute for six months, and that I was determined to be used so no longer. With that, he strove to drag me to a stick that was lying just out of the stable door. He meant to knock me down. But just as he was leaning over to get the stick, I seized him with both hands by his collar, and brought him by a sudden snatch to the ground. By this time, Bill came. Covey called upon him for assistance. Bill wanted to know what he could do. Covey said, "Take hold of him, take hold of him!" Bill said his master hired him out to work, and not to help to whip me; so he left Covey and myself to fight our own battle out. We were at it for nearly two hours. Covey at length let me go, puffing and blowing at a great rate, saying that if I had not resisted, he would not have whipped me half so much. The truth was, that he had not whipped me at all. I considered him as getting entirely the worst end of the bargain; for he had drawn no blood from me, but I had from him. The whole six months afterwards, that I spent with Mr. Covey, he never laid the weight of his finger upon me in anger. He would occasionally say, he didn't want to get hold of me again. "No," thought I, "you need not; for you will come off worse than you did before."

This battle with Mr. Covey was the turning-point in my career as a slave. It rekindled the few expiring embers of freedom, and revived within me a sense of my own manhood. It recalled the departed self-confidence, and inspired me again with a determination to be free. The gratification afforded by the triumph was a full compensation for whatever else might follow, even death itself. He only can understand the deep satisfaction which I experienced, who has himself repelled by force the bloody arm of slavery. I felt as I never felt before. It was a glorious resurrection, from the tomb of slavery, to the heaven of freedom. My long-crushed spirit rose, cowardice departed, bold defiance took its place; and I now resolved that, however long I might remain a slave in form, the day had passed forever when I could be a slave in fact. I did not hesitate to let it be known of me, that the white man who expected to succeed in whipping, must also succeed in killing me.

From this time I was never again what might be called fairly whipped, though I remained a slave four years afterwards. I had several fights, but was never whipped.

It was for a long time a matter of surprise to me why Mr. Covey did not immediately have me taken by the constable to the whipping-post, and there regularly whipped for the crime of raising my hand against a white man in defence of myself. And the only explanation I can now think of does not entirely satisfy me; but such as it is, I will give it. Mr. Covey enjoyed the most unbounded reputation for being a first-rate overseer and negro-breaker. It was of considerable importance to him. That reputation was at stake; and had he sent me—a boy about sixteen years old—to the public whipping-post, his reputation would have been lost; so, to save his reputation, he suffered me to go unpunished.

My term of actual service to Mr. Edward Covey ended on Christmas day, 1833. The days between Christmas and New Year's day are allowed as holidays; and, accordingly, we were not required to perform any labor, more than to feed and take care of the stock. This time we regarded as our own, by the grace of our masters; and we therefore used or abused it nearly as we pleased. Those of us who had families at a distance, were generally allowed to spend the whole six days in their society. This time, however, was spent in various ways. The staid, sober, thinking and industrious ones of our number would employ themselves in making corn-brooms, mats, horse-collars, and baskets; and another class of us would spend the time hunting opossums, hares, and coons. But by far the larger part engaged in such sports and merriments as playing ball, wrestling, running foot-races, fiddling, dancing, and drinking whisky; and this latter mode of spending the time was by far the most agreeable to the feelings of our master. A slave who would work during the holidays was considered by our masters as scarcely deserving them. He was regarded as one who rejected the favor of his master. It was deemed a disgrace not to get drunk at Christmas; and he was regarded as lazy indeed, who had not provided himself with the necessary means, during the year, to get whisky enough to last him through Christmas.

From what I know of the effect of these holidays upon the slave, I believe them to be among the most effective means in the hands of the slaveholder in keeping down the spirit of insurrection. Were the slaveholders at once to abandon this practice, I have not the slightest doubt it would lead to an immediate insurrection among the slaves. These holidays serve as conductors, or safety-valves, to carry off the rebellious spirit of enslaved humanity. But for these, the slave would be forced up to the wildest desperation; and woe betide the slaveholder, the day he ventures to remove or hinder the operation of those conductors! I warn him that, in such an event, a spirit will go forth in their midst, more to be dreaded than the most appalling earthquake.

The holidays are part and parcel of the gross fraud, wrong, and inhumanity of slavery. They are professedly a custom established by the benevolence of the slaveholders; but I undertake to say, it is the result of selfishness, and one of the grossest frauds committed upon the downtrodden slave. They do not give the slaves this time because they would not like to have their work during its continuance, but because they know it would be unsafe to deprive them of it. This will be seen by the fact, that the slaveholders like to have their slaves spend those days just in such a manner as to make them as glad of their ending as of their beginning. Their object seems to be, to disgust their slaves with freedom, by plunging them into the lowest depths of dissipation. For instance, the slaveholders not only like to see the slave drink of his own accord, but will adopt various plans to make him drunk. One plan is, to make bets on their slaves, as to who can drink the most whisky without getting drunk; and in this way they succeed in getting whole multitudes to drink to excess. Thus, when the slave asks for virtuous freedom, the cunning slaveholder, knowing his ignorance, cheats him with a dose of vicious dissipation, artfully labelled with the name of liberty. The most of us used to drink it down, and the result was just what might be supposed: many of us were led to think that there was little to choose between liberty and slavery. We felt, and very properly too, that we had almost as well be slaves to man as to rum. So, when the holidays ended, we staggered up from the filth of our wallowing, took a long breath, and marched to the field,—feeling, upon the whole, rather glad to go, from what our master had deceived us into a belief was freedom, back to the arms of slavery.

I have said that this mode of treatment is a part of the whole system of fraud and inhumanity of slavery. It is so. The mode here adopted to disgust the slave with freedom, by allowing him to see only the abuse of it, is carried out in other things. For instance, a slave loves molasses; he steals some. His master, in many cases, goes off to town, and buys a large quantity; he returns, takes his whip, and commands the slave to eat the molasses, until the poor fellow is made sick at the very mention of it. The same mode is sometimes adopted to make the slaves refrain from asking for more food than their regular allowance. A slave runs through his allowance, and applies for more. His master is enraged at him; but, not willing to send him off without food, gives him more than is necessary, and compels him to eat it within a given time. Then, if he complains that he cannot eat it, he is said to be satisfied neither full nor fasting, and is whipped for being hard to please! I have an abundance of such illustrations of the same principle, drawn from my own observation, but think the cases I have cited sufficient. The practice is a very common one.

On the first of January, 1834, I left Mr. Covey, and went to live with Mr. William Freeland, who lived about three miles from St. Michael's.

I soon found Mr. Freeland a very different man from Mr. Covey. Though not rich, he was what would be called an educated southern gentleman. Mr. Covey, as I have shown, was a well-trained negro-breaker and slave-driver. The former (slaveholder though he was) seemed to possess some regard for honor, some reverence for justice, and some respect for humanity. The latter seemed totally insensible to all such sentiments. Mr. Freeland had many of the faults peculiar to slaveholders, such as being very passionate and fretful; but I must do him the justice to say, that he was exceedingly free from those degrading vices to which Mr. Covey was constantly addicted. The one was open and frank, and we always knew where to find him. The other was a most artful deceiver, and could be understood only by such as were skilful enough to detect his cunningly-devised frauds. Another advantage I gained in my new master was, he made no pretensions to, or profession of, religion; and this, in my opinion, was truly a great advantage. I assert most unhesitatingly, that the religion of the south is a mere covering for the most horrid crimes,—a justifier of the most appalling barbarity,—a sanctifier of the most hateful frauds,—and a dark shelter under which the darkest, foulest, grossest, and most infernal deeds of slaveholders find the strongest protection. Were I to be again reduced to the chains of slavery, next to that enslavement, I should regard being the slave of a religious master the greatest calamity that could befall me. For of all slaveholders with whom I have ever met, religious slaveholders are the worst. I have ever found them the meanest and basest, the most cruel and cowardly, of all others. It was my unhappy lot not only to belong to a religious slaveholder, but to live in a community of such religionists. Very near Mr. Freeland lived the Rev. Daniel Weeden, and in the same neighborhood lived the Rev. Rigby Hopkins. These were members and ministers in the Reformed Methodist Church. Mr. Weeden owned, among others, a woman slave, whose name I have forgotten. This woman's back, for weeks, was kept literally raw, made so by the lash of this merciless, *religious* wretch. He used to hire hands. His maxim was, Behave well or behave ill, it is the duty of a master occasionally to whip a slave, to remind him of his master's authority. Such was his theory, and such his practice.

Mr. Hopkins was even worse than Mr. Weeden. His chief boast was his ability to manage slaves. The peculiar feature of his government was that of whipping slaves in advance of deserving it. He always managed to have one or more of his slaves to whip every Monday morning. He did this to alarm their fears, and strike terror into those who escaped. His plan was to whip for the smallest offences, to prevent the commission of large ones. Mr. Hopkins could always find some excuse for whipping a slave. It would astonish one, unaccustomed to a slaveholding life, to see with what wonderful ease a slaveholder can find things, of which to make occasion to whip a slave. A mere look, word, or motion,—a mistake, accident, or want of power,—are all matters for which a slave may be whipped at any time. Does a slave look dissatisfied? It is said, he has the devil in him, and it must be whipped out. Does he speak loudly when spoken to by his master? Then he is getting high-minded, and should be taken down a button-hole lower. Does he forget to pull off his hat at the approach of a white person? Then he is wanting in rever-ence, and should be whipped for it. Does he ever venture to vindicate his conduct, when censured for it? Then he is guilty of impudence,— one of the greatest crimes of which a slave can be guilty. Does he ever venture to suggest a different mode of doing things from that pointed out by his master? He is indeed presumptuous, and getting above him-self; and nothing less than a flogging will do for him. Does he, while ploughing, break a plough,—or, while hoeing, break a hoe? It is owing to his carelessness, and for it a slave must always be whipped. Mr. Hop-kins could always find something of this sort to justify the use of the lash, and he seldom failed to embrace such opportunities. There was not a man in the whole county, with whom the slaves who had the getting their own home, would not prefer to live, rather than with this Rev. Mr. Hopkins. And yet there was not a man any where round, who made higher professions of religion, or was more active in revivals— more attentive to the class, love-feast, prayer and preaching meetings, or more devotional in his family,—that prayed earlier, later, louder, and longer,—than this same reverend slave-driver, Rigby Hopkins.

But to return to Mr. Freeland, and to my experience while in his employment. He, like Mr. Covey, gave us enough to eat; but unlike Mr. Covey, he also gave us sufficient time to take our meals. He worked us hard, but always between sunrise and sunset. He required a good deal of work to be done, but gave us good tools with which to work. His farm was large, but he employed hands enough to work it, and with ease, compared with many of his neighbors. My treatment, while in his employment, was heavenly, compared with what I experienced at the hands of Mr. Edward Covey.

Mr. Freeland was himself the owner of but two slaves. Their names were Henry Harris and John Harris. The rest of his hands he hired. These consisted of myself, Sandy Jenkins[6] and Handy Caldwell. Henry and John were quite intelligent, and in a very little while after I went there, I succeeded in creating in them a strong desire to learn how to read. This desire soon sprang up in the others also. They very soon mustered up some old spelling-books, and nothing would do but that I must keep a Sabbath school. I agreed to do so, and accordingly devoted

6. "This is the same man who gave me the roots to prevent my being whipped by Mr. Covey. He was a 'clever soul.' We used frequently to talk about the fight with Covey, and as often as we did so, he would claim my success as the result of the roots he gave me. This superstition is very common among the more ignorant slaves. A slave seldom dies but that his death is attrib-uted to trickery" [Douglass's note].

my Sundays to teaching these my loved fellow-slaves how to read. Neither of them knew his letters when I went there. Some of the slaves of the neighboring farms found what was going on, and also availed themselves of this little opportunity to learn to read. It was understood, among all who came, that there must be as little display about it as possible. It was necessary to keep our religious masters at St. Michael's unacquainted with the fact, that, instead of spending the Sabbath in wrestling, boxing, and drinking whisky, we were trying to learn how to read the will of God; for they had much rather see us engaged in those degrading sports, than to see us behaving like intellectual, moral, and accountable beings. My blood boils as I think of the bloody manner in which Messrs. Wright Fairbanks and Garrison West, both class-leaders, in connection with many others, rushed in upon us with sticks and stones, and broke up our virtuous little Sabbath school, at St. Michael's—all calling themselves Christians! humble followers of the Lord Jesus Christ! But I am again digressing.

I held my Sabbath school at the house of a free colored man, whose name I deem it imprudent to mention; for should it be known, it might embarrass him greatly, though the crime of holding the school was committed ten years ago. I had at one time over forty scholars, and those of the right sort, ardently desiring to learn. They were of all ages, though mostly men and women. I look back to those Sundays with an amount of pleasure not to be expressed. They were great days to my soul. The work of instructing my dear fellow-slaves was the sweetest engagement with which I was ever blessed. We loved each other, and to leave them at the close of the Sabbath was a severe cross indeed. When I think that those precious souls are to-day shut up in the prison-house of slavery, my feelings overcome me, and I am almost ready to ask, "Does a righteous God govern the universe? and for what does he hold the thunders in his right hand, if not to smite the oppressor, and deliver the spoiled out of the hand of the spoiler?" These dear souls came not to Sabbath school because it was popular to do so, nor did I teach them because it was reputable to be thus engaged. Every moment they spent in that school, they were liable to be taken up, and given thirty-nine lashes. They came because they wished to learn. Their minds had been starved by their cruel masters. They had been shut up in mental darkness. I taught them, because it was the delight of my soul to be doing something that looked like bettering the condition of my race. I kept up my school nearly the whole year I lived with Mr. Freeland; and, beside my Sabbath school, I devoted three evenings in the week, during the winter, to teaching the slaves at home. And I have the happiness to know, that several of those who came to Sabbath school learned how to read; and that one, at least, is now free through my agency.

The year passed off smoothly. It seemed only about half as long as the year which preceded it. I went through it without receiving a single blow. I will give Mr. Freeland the credit of being the best master I ever had, *till I became my own master.* For the ease with which I passed the year, I was; however, somewhat indebted to the society of my fellow-slaves. They were noble souls; they not only possessed loving hearts, but brave ones. We were linked and interlinked with each other. I loved them with a love stronger than any thing I have experienced since. It is sometimes said that we slaves do not love and confide in each other. In answer to this assertion, I can say, I never loved any or confided in any people more than my fellow-slaves, and especially those with whom I lived at Mr. Freeland's. I believe we would have died for each other. We never undertook to do any thing, of any importance, without a mutual consultation. We never moved separately. We were one; and as much so by our tempers and dispositions, as by the mutual hardships to which we were necessarily subjected by our condition as slaves.

At the close of the year 1834, Mr. Freeland again hired me of my master, for the year 1835. But, by this time, I began to want to live *upon free land* as well as *with Freeland*; and I was no longer content, there-fore, to live with him or any other slaveholder. I began, with the com-mencement of the year, to prepare myself for a final struggle, which should decide my fate one way or the other. My tendency was upward. I was fast approaching manhood, and year after year had passed, and I was still a slave. These thoughts roused me—I must do something. I therefore resolved that 1835 should not pass without witnessing an attempt, on my part, to secure my liberty. But I was not willing to cher-ish this determination alone. My fellow-slaves were dear to me. I was anxious to have them participate with me in this, my life-giving determi-nation. I therefore, though with great prudence, commenced early to ascertain their views and feelings in regard to their condition, and to imbue their minds with thoughts of freedom. I bent myself to devising ways and means for our escape, and meanwhile strove, on all fitting occasions, to impress them with the gross fraud and inhumanity of slav-ery. I went first to Henry, next to John, then to the others. I found, in them all, warm hearts and noble spirits. They were ready to hear, and ready to act when a feasible plan should be proposed. This was what I wanted. I talked to them of our want of manhood, if we submitted to our enslavement without at least one noble effort to be free. We met often, and consulted frequently, and told our hopes and fears, recounted the difficulties, real and imagined, which we should be called on to meet. At times we were almost disposed to give up, and try to content ourselves with our wretched lot; at others, we were firm and unbending in our determination to go. Whenever we suggested any plan, there was shrinking—the odds were fearful. Our path was beset with the greatest obstacles; and if we succeeded in gaining the end of it, our right to be free was yet questionable—we were yet liable to be returned to bondage. We could see no spot, this side of the ocean, where we could be free.

We knew nothing about Canada. Our knowledge of the north did not extend farther than New York; and to go there, and be forever harassed with the frightful liability of being returned to slavery—with the certainty of being treated tenfold worse than before—the thought was truly a horrible one, and one which it was not easy to overcome. The case sometimes stood thus: At every gate through which we were to pass, we saw a watchman—at every ferry a guard—on every bridge a sentinel—and in every wood a patrol. We were hemmed in upon every side. Here were the difficulties, real or imagined—the good to be sought, and the evil to be shunned. On the one hand, there stood slavery, a stern reality, glaring frightfully upon us,—its robes already crimsoned with the blood of millions, and even now feasting itself greedily upon our own flesh. On the other hand, away back in the dim distance, under the flickering light of the north star, behind some craggy hill or snow-covered mountain, stood a doubtful freedom—half frozen—beckoning us to come and share its hospitality. This in itself was sometimes enough to stagger us; but when we permitted ourselves to survey the road, we were frequently appalled. Upon either side we saw grim death, assuming the most horrid shapes. Now it was starvation, causing us to eat our own flesh;—now we were contending with the waves, and were drowned;—now we were overtaken, and torn to pieces by the fangs of the terrible bloodhound. We were stung by scorpions, chased by wild beasts, bitten by snakes, and finally, after having nearly reached the desired spot,—after swimming rivers, encountering wild beasts, sleeping in the woods, suffering hunger and nakedness,—we were overtaken by our pursuers, and in our resistance, we were shot dead upon the spot! I say, this picture sometimes appalled us, and made us

> "rather bear those ills we had,
> Than fly to others, that we knew not of." [7]

In coming to a fixed determination to run away, we did more than Patrick Henry, when he resolved upon liberty or death. With us it was a doubtful liberty at most, and almost certain death if we failed. For my part, I should prefer death to hopeless bondage.

Sandy, one of our number, gave up the notion, but still encouraged us. Our company then consisted of Henry Harris, John Harris, Henry Bailey, Charles Roberts, and myself. Henry Bailey was my uncle, and belonged to my master. Charles married my aunt: he belonged to my master's father-in-law, Mr. William Hamilton.

The plan we finally concluded upon was, to get a large canoe belonging to Mr. Hamilton, and upon the Saturday night previous to Easter holidays, paddle directly up the Chesapeake Bay. On our arrival at the head of the bay, a distance of seventy or eighty miles from where we

---

7. Shakespeare, *Hamlet* 3.1.81–82.

lived, it was our purpose to turn our canoe adrift, and follow the guidance of the north star till we got beyond the limits of Maryland. Our reason for taking the water route was, that we were less liable to be suspected as runaways; we hoped to be regarded as fishermen; whereas, if we should take the land route, we should be subjected to interruptions of almost every kind. Any one having a white face, and being so disposed, could stop us, and subject us to examination.

The week before our intended start, I wrote several protections, one for each of us. As well as I can remember, they were in the following words, to wit: —

"This is to certify that I, the undersigned, have given the bearer, my servant, full liberty to go to Baltimore, and spend the Easter holidays. Written with mine own hand, &c., 1835.

"WILLIAM HAMILTON,
"Near St. Michael's, in Talbot county, Maryland."

We were not going to Baltimore; but, in going up the bay, we went toward Baltimore, and these protections were only intended to protect us while on the bay.

As the time drew near for our departure, our anxiety became more and more intense. It was truly a matter of life and death with us. The strength of our determination was about to be fully tested. At this time, I was very active in explaining every difficulty, removing every doubt, dispelling every fear, and inspiring all with the firmness indispensable to success in our undertaking; assuring them that half was gained the instant we made the move; we had talked long enough; we were now ready to move; if not now, we never should be; and if we did not intend to move now, we had as well fold our arms, sit down, and acknowledge ourselves fit only to be slaves. This, none of us were prepared to acknowledge. Every man stood firm; and at our last meeting, we pledged ourselves afresh, in the most solemn manner, that, at the time appointed, we would certainly start in pursuit of freedom. This was in the middle of the week, at the end of which we were to be off. We went, as usual, to our several fields of labor, but with bosoms highly agitated with thoughts of our truly hazardous undertaking. We tried to conceal our feelings as much as possible; and I think we succeeded very well.

After a painful waiting, the Saturday morning, whose night was to witness our departure, came. I hailed it with joy, bring what of sadness it might. Friday night was a sleepless one for me. I probably felt more anxious than the rest, because I was, by common consent, at the head of the whole affair. The responsibility of success or failure lay heavily upon me. The glory of the one, and the confusion of the other, were alike mine. The first two hours of that morning were such as I never experienced before, and hope never to again. Early in the morning, we went, as usual, to the field. We were spreading manure; and all at once, while thus engaged, I was overwhelmed with an indescribable feeling, in the fulness of which I turned to Sandy, who was near by, and said, "We are betrayed!" "Well," said he, "that thought has this moment struck me." We said no more. I was never more certain of any thing. The horn was blown as usual, and we went up from the field to the house for breakfast. I went for the form, more than for want of any thing to eat that morning. Just as I got to the house, in looking out at the lane gate, I saw four white men, with two colored men. The white men were on horseback, and the colored ones were walking behind, as if tied. I watched them a few moments till they got up to our lane gate. Here they halted, and tied the colored men to the gate-post. I was not yet certain as to what the matter was. In a few moments, in rode Mr. Hamilton, with a speed betokening great excitement. He came to the door, and inquired if Master William was in. He was told he was at the barn. Mr. Hamilton, without dismounting, rode up to the barn with extraordinary speed. In a few moments, he and Mr. Freeland returned to the house. By this time, the three constables rode up, and in great haste dismounted, tied their horses, and met Master William and Mr. Hamilton returning from the barn; and after talking awhile, they all walked up to the kitchen door. There was no one in the kitchen but myself and John. Henry and Sandy were up at the barn. Mr. Freeland put his head in at the door, and called me by name, saying, there were some gentlemen at the door who wished to see me. I stepped to the door, and inquired what they wanted. They at once seized me, and, without giving me any satisfaction, tied me—lashing my hands closely together. I insisted upon knowing what the matter was. They at length said, that they had learned I had been in a "scrape," and that I was to be examined before my master; and if their information proved false, I should not be hurt.

In a few moments, they succeeded in tying John. They then turned to Henry, who had by this time returned, and commanded him to cross his hands. "I won't!" said Henry, in a firm tone, indicating his readiness to meet the consequences of his refusal. "Won't you?" said Tom Graham, the constable. "No, I won't!" said Henry, in a still stronger tone. With this, two of the constables pulled out their shining pistols, and swore, by their Creator, that they would make him cross his hands or kill him. Each cocked his pistol, and, with fingers on the trigger, walked up to Henry, saying, at the same time, if he did not cross his hands, they would blow his damned heart out. "Shoot me, shoot me!" said Henry; "you can't kill me but once. Shoot, shoot,—and be damned! *I won't be tied!*" This he said in a tone of loud defiance; and at the same time, with a motion as quick as lightning, he with one single stroke dashed the pistols from the hand of each constable. As he did this, all hands fell upon him, and, after beating him some time, they finally overpowered him, and got him tied.

During the scuffle, I managed, I know not how, to get my pass out, and, without being discovered, put it into the fire. We were all now tied; and just as we were to leave for Easton jail, Betsy Freeland, mother of William Freeland, came to the door with her hands full of biscuits, and divided them between Henry and John. She then delivered herself of a speech, to the following effect:—addressing herself to me, she said, "You devil! You yellow devil! it was you that put it into the heads of Henry and John to run away. But for you, you long-legged mulatto devil! Henry nor John would never have thought of such a thing." I made no reply, and was immediately hurried off towards St. Michael's. Just a moment previous to the scuffle with Henry, Mr. Hamilton suggested the propriety of making a search for the protections which he had understood Frederick had written for himself and the rest. But, just at the moment he was about carrying his proposal into effect, his aid was needed in helping to tie Henry; and the excitement attending the scuffle caused them either to forget, or to deem it unsafe, under the circumstances, to search. So we were not yet convicted of the intention to run away.

When we got about half way to St. Michael's, while the constables having us in charge were looking ahead, Henry inquired of me what he should do with his pass. I told him to eat it with his biscuit, and own nothing; and we passed the word around, "Own nothing;" and "Own nothing!" said we all. Our confidence in each other was unshaken. We were resolved to succeed or fail together, after the calamity had befallen us as much as before. We were now prepared for any thing. We were to be dragged that morning fifteen miles behind horses, and then to be placed in the Easton jail. When we reached St. Michael's, we underwent a sort of examination. We all denied that we ever intended to run away. We did this more to bring out the evidence against us, than from any hope of getting clear of being sold; for, as I have said, we were ready for that. The fact was, we cared but little where we went, so we went together. Our greatest concern was about separation. We dreaded that more than any thing this side of death. We found the evidence against us to be the testimony of one person; our master would not tell who it was; but we came to a unanimous decision among ourselves as to who their informant was. We were sent off to the jail at Easton. When we got there, we were delivered up to the sheriff, Mr. Joseph Graham, and by him placed in jail. Henry, John, and myself, were placed in one room together—Charles, and Henry Bailey, in another. Their object in separating us was to hinder concert.

We had been in jail scarcely twenty minutes, when a swarm of slave traders, and agents for slave traders, flocked into jail to look at us, and to ascertain if we were for sale. Such a set of beings I never saw before! I felt myself surrounded by so many fiends from perdition. A band of pirates never looked more like their father, the devil. They laughed and grinned over us, saying, "Ah, my boys! we have got you, haven't we?"

And after taunting us in various ways, they one by one went into an examination of us, with intent to ascertain our value. They would impudently ask us if we would not like to have them for our masters. We would make them no answer, and leave them to find out as best they could. Then they would curse and swear at us, telling us that they could take the devil out of us in a very little while, if we were only in their hands.

While in jail, we found ourselves in much more comfortable quarters than we expected when we went there. We did not get much to eat, nor that which was very good; but we had a good clean room, from the windows of which we could see what was going on in the street, which was very much better than though we had been placed in one of the dark, damp cells. Upon the whole, we got along very well, so far as the jail and its keeper were concerned. Immediately after the holidays were over, contrary to all our expectations, Mr. Hamilton and Mr. Freeland came up to Easton, and took Charles, the two Henrys, and John, out of jail, and carried them home, leaving me alone. I regarded this separation as a final one. It caused me more pain than any thing else in the whole transaction. I was ready for any thing rather than separation. I supposed that they had consulted together, and had decided that, as I was the whole cause of the intention of the others to run away, it was hard to make the innocent suffer with the guilty; and that they had, therefore, concluded to take the others home, and sell me, as a warning to the others that remained. It is due to the noble Henry to say, he seemed almost as reluctant at leaving the prison as at leaving home to come to the prison. But we knew we should, in all probability, be separated, if we were sold; and since he was in their hands, he concluded to go peaceably home.

I was now left to my fate. I was all alone, and within the walls of a stone prison. But a few days before, and I was full of hope. I expected to have been safe in a land of freedom; but now I was covered with gloom, sunk down to the utmost despair. I thought the possibility of freedom was gone. I was kept in this way about one week, at the end of which, Captain Auld, my master, to my surprise and utter astonishment, came up, and took me out, with the intention of sending me, with a gentleman of his acquaintance, into Alabama. But, from some cause or other, he did not send me to Alabama, but concluded to send me back to Baltimore, to live again with his brother Hugh, and to learn a trade.

Thus, after an absence of three years and one month, I was once more permitted to return to my old home at Baltimore. My master sent me away, because there existed against me a very great prejudice in the community, and he feared I might be killed.

In a few weeks after I went to Baltimore, Master Hugh hired me to Mr. William Gardner, an extensive ship-builder, on Fell's Point. I was put there to learn how to calk. It, however, proved a very unfavorable place for the accomplishment of this object. Mr. Gardner was engaged that spring in building two large man-of-war brigs, professedly for the Mexican government. The vessels were to be launched in the July of that year, and in failure thereof, Mr. Gardner was to lose a considerable sum; so that when I entered, all was hurry. There was no time to learn any thing. Every man had to do that which he knew how to do. In entering the ship-yard, my orders from Mr. Gardner were, to do whatever the carpenters commanded me to do. This was placing me at the beck and call of about seventy-five men. I was to regard all these as masters. Their word was to be my law. My situation was a most trying one. At times I needed a dozen pair of hands. I was called a dozen ways in the space of a single minute. Three or four voices would strike my ear at the same moment. It was—"Fred., come help me to cant this timber here."—"Fred., come carry this timber yonder."—"Fred., bring that roller here."—"Fred., go get a fresh can of water."—"Fred., come help saw off the end of this timber."—"Fred., go quick, and get the crowbar."—"Fred., hold on the end of this fall."[8]—"Fred., go to the blacksmith's shop, and get a new punch."—"Hurra, Fred.! run and bring me a cold chisel."—"I say, Fred., bear a hand, and get up a fire as quick as lightning under that steam-box."—"Halloo, nigger! come, turn this grindstone."—"Come, come! move, move! and bowse[9] this timber forward."—"I say, darky, blast your eyes, why don't you heat up some pitch?"—"Halloo! halloo! halloo!" (Three voices at the same time.) "Come here!—Go there!—Hold on where you are! Damn you, if you move, I'll knock your brains out!"

This was my school for eight months; and I might have remained there longer, but for a most horrid fight I had with four of the white apprentices, in which my left eye was nearly knocked out, and I was horribly mangled in other respects. The facts in the case were these: Until a very little while after I went there, white and black ship-carpenters worked side by side, and no one seemed to see any impropriety in it. All hands seemed to be very well satisfied. Many of the black carpenters were freemen. Things seemed to be going on very well. All at once, the white carpenters knocked off, and said they would not work with free colored workmen. Their reason for this, as alleged, was, that if free colored carpenters were encouraged, they would soon take the trade into their own hands, and poor white men would be thrown out of employment. They therefore felt called upon at once to put a stop to it. And, taking advantage of Mr. Gardner's necessities, they broke off, swearing they would work no longer, unless he would discharge his black carpenters. Now, though this did not extend to me in form, it did reach me in fact. My fellow-apprentices very soon began to feel it

8. Nautical term for the free end of a rope of a tackle or hoisting device.
9. To haul the timber by pulling on the rope.

degrading to them to work with me. They began to put on airs, and talk about the "niggers" taking the country, saying we all ought to be killed; and, being encouraged by the journeymen, they commenced making my condition as hard as they could, by hectoring me around, and sometimes striking me. I, of course, kept the vow I made after the fight with Mr. Covey, and struck back again, regardless of consequences; and while I kept them from combining, I succeeded very well; for I could whip the whole of them, taking them separately. They, however, at length combined, and came upon me, armed with sticks, stones, and heavy handspikes. One came in front with a half brick. There was one at each side of me, and one behind me. While I was attending to those in front, and on either side, the one behind ran up with the handspike, and struck me a heavy blow upon the head. It stunned me. I fell, and with this they all ran upon me, and fell to beating me with their fists. I let them lay on for a while, gathering strength. In an instant, I gave a sudden surge, and rose to my hands and knees. Just as I did that, one of their number gave me, with his heavy boot, a powerful kick in the left eye. My eyeball seemed to have burst. When they saw my eye closed, and badly swollen, they left me. With this I seized the handspike, and for a time pursued them. But here the carpenters interfered, and I thought I might as well give it up. It was impossible to stand my hand against so many. All this took place in sight of not less than fifty white ship-carpenters, and not one interposed a friendly word; but some cried, "Kill the damned nigger! Kill him! kill him! He struck a white person." I found my only chance for life was in flight. I succeeded in getting away without an additional blow, and barely so; for to strike a white man is death by Lynch law,[1]—and that was the law in Mr. Gardner's ship yard; nor is there much of any other out of Mr. Gardner's ship-yard.

I went directly home, and told the story of my wrongs to Master Hugh; and I am happy to say of him, irreligious as he was, his conduct was heavenly, compared with that of his brother Thomas under similar circumstances. He listened attentively to my narration of the circumstances leading to the savage outrage, and gave many proofs of his strong indignation at it. The heart of my once overkind mistress was again melted into pity. My puffed-out eye and blood-covered face moved her to tears. She took a chair by me, washed the blood from my face, and, with a mother's tenderness, bound up my head, covering the wounded eye with a lean piece of fresh beef. It was almost compensation for my suffering to witness, once more, a manifestation of kindness from this, my once affectionate old mistress. Master Hugh was very much enraged. He gave expression to his feelings by pouring out curses upon the heads of those who did the deed. As soon as I got a little the better of my bruises, he took me with him to Esquire Watson's, on Bond Street, to

1. I.e., to be subject to lynching, without benefit of legal procedures.

see what could be done about the matter. Mr. Watson inquired who saw the assault committed. Master Hugh told him it was done in Mr. Gardner's ship-yard, at midday, where there were a large company of men at work. "As to that," he said, "the deed was done, and there was no question as to who did it." His answer was, he could do nothing in the case, unless some white man would come forward and testify. He could issue no warrant on my word. If I had been killed in the presence of a thousand colored people, their testimony combined would have been insufficient to have arrested one of the murderers. Master Hugh, for once, was compelled to say this state of things was too bad. Of course, it was impossible to get any white man to volunteer his testimony in my behalf, and against the white young men. Even those who may have sympathized with me were not prepared to do this. It required a degree of courage unknown to them to do so; for just at that time, the slightest manifestation of humanity toward a colored person was denounced as abolitionism, and that name subjected its bearer to frightful liabilities. The watchwords of the bloody-minded in that region, and in those days, were, "Damn the abolitionists!" and "Damn the niggers!" There was nothing done, and probably nothing would have been done if I had been killed. Such was, and such remains, the state of things in the Christian city of Baltimore.

Master Hugh, finding he could get no redress, refused to let me go back again to Mr. Gardner. He kept me himself, and his wife dressed my wound till I was again restored to health. He then took me into the ship-yard of which he was foreman, in the employment of Mr. Walter Price. There I was immediately set to calking, and very soon learned the art of using my mallet and irons. In the course of one year from the time I left Mr. Gardner's, I was able to command the highest wages given to the most experienced calkers. I was now of some importance to my master. I was bringing him from six to seven dollars per week. I sometimes brought him nine dollars per week: my wages were a dollar and a half a day. After learning how to calk, I sought my own employment, made my own contracts, and collected the money which I earned. My pathway became much more smooth than before; my condition was now much more comfortable. When I could get no calking to do, I did nothing. During these leisure times, those old notions about freedom would steal over me again. When in Mr. Gardner's employment, I was kept in such a perpetual whirl of excitement, I could think of nothing, scarcely, but my life; and in thinking of my life, I almost forgot my liberty. I have observed this in my experience of slavery,—that whenever my condition was improved, instead of its increasing my contentment, it only increased my desire to be free, and set me to thinking of plans to gain my freedom. I have found that, to make a contented slave, it is necessary to make a thoughtless one. It is necessary to darken his moral and mental vision, and, as far as possible, to annihilate the power of reason. He must be able to detect no inconsistencies in slavery; he must be made to feel that slavery is right; and he can be brought to that only when he ceases to be a man.

I was now getting, as I have said, one dollar and fifty cents per day. I contracted for it; I earned it; it was paid to me; it was rightfully my own; yet, upon each returning Saturday night, I was compelled to deliver every cent of that money to Master Hugh. And why? Not because he earned it,—not because he had any hand in earning it,—not because I owed it to him,—nor because he possessed the slightest shadow of a right to it; but solely because he had the power to compel me to give it up. The right of the grim-visaged pirate upon the high seas is exactly the same.

Chapter XI

I now come to that part of my life during which I planned, and finally succeeded in making, my escape from slavery. But before narrating any of the peculiar circumstances, I deem it proper to make known my intention not to state all the facts connected with the transaction. My reasons for pursuing this course may be understood from the following: First, were I to give a minute statement of all the facts, it is not only possible, but quite probable, that others would thereby be involved in the most embarrassing difficulties. Secondly, such a statement would most undoubtedly induce greater vigilance on the part of slaveholders than has existed heretofore among them; which would, of course, be the means of guarding a door whereby some dear brother bondman might escape his galling chains. I deeply regret the necessity that impels me to suppress any thing of importance connected with my experience in slavery. It would afford me great pleasure indeed, as well as materially add to the interest of my narrative, were I at liberty to gratify a curiosity, which I know exists in the minds of many, by an accurate statement of all the facts pertaining to my most fortunate escape. But I must deprive myself of this pleasure, and the curious of the gratification which such a statement would afford. I would allow myself to suffer under the greatest imputations which evil-minded men might suggest, rather than exculpate myself, and thereby run the hazard of closing the slightest avenue by which a brother slave might clear himself of the chains and fetters of slavery.

I have never approved of the very public manner in which some of our western friends have conducted what they call the *underground railroad*, but which, I think, by their own declarations, has been made most emphatically the *upperground railroad*. I honor those good men and women for their noble daring, and applaud them for willingly subjecting themselves to bloody persecution, by openly avowing their participation in the escape of slaves. I, however, can see very little good resulting from such a course, either to themselves or the slaves escaping; while, upon the other hand, I see and feel assured that those open declarations are a positive evil to the slaves remaining, who are seeking to escape. They do nothing towards enlightening the slave, whilst they do much towards enlightening the master. They stimulate him to greater watchfulness, and enhance his power to capture his slave. We owe something to the slaves south of the line as well as to those north of it; and in aiding the latter on their way to freedom, we should be careful to do nothing which would be likely to hinder the former from escaping from slavery. I would keep the merciless slaveholder profoundly ignorant of the means of flight adopted by the slave. I would leave him to imagine himself surrounded by myriads of invisible tormentors, ever ready to snatch from his infernal grasp his trembling prey. Let him be left to feel his way in the dark; let darkness commensurate with his crime hover over him; and let him feel that at every step he takes, in pursuit of the flying bondman, he is running the frightful risk of having his hot brains dashed out by an invisible agency. Let us render the tyrant no aid; let us nòt hold the light by which he can trace the footprints of our flying brother. But enough of this. I will now proceed to the statement of those facts, connected with my escape, for which I am alone responsible, and for which no one can be made to suffer but myself.

In the early part of the year 1838, I became quite restless. I could see no reason why I should, at the end of each week, pour the reward of my toil into the purse of my master. When I carried to him my weekly wages, he would, after counting the money, look me in the face with a robber-like fierceness, and say, "Is this all?" He was satisfied with nothing less than the last cent. He would, however, when I made him six dollars, sometimes give me six cents, to encourage me. It had the opposite effect. I regarded it as a sort of admission of my right to the whole. The fact that he gave me any part of my wages was proof, to my mind, that he believed me entitled to the whole of them. I always felt worse for having received any thing; for I feared that the giving me a few cents would ease his conscience, and make him feel himself to be a pretty honorable sort of robber. My discontent grew upon me. I was ever on the look-out for means of escape; and, finding no direct means, I determined to try to hire my time, with a view of getting money with which to make my escape. In the spring of 1838, when Master Thomas came to Baltimore to purchase his spring goods, I got an opportunity, and applied to him to allow me to hire my time. He unhesitatingly refused my request, and told me this was another stratagem by which to escape. He told me I could go nowhere but that he could get me; and that, in the event of my running away, he should spare no pains in his efforts to catch me. He exhorted me to content myself, and be obedient. He told me, if I would be happy, I must lay out no plans for the future. He said, if I behaved myself properly, he would take care of me. Indeed, he advised me to complete thoughtlessness of the future, and taught me to depend solely upon him for happiness. He seemed to see fully the pressing necessity of setting aside my intellectual nature, in order to [insure] contentment in slavery. But in spite of him, and even in spite of myself, I continued to think, and to think about the injustice of my enslavement, and the means of escape.

About two months after this, I applied to Master Hugh for the privilege of hiring my time. He was not acquainted with the fact that I had applied to Master Thomas, and had been refused. He too, at first, seemed disposed to refuse; but, after some reflection, he granted me the privilege, and proposed the following terms: I was to be allowed all my time, make all contracts with those for whom I worked, and find my own employment; and, in return for this liberty, I was to pay him three dollars at the end of each week; find myself in calking tools, and in board and clothing. My board was two dollars and a half per week. This, with the wear and tear of clothing and calking tools, made my regular expenses about six dollars per week. This amount I was compelled to make up, or relinquish the privilege of hiring my time. Rain or shine, work or no work, at the end of each week the money must be forthcoming, or I must give up my privilege. This arrangement, it will be perceived, was decidedly in my master's favor. It relieved him of all need of looking after me. His money was sure. He received all the benefits of slaveholding without its evils; while I endured all the evils of a slave, and suffered all the care and anxiety of a freeman. I found it a hard bargain. But, hard as it was, I thought it better than the old mode of getting along. It was a step towards freedom to be allowed to bear the responsibilities of a freeman, and I was determined to hold on upon it. I bent myself to the work of making money. I was ready to work at night as well as day, and by the most untiring perseverance and industry, I made enough to meet my expenses, and lay up a little money every week. I went on thus from May till August. Master Hugh then refused to allow me to hire my time longer. The ground for his refusal was a failure on my part, one Saturday night, to pay him for my week's time. This failure was occasioned by my attending a camp meeting about ten miles from Baltimore. During the week, I had entered into an engagement with a number of young friends to start from Baltimore to the camp ground early Saturday evening; and being detained by my employer, I was unable to get down to Master Hugh's without disappointing the company. I knew that Master Hugh was in no special need of the money that night. I therefore decided to go to camp meeting, and upon my return pay him the three dollars. I staid at the camp meeting one day longer than I intended when I left. But as soon as I returned, I called upon him to pay him what he considered his due. I found him very angry; he could scarce restrain his wrath. He said he had a great mind to give me a severe whipping. He wished to know how I dared go out of the city without asking his permission. I told him I hired my time, and while I paid him the price which he asked for it, I did not know that I was bound to ask him when and where I should go. This reply troubled him; and, after reflecting a few moments, he turned to me, and said I should hire my time no longer; that the next thing he should know of, I would be running away. Upon the same plea, he told me to bring my tools and clothing home forthwith. I did so; but instead of seeking work, as I had been accustomed to do previously to hiring my time, I spent the whole week without the performance of a single stroke of work. I did this in retaliation. Saturday night, he called upon me as usual for my week's wages. I told him I had no wages; I had done no work that week. Here we were upon the point of coming to blows. He raved, and swore his determination to get hold of me. I did not allow myself a single word; but was resolved, if he laid the weight of his hand upon me, it should be blow for blow. He did not strike me, but told me that he would find me in constant employment in future. I thought the matter over during the next day, Sunday, and finally resolved upon the third day of September, as the day upon which I would make a second attempt to secure my freedom. I now had three weeks during which to prepare for my journey. Early on Monday morning, before Master Hugh had time to make any engagement for me, I went out and got employment of Mr. Butler, at his ship-yard near the drawbridge, upon what is called the City Block, thus making it unnecessary for him to seek employment for me. At the end of the week, I brought him between eight and nine dollars. He seemed very well pleased, and asked me why I did not do the same the week before. He little knew what my plans were. My object in working steadily was to remove any suspicion he might entertain of my intent to run away; and in this I succeeded admirably. I suppose he thought I was never better satisfied with my condition than at the very time during which I was planning my escape. The second week passed, and again I carried him my full wages; and so well pleased was he, that he gave me twenty-five cents, (quite a large sum for a slaveholder to give a slave), and bade me to make a good use of it. I told him I would.

Things went on without very smoothly indeed, but within there was trouble. It is impossible for me to describe my feelings as the time of my contemplated start drew near. I had a number of warm-hearted friends in Baltimore,—friends that I loved almost as I did my life,—and the thought of being separated from them forever was painful beyond expression. It is my opinion that thousands would escape from slavery, who now remain, but for the strong cords of affection that bind them to their friends. The thought of leaving my friends was decidedly the most painful thought with which I had to contend. The love of them was my tender point, and shook my decision more than all things else. Besides the pain of separation, the dread and apprehension of a failure exceeded what I had experienced at my first attempt. The appalling defeat I then sustained returned to torment me. I felt assured that, if I failed in this attempt, my case would be a hopeless one—it would seal my fate as a slave forever. I could not hope to get off with any thing less than the severest punishment, and being placed beyond the means of escape. It required no very vivid imagination to depict the most frightful scenes through which I should have to pass, in case I failed. The wretchedness of slavery, and the blessedness of freedom, were perpetually before me. It was life and death with me. But I remained firm, and, according to my resolution, on the third day of September, 1838, I left my chains, and succeeded in reaching New York without the slightest interruption of any kind.[2] How I did so,—what means I adopted,—what direction I travelled, and by what mode of conveyance,—I must leave unexplained, for the reasons before mentioned.

I have been frequently asked how I felt when I found myself in a free State. I have never been able to answer the question with any satisfaction to myself. It was a moment of the highest excitement I ever experienced. I suppose I felt as one may imagine the unarmed mariner to feel when he is rescued by a friendly man-of-war from the pursuit of a pirate. In writing to a dear friend, immediately after my arrival at New York, I said I felt like one who had escaped a den of hungry lions. This state of mind, however, very soon subsided; and I was again seized with a feeling of great insecurity and loneliness. I was yet liable to be taken back, and subjected to all the tortures of slavery. This in itself was enough to damp the ardor of my enthusiasm. But the loneliness overcame me. There I was in the midst of thousands, and yet a perfect stranger; without home and without friends, in the midst of thousands of my own brethren— children of a common Father, and yet I dared not to unfold to any one of them my sad condition. I was afraid to speak to any one for fear of speaking to the wrong one, and thereby falling into the hands of money-loving kidnappers, whose business it was to lie in wait for the panting fugitive, as the ferocious beasts of the forest lie in wait for their prey. The motto which I adopted when I started from slavery was this—"Trust no man!" I saw in every white man an enemy, and in almost every colored man cause for distrust. It was a most painful situation; and, to understand it, one must needs experience it, or imagine himself in similar circumstances. Let him be a fugitive slave in a strange land—a land given up to be the hunting-ground for slaveholders—whose inhabitants are legalized kidnappers—where he is every moment subjected to the terrible liability of being seized upon by his fellow-men, as the hideous crocodile seizes upon his prey!—I say, let him place himself in my situa-

---

2. See "Douglass on His Escape from Slavery," below, pp. 104–11.

tion—without home or friends—without money or credit—wanting shelter, and no one to give it—wanting bread, and no money to buy it,—and at the same time let him feel that he is pursued by merciless men-hunters, and in total darkness as to what to do, where to go, or where to stay,—perfectly helpless both as to the means of defence and means of escape,—in the midst of plenty, yet suffering the terrible gnaw-ings of hunger,—in the midst of houses, yet having no home,—among fellow-men, yet feeling as if in the midst of wild beasts, whose greediness to swallow up the trembling and half-famished fugitive is only equalled by that with which the monsters of the deep swallow up the helpless fish upon which they subsist,—I say, let him be placed in this most trying situation,—the situation in which I was placed,—then, and not till then, will he fully appreciate the hardships of, and know how to sympathize with, the toil-worn and whip-scarred fugitive slave.

Thank Heaven, I remained but a short time in this distressed situa-tion. I was relieved from it by the humane hand of MR. DAVID RUG-GLES,[3] whose vigilance, kindness, and perseverance, I shall never forget. I am glad of an opportunity to express, as far as words can, the love and gratitude I bear him. Mr. Ruggles is now afflicted with blindness, and is himself in need of the same kind offices which he was once so forward in the performance of toward others. I had been in New York but a few days, when Mr. Ruggles sought me out, and very kindly took me to his boarding-house at the corner of Church and Lespenard Streets. Mr. Ruggles was then very deeply engaged in the memorable *Darg* case,[4] as well as attending to a number of other fugitive slaves; devising ways and means for their successful escape; and, though watched and hemmed in on almost every side, he seemed to be more than a match for his enemies.

Very soon after I went to Mr. Ruggles, he wished to know of me where I wanted to go; as he deemed it unsafe for me to remain in New York. I told him I was a calker, and should like to go where I could get work. I thought of going to Canada; but he decided against it, and in favor of my going to New Bedford, thinking I should be able to get work there at my trade. At this time, Anna,[5] my intended wife, came on; for I wrote to her immediately after my arrival at New York, (notwithstanding my homeless, houseless, and helpless condition,) informing her of my suc-cessful flight, and wishing her to come on forthwith. In a few days after her arrival, Mr. Ruggles called in the Rev. J. W. C. Pennington,[6] who,

3. A black journalist and abolitionist famous for his aid to fugitive slaves (1810–1849); Douglass stayed in Ruggles's house on his way to New Bedford in 1838.
4. Ruggles had been arrested in 1839 and charged with harboring a fugitive slave who had escaped from John P. Darg of Arkansas.
5. "She was free" [Douglass's note]. Anna Murray (d. 1882) had been a self-supporting domestic worker and a member of the East Baltimore Mental Improvement Society before moving to New York to marry.
6. Fugitive slave (also from Maryland's Eastern Shore), abolitionist orator, and Congregationalist pastor (1807–1870).

in the presence of Mr. Ruggles, Mrs. Michaels, and two or three others, performed the marriage ceremony, and gave us a certificate, of which the following is an exact copy:—

"This may certify, that I joined together in holy matrimony Frederick Johnson[7] and Anna Murray, as man and wife, in the presence of Mr. David Ruggles and Mrs. Michaels.

"James W. C. Pennington
"New York, Sept. 15, 1838."

Upon receiving this certificate, and a five-dollar bill from Mr. Ruggles, I shouldered one part of our baggage, and Anna took up the other, and we set out forthwith to take passage on board of the steamboat John W. Richmond for Newport, on our way to New Bedford. Mr. Ruggles gave me a letter to a Mr. Shaw in Newport, and told me, in case my money did not serve me to New Bedford, to stop in Newport and obtain further assistance; but upon our arrival at Newport, we were so anxious to get to a place of safety, that, notwithstanding we lacked the necessary money to pay our fare, we decided to take seats in the stage, and promise to pay when we got to New Bedford. We were encouraged to do this by two excellent gentlemen, residents of New Bedford, whose names I afterward ascertained to be Joseph Ricketson and William C. Taber. They seemed at once to understand our circumstances, and gave us such assurance of their friendliness as put us fully at ease in their presence. It was good indeed to meet with such friends, at such a time. Upon reaching New Bedford, we were directed to the house of Mr. Nathan Johnson, by whom we were kindly received, and hospitably provided for. Both Mr. and Mrs. Johnson took a deep and lively interest in our welfare. They proved themselves quite worthy of the name of abolitionists. When the stage-driver found us unable to pay our fare, he held on upon our baggage as security for the debt. I had but to mention the fact to Mr. Johnson, and he forthwith advanced the money.

We now began to feel a degree of safety, and to prepare ourselves for the duties and responsibilities of a life of freedom. On the morning after our arrival at New Bedford, while at the breakfast-table, the question arose as to what name I should be called by. The name given me by my mother was, "Frederick Augustus Washington Bailey." I, however, had dispensed with the two middle names long before I left Maryland so that I was generally known by the name of "Frederick Bailey." I started from Baltimore bearing the name of "Stanley." When I got to New York, I again changed my name to "Frederick Johnson," and thought that would be the last change. But when I got to New Bedford, I found it necessary again to change my name. The reason of this necessity was, that there were so many Johnsons in New Bedford, it was already quite

7. "I had changed my name from Frederick *Bailey* to that of *Johnson*" [Douglass's note].

difficult to distinguish between them. I gave Mr. Johnson the privilege of choosing me a name, but told him he must not take from me the name of "Frederick." I must hold on to that, to preserve a sense of my identity. Mr. Johnson had just been reading the "Lady of the Lake,"[8] and at once suggested that my name be "Douglass." From that time until now I have been called "Frederick Douglass;" and as I am more widely known by that name than by either of the others, I shall continue to use it as my own.

I was quite disappointed at the general appearance of things in New Bedford. The impression which I had received respecting the character and condition of the people of the north, I found to be singularly erroneous. I had very strangely supposed, while in slavery, that few of the comforts, and scarcely any of the luxuries, of life were enjoyed at the north, compared with what were enjoyed by the slaveholders of the south. I probably came to this conclusion from the fact that northern people owned no slaves. I supposed that they were about upon a level with the non-slaveholding population of the south. I knew *they* were exceedingly poor, and I had been accustomed to regard their poverty as the necessary consequence of their being non-slaveholders. I had somehow imbibed the opinion that, in the absence of slaves, there could be no wealth, and very little refinement. And upon coming to the north, I expected to meet with a rough, hard-handed, and uncultivated population, living in the most Spartan-like simplicity, knowing nothing of the ease, luxury, pomp, and grandeur of southern slaveholders. Such being my conjectures, any one acquainted with the appearance of New Bedford may very readily infer how palpably I must have seen my mistake.

In the afternoon of the day when I reached New Bedford, I visited the wharves, to take a view of the shipping. Here I found myself surrounded with the strongest proofs of wealth. Lying at the wharves, and riding in the stream, I saw many ships of the finest model, in the best order, and of the largest size. Upon the right and left, I was walled in by granite warehouses of the widest dimensions, stowed to their utmost capacity with the necessaries and comforts of life. Added to this, almost every body seemed to be at work, but noiselessly so, compared with what I had been accustomed to in Baltimore. There were no loud songs heard from those engaged in loading and unloading ships. I heard no deep oaths or horrid curses on the laborer. I saw no whipping of men; but all seemed to go smoothly on. Every man appeared to understand his work, and went at it with a sober, yet cheerful earnestness, which betokened the deep interest which he felt in what he was doing, as well as a sense of his own dignity as a man. To me this looked exceedingly

---

8. Sir Walter Scott's (1771–1832) poem *Lady of the Lake* (1810), a historical romance set in the Scottish highlands in the 16th century. Douglass's namesake is the wrongfully exiled Lord James of Douglas, a Scottish chieftain revered for his bravery and virtue. There is also the famous "black Douglas" in Scott's *Fair Maid of Perth*. The novelist was one of Douglass's favorites.

strange. From the wharves I strolled around and over the town, gazing with wonder and admiration at the splendid churches, beautiful dwellings, and finely-cultivated gardens; evincing an amount of wealth, comfort, taste, and refinement, such as I had never seen in any part of slaveholding Maryland.

Every thing looked clean, new, and beautiful. I saw few or no dilapidated houses, with poverty-stricken inmates; no half-naked children and barefooted women, such as I had been accustomed to see in Hillsborough, Easton, St. Michael's, and Baltimore. The people looked more able, stronger, healthier, and happier, than those of Maryland. I was for once made glad by a view of extreme wealth, without being saddened by seeing extreme poverty. But the most astonishing as well as the most interesting thing to me was the condition of the colored people, a great many of whom, like myself, had escaped thither as a refuge from the hunters of men. I found many, who had not been seven years out of their chains, living in finer houses, and evidently enjoying more of the comforts of life, than the average of slaveholders in Maryland. I will venture to assert that my friend Mr. Nathan Johnson (of whom I can say with a grateful heart, "I was hungry, and he gave me meat; I was thirsty, and he gave me drink; I was a stranger, and he took me in"[9]) lived in a neater house; dined at a better table; took, paid for, and read, more newspapers; better understood the moral, religious, and political character of the nation,—than nine tenths of the slaveholders in Talbot county Maryland. Yet Mr. Johnson was a working man. His hands were hardened by toil, and not his alone, but those also of Mrs. Johnson. I found the colored people much more spirited than I had supposed they would be. I found among them a determination to protect each other from the blood-thirsty kidnapper, at all hazards. Soon after my arrival, I was told of a circumstance which illustrated their spirit. A colored man and a fugitive slave were on unfriendly terms. The former was heard to threaten the latter with informing his master of his whereabouts. Straightway a meeting was called among the colored people, under the stereotyped notice, "Business of importance!" The betrayer was invited to attend. The people came at the appointed hour, and organized the meeting by appointing a very religious old gentleman as president, who, I believe, made a prayer, after which he addressed the meeting as follows: *"Friends, we have got him here, and I would recommend that you young men just take him outside the door, and kill him!"* With this, a number of them bolted at him; but they were intercepted by some more timid than themselves, and the betrayer escaped their vengeance, and has not been seen in New Bedford since. I believe there have been no more such threats, and should there be hereafter, I doubt not that death would be the consequence.

9. Cf. Matthew 25.35.

I found employment, the third day after my arrival, in stowing a sloop with a load of oil. It was new, dirty, and hard work for me; but I went at it with a glad heart and a willing hand. I was now my own master. It was a happy moment, the rapture of which can be understood only by those who have been slaves. It was the first work, the reward of which was to be entirely my own. There was no Master Hugh standing ready, the moment I earned the money, to rob me of it. I worked that day with a pleasure I had never before experienced. I was at work for myself and newly-married wife. It was to me the starting-point of a new existence. When I got through with that job, I went in pursuit of a job of calking; but such was the strength of prejudice against color, among the white calkers, that they refused to work with me, and of course I could get no employment.[1] Finding my trade of no immediate benefit, I threw off my calking habiliments, and prepared myself to do any kind of work I could get to do. Mr. Johnson kindly let me have his wood-horse and saw, and I very soon found myself a plenty of work. There was no work too hard—none too dirty. I was ready to saw wood, shovel coal, carry the hod, sweep the chimney, or roll oil casks,—all of which I did for nearly three years in New Bedford, before I became known to the anti-slavery world.

In about four months after I went to New Bedford, there came a young man to me, and inquired if I did not wish to take the "Liberator."[2] I told him I did; but, just having made my escape from slavery, I remarked that I was unable to pay for it then. I, however, finally became a subscriber to it. The paper came, and I read it from week to week with such feelings as it would be quite idle for me to attempt to describe. The paper became my meat and my drink. My soul was set all on fire. Its sympathy for my brethren in bonds—its scathing denunciations of slaveholders—its faithful exposures of slavery—and its powerful attacks upon the upholders of the institution—sent a thrill of joy through my soul, such as I had never felt before!

I had not long been a reader of the "Liberator," before I got a pretty correct idea of the principles, measures and spirit of the anti-slavery reform. I took right hold of the cause. I could do but little; but what I could, I did with a joyful heart, and never felt happier than when in an anti-slavery meeting. I seldom had much to say at the meetings, because what I wanted to say was said so much better by others. But, while attending an anti-slavery convention at Nantucket, on the 11th of August, 1841, I felt strongly moved to speak, and was at the same time much urged to do so by Mr. William C. Coffin, a gentleman who had

1. "I am told that colored persons can now get employment at calking in New Bedford—a result of anti-slavery effort" [Douglass's note].
2. The first issue of Garrison's *Liberator* appeared in January 1831. Initially dependent on its black readership for support, it became the most eloquent and widely read of the abolitionist organs during more than thirty years of publication.

heard me speak in the colored people's meeting at New Bedford.[3] It was a severe cross, and I took it up reluctantly. The truth was, I felt myself a slave, and the idea of speaking to white people weighed me down. I spoke but a few moments, when I felt a degree of freedom, and said what I desired with considerable ease. From that time until now, I have been engaged in pleading the cause of my brethren—with what success, and with what devotion, I leave those acquainted with my labors to decide.

Appendix

I find, since reading over the foregoing Narrative, that I have, in several instances, spoken in such a tone and manner, respecting religion, as may possibly lead those unacquainted with my religious views to suppose me an opponent of all religion. To remove the liability of such misapprehension, I deem it proper to append the following brief explanation. What I have said respecting and against religion, I mean strictly to apply to the *slaveholding religion* of this land, and with no possible reference to Christianity proper; for, between the Christianity of this land, and the Christianity of Christ, I recognize the widest possible difference—so wide, that to receive the one as good, pure, and holy, is of necessity to reject the other as bad, corrupt, and wicked. To be the friend of the one, is of necessity to be the enemy of the other. I love the pure, peaceable, and impartial Christianity of Christ: I therefore hate the corrupt, slaveholding, women whipping, cradle-plundering, partial and hypocritical Christianity of this land. Indeed, I can see no reason, but the most deceitful one, for calling the religion of this land Christianity. I look upon it as the climax of all misnomers, the boldest of all frauds, and the grossest of all libels. Never was there a clearer case of "stealing the livery of the court of heaven to serve the devil in."[4] I am filled with unutterable loathing when I contemplate the religious pomp and show, together with the horrible inconsistencies, which every where surround me. We have men-stealers for ministers, women-whippers for missionaries, and cradle-plunderers for church members. The man who wields the blood-clotted cowskin during the week fills the pulpit on Sunday, and claims to be a minister of the meek and lowly Jesus. The man who robs me of my earnings at the end of each week meets me as a class-leader on Sunday morning, to show me the way of life, and the path of salvation. He who sells my sister, for purposes of prostitution, stands forth as the pious advocate of purity. He who proclaims it a religious duty to read the Bible denies me the right of learning to read the name of the God who made me. He who is the religious advocate of

---

3. Douglass was licensed to preach in the African Methodist Episcopal Zion church in 1839.
4. From Rev. Robert Pollok, *The Course of Time* (1827), book 8, 616–18.

marriage robs whole millions of its sacred influence, and leaves them to the ravages of wholesale pollution. The warm defender of the sacredness of the family relation is the same that scatters whole families,—sundering husbands and wives, parents and children, sisters and brothers,— leaving the hut vacant, and the hearth desolate. We see the thief preaching against theft, and the adulterer against adultery. We have men sold to build churches, women sold to support the gospel, and babes sold to purchase Bibles for the *poor heathen! all for the glory of God and the good of souls!* The slave auctioneer's bell and the church-going bell chime in with each other, and the bitter cries of the heart-broken slave are drowned in the religious shouts of his pious master. Revivals of religion and revivals in the slave-trade go hand in hand together. The slave prison and the church stand near each other. The clanking of fetters and the rattling of chains in the prison, and the pious psalm and solemn prayer in the church, may be heard at the same time. The dealers in the bodies and souls of men erect their stand in the presence of the pulpit, and they mutually help each other. The dealer gives his blood-stained gold to support the pulpit, and the pulpit, in return, covers his infernal business with the garb of Christianity. Here we have religion and robbery the allies of each other—devils dressed in angels' robes, and hell presenting the semblance of paradise.

> "Just God! and these are they,
>   Who minister at thine altar, God of right!
> Men who their hands, with prayer and blessing, lay
>   On Israel's ark of light.[5]
>
> "What! preach, and kidnap men?
>   Give thanks, and rob thy own afflicted poor?
> Talk of thy glorious liberty, and then
>   Bolt hard the captive's door?
>
> "What! servants of thy own
>   Merciful Son, who came to seek and save
> The homeless and the outcast, fettering down
>   The tasked and plundered slave!
>
> "Pilate and Herod[6] friends!
>   Chief priests and rulers, as of old, combine!
> Just God and holy! is that church which lends
>   Strength to the spoiler thine?"[7]

5. I.e., the Holy Ark containing the Torah; by extension, the entire body of law as contained in the Old Testament and Talmud.
6. Herod Antipas, ruler of Galilee, ordered the execution of John the Baptist and participated in the trial of Christ. Pontius Pilate was the Roman authority who condemned Christ to death.
7. These stanzas are from Whittier's antislavery poem *Clerical Oppressors* (1836).

The Christianity of America is a Christianity, of whose votaries it may be as truly said, as it was of the ancient scribes and Pharisees,[8] "They bind heavy burdens, and grievous to be borne, and lay them on men's shoulders, but they themselves will not move them with one of their fingers. All their works they do for to be seen of men. —— They love the uppermost rooms at feasts, and the chief seats in the synagogues, ... and to be called of men, Rabbi, Rabbi. —— But woe unto you, scribes and Pharisees, hypocrites! for ye shut up the kingdom of heaven against men; for ye neither go in yourselves, neither suffer ye them that are entering to go in. Ye devour widows' houses, and for a pretence make long prayers; therefore ye shall receive the greater damnation. Ye compass sea and land to make one proselyte, and when he is made, ye make him twofold more the child of hell than yourselves. —— Woe unto you, scribes and Pharisees, hypocrites! for ye pay tithe of mint, and anise, and cumin, and have omitted the weightier matters of the law, judgment, mercy, and faith; these ought ye to have done, and not to leave the other undone. Ye blind guides! which strain at a gnat, and swallow a camel. Woe unto you, scribes and Pharisees, hypocrites! for ye make clean the outside of the cup and of the platter; but within, they are full of extortion and excess. —— Woe unto you, scribes and Pharisees, hypocrites! for ye are like unto whited sepulchres, which indeed appear beautiful outward, but are within full of dead men's bones, and of all uncleanness. Even so ye also outwardly appear righteous unto men, but within ye are full of hypocrisy and iniquity."[9]

Dark and terrible as is this picture, I hold it to be strictly true of the overwhelming mass of professed Christians in America. They strain at a gnat, and swallow a camel. Could any thing be more true of our churches? They would be shocked at the proposition of fellowshipping a *sheep*-stealer; and at the same time they hug to their communion a *man*-stealer, and brand me with being an infidel, if I find fault with them for it. They attend with Pharisaical strictness to the outward forms of religion, and at the same time neglect the weightier matters of the law, judgment, mercy, and faith. They are always ready to sacrifice, but seldom to show mercy. They are they who are represented as professing to love God whom they have not seen, whilst they hate their brother whom they have seen. They love the heathen on the other side of the globe. They can pray for him, pay money to have the Bible put into his hand, and missionaries to instruct him; while they despise and totally neglect the heathen at their own doors.

Such is, very briefly, my view of the religion of this land; and to avoid any misunderstanding, growing out of the use of general terms, I mean,

---

8. Members of a powerful Jewish sect that insisted on strict observance of written and oral religious laws. The scribes were the Jewish scholars who taught Jewish law and edited and interpreted the Bible.
9. Cf. Matthew 23.4–28.

by the religion of this land, that which is revealed in the words, deeds, and actions, of those bodies, north and south, calling themselves Christian churches, and yet in union with slaveholders. It is against religion, as presented by these bodies, that I have felt it my duty to testify.

I conclude these remarks by copying the following portrait of the religion of the south, (which is, by communion and fellowship, the religion of the north,) which I soberly affirm is "true to the life," and without caricature or the slightest exaggeration. It is said to have been drawn, several years before the present anti-slavery agitation began, by a northern Methodist preacher, who, while residing at the south, had an opportunity to see slaveholding morals, manners, and piety, with his own eyes. "Shall I not visit for these things? saith the Lord. Shall not my soul be avenged on such a nation as this?"[1]

A PARODY[2]

"Come, saints and sinners, hear me tell
How pious priests whip Jack and Nell,
And women buy and children sell,
And preach all sinners down to hell,
   And sing of heavenly union.

"They'll bleat and baa, dona like goats,
Gorge down black sheep, and strain at motes,
Array their backs in fine black coats,
Then seize their negroes by their throats,
   And choke, for heavenly union.

"They'll church you if you sip a dram,
And damn you if you steal a lamb;
Yet rob old Tony, Doll, and Sam,
Of human rights, and bread and ham;
   Kidnapper's heavenly union.

"They'll loudly talk of Christ's reward,
And bind his image with a cord,
And scold, and swing the lash abhorred,
And sell their brother in the Lord
   To handcuffed heavenly union.

"They'll read and sing a sacred song,
And make a prayer both loud and long,

---

1. Jeremiah speaks God's charges against the sins of the House of Israel (Jeremiah 5–9).
2. Douglass is parodying "Heavenly Union," a hymn sung in many Southern churches at the time. Douglass was famous for his sharp sense of humor and ability to mimic the Southern clergy.

And teach the right and do the wrong,
Hailing the brother, sister throng,
    With words of heavenly union.

"We wonder how such saints can sing,
Or praise the Lord upon the wing,
Who roar, and scold, and whip, and sting,
And to their slaves and mammon cling,
    In guilty conscience union.

"They'll raise tobacco, corn, and rye,
And drive, and thieve, and cheat, and lie,
And lay up treasures in the sky,
By making switch and cowskin fly,
    In hope of heavenly union.

"They'll crack old Tony on the skull,
And preach and roar like Bashan[3] bull,
Or braying ass, of mischief full,
Then seize old Jacob by the wool,
    And pull for heavenly union.

"A roaring, ranting, sleek man-thief,
Who lived on mutton, veal, and beef,
Yet never would afford relief
To needy, sable sons of grief,
    Was big with heavenly union.

" 'Love not the world,' the preacher said,
And winked his eye, and shook his head;
He seized on Tom, and Dick, and Ned,
Cut short their meat, and clothes, and bread,
    Yet still loved heavenly union.

"Another preacher whining spoke
Of One whose heart for sinners broke:
He tied old Nanny to an oak,
And drew the blood at every stroke,
    And prayed for heavenly union.

"Two others oped their iron jaws,
And waved their children-stealing paws;
There sat their children in gewgaws;
By stinting negroes' backs and maws,
    They kept up heavenly union.

3. Strong bulls mentioned in the Old Testament.

> "All good from Jack another takes,
> And entertains their flirts and rakes,
> Who dress as sleek as glossy snakes,
> And cram their mouths with sweetened cakes;
> And this goes down for union."

Sincerely and earnestly hoping that this little book may do something toward throwing light on the American slave system, and hastening the glad day of deliverance to the millions of my brethren in bonds—faithfully relying upon the power of truth, love, and justice, for success in my humble efforts—and solemnly pledging my self anew to the sacred cause,—I subscribe myself,

FREDERICK DOUGLASS.

LYNN, *Mass., April* 28, 1845.

1845

CONTEXTS

MARGARET FULLER

[Review of the *Narrative*]

[Margaret Fuller (1810–1850), one of the leading intellectuals of her day, had been editor of the literary journal *The Dial* before joining Horace Greeley's *New York Tribune*. It was a mark of the importance attached to Douglass's *Narrative* that Fuller, perhaps the most prominent book review critic of the era, reviewed the book for her influential newspaper. The review appeared in the *Tribune* on June 10, 1845.]

Frederick Douglass has been for some time a prominent member of the Abolition party. He is said to be an excellent speaker—can speak from a thorough personal experience—and has upon the audience, beside, the influence of a strong character and uncommon talents. In the book before us he has put into the story of his life the thoughts, the feelings, and the adventures that have been so affecting through the living voice; nor are they less so from the printed page. He has had the courage to name the persons, times and places, thus exposing himself to obvious danger, and setting the seal on his deep convictions as to the religious need of speaking the whole truth. Considered merely as a narrative, we have never read one more simple, true, coherent, and warm with genuine feeling. It is an excellent piece of writing, and on that score to be prized as a specimen of the powers of the Black Race, which Prejudice persists in disputing. We prize highly all evidence of this kind, and it is becoming more abundant. The Cross of the Legion of Honor has just been conferred in France on Dumas and Soulie, both celebrated in the paths of light and literature. Dumas, whose father was a General in the French Army, is a Mulatto; Soulie, a Quadroon. He went from New Orleans, where, though to the eye a white man, yet as known to have African blood in his veins, he could never have enjoyed the privileges due to a human being. Leaving the Land of Freedom, he found himself free to develop the powers that God had given.

Two wise and candid thinkers,—the Scotchman, Kinment, prematurely lost to this country, of which he was so faithful and generous a student, and the late Dr. Channing,—both thought that the African Race had in them a peculiar element, which, if it could be assimilated with those imported among us from Europe would give to genius a development, and to the energies of character a balance and harmony beyond what has been seen heretofore in the history of the world. Such an element is indicated in their lowest estate by a talent for melody, a ready skill at imitation and adaptation, an almost indestructible elasticity of nature. It is to be remarked in the writings both of Soulie and Dumas, full of faults but glowing with plastic life and fertile in invention. The same torrid energy and saccharine fulness may be felt in the writings of this Douglass, though his life being one of action or resistance, was less favorable to SUCH powers than one of a more joyous flow might have been.

The book is prefaced by two communications—one from Garrison and one from Wendell Phillips. That from the former is in his usual over-emphatic style. His motives and his course have been noble and generous. We look upon him with high respect, but he has indulged in violent invective and denunciation till he has spoiled the temper of his mind. Like a man who has been in the habit of screaming himself hoarse to make the deaf better, he can no longer pitch his voice on a key agreeable to common ears. Mr. Phillips's remarks are equally decided, without this exaggeration in the tone. Douglass himself seems very just and temperate. We feel that his view, even of those who have injured him most, may be relied upon. He knows how to allow for motives and influences. Upon the subject of Religion, he speaks with great force, and not more than our own sympathies can respond to. The inconsistencies of Slaveholding professors of religion cry to Heaven. We are not disposed to detest, or refuse communion with them. Their blindness is but one form of that prevalent fallacy which substitutes a creed for a faith, a ritual for life. We have seen too much of this system of atonement not to know that those who adopt it often began with good intentions, and are, at any rate, in their mistakes worthy of the deepest pity. But that is no reason why the truth should not be uttered, trumpet-tongued, about the thing. "Bring no more vain oblations": sermons must daily be preached anew on that text. Kings, five hundred years ago, built churches with the spoils of war; Clergymen to-day command Slaves to obey a Gospel which they will not allow them to read, and call themselves Christians amid the curses of their fellow men. The world ought to get on a little faster than that, if there be really any principle of movement in it. The Kingdom of Heaven may not at the beginning have dropped seed larger than a mustard seed, but even from that we had a right to expect a fuller growth than can be believed to exist, when we read such a book as this of Douglass. Unspeakably affecting is the fact that he never saw his mother at all by day light. "I do not recollect of ever seeing my mother by the light of day. She was with me in the night. She would lie down with me, and get me to sleep, but long before I waked she was gone."

The following extract presents a suitable answer to the background argument drawn by the defender of Slavery from the songs of the Slave, and it is also a good specimen of the powers of observation and manly heart of the writer. We wish that every one may read his book and see what a mind might have been stifled in bondage—what a man may be subjected to the insults of spendthrift dandies, or the blows of mercenary brutes, in whom there is no whiteness except of the skin, no humanity except in the outward form, and of whom the Avenger will not fail yet to demand—"where is thy brother?"[1]

ANONYMOUS

[Review of the Narrative] †

[The *Spectator*, an English journal first published in 1828, while not radical, generally supported reform movements. This review appeared on November 29, 1845. It was the custom for such reviews not to be signed.

The European edition of the *Narrative* had been published in Dublin in 1845 and was widely read.]

Frederick Douglass appears as a Maryland slave, who escaped from his master in 1838, and, after working as a free labourer in the Northeastern States till 1841, was engaged by an American Anti-Slavery Society as itinerant lecturer. Having a natural force and fluency of language, and dealing with things within his own experience, he appears to have spoken with so much acceptance as to have been stimulated to commit to paper the autobiographical portion of his addresses, which is before us in a Dublin reprint.

In his life there is not much of hairbreadth escape. He is a Mulatto, and supposes that his first owner was his father. Time, to a slave, is not known in its particulars, such as birthdays and exact dates; so that he does not know his own age, but supposes it now to be about seven-and-twenty. According to this reckoning, he was sent in his sixth year from the estate where he was born to wait upon a little boy in Baltimore. Here he was treated kindly; and his mistress began to teach him to read, till his master forbade it: but Frederick, having, as he says, had his mind a little opened, persevered in teaching himself, and succeeded by dint of casual assistance from poor White boys in the street: and to reading, at a subsequent period, he added writing. When about fifteen, his owner in the country took him from his master in town, in consequence of a family quarrel; and Frederick was transformed from a sort of page or footman to a field-labourer. His first two country masters were religious men, but very cruel and exacting; so that he had no time to think of anything but work. His third master was more liberal; and, having time to meditate, he planned an escape, with some fellow-slaves: but it was

---

1. See Genesis 4.9. This review concludes by quoting the last four paragraphs of chapter 2 of the *Narrative* [Editors].
† Bracketed page numbers refer to this Norton Critical Edition.

detected; and Frederick, after being imprisoned and threatened with sale, was sent back to his old quarters in Baltimore, whence he finally managed to escape in reality. Up to this point his narrative is pretty full; but he designedly suppresses the particulars of his escape, lest he should expose others to danger, and prevent some unfortunates from attaining their freedom. In plain English, he was assisted by those secret agents who are scattered through some of the Southern States for the especial purpose of aiding the escape of runaway slaves.

We assume that Frederick Douglass is really what he professes, and not a Coloured free man in masquerade, upon the Jesuit's principle that the end justifies the means. On the one hand, we note the very extraordinary manner in which he taught himself to read; some contentions with different masters, in one case proceeding to a fight,—which seems an improbable insubordination in a slave country, though it may have been heightened to add dignity to Douglass; and a precocious air in the more youthful part of his career, but which also may have been unconsciously coloured by his feelings at the period of composition. On the other hand, the facts and incidents have a strong character of truth. Frederick deals a little in atrocities, though he admits them to be exceptions; but they do not make the greatest impression on the reader as to the horrors of slavery. This appears rather in the brutish degradation to which the mind of the slave is reduced, the destruction of all family ties which is systematically aimed at, and the reaction of the "institution" upon the whites themselves, lowering their character, and often, according to Douglass, wringing their affections in the case of their Coloured children.

> "It is worthy of remark, that such slaves [children of the planter] invariably suffer greater hardships, and have more to contend with than others. They are, in the first place, a constant offence to their mistress. She is ever disposed to find fault with them; they can seldom do anything to please her; she is never better pleased than when she sees them under the lash, especially when she suspects her husband of showing to his Mulatto children favours which he withholds from his Black slaves. The master is frequently compelled to sell this class of his slaves, out of deference to the feelings of his White wife; and, cruel as the deed may strike any one to be for a man to sell his own children to human fleshmongers, it is often the dictate of humanity for him to do so; for unless he does this, he must not only whip them himself, but must stand by and see one White son tie up his brother of but few shades darker complexion than himself, and ply the gory lash to his naked back; and if he lisp one word of disapproval, it is set down to his parental partiality, and only makes a bad matter worse both for himself and the slave whom he would protect and defend." [13–14]

There is something natural and touching in this instance of maternal feeling.

> "My mother and I were separated when I was but an infant—before I knew her as my mother. It is a common custom, in the part of Maryland from which I ran away, to part children from their mothers at a very early age. Frequently, before the child has reached its twelfth month, its mother is taken from it, and hired out on some farm a considerable distance off; and the child is placed under the care of an old woman, too old for field-labour. For what this separation is done I do not know, unless it be to hinder the development of the child's affection toward its mother, and to blunt and destroy the natural affection of the mother for the child. This is the inevitable result.
>
> "I never saw my mother, to know her as such, more than four or five times in my life; and each of these times was very short in duration, and at night. She was hired by a Mr. Stewart, who lived about twelve miles from my home. She made her journey to see me in the night, travelling the whole distance on foot, after the performance of her day's work. She was a field hand, and a whipping is the penalty of not being in the field at sunrise, unless a slave has special permission from his or her master to the contrary; a permission which they seldom get, and one that gives to him that gives it the proud name of being a kind master. I do not recollect of ever seeing my mother by the light of day. She was with me in the night. She would lie down with me, and get me to sleep; but long before I waked she was gone." [12–13]

According to Frederick, slaveholders professing religion are a great deal worse than others; more gravely cruel, more exacting, and very mean—not even giving their people enough to eat, which in Maryland is very contrary to public opinion. "Not to give a slave enough to eat, is regarded as the most aggravated development of meanness even among slaveholders. The rule is, no matter how coarse the food, only let there be enough of it." This meanness the professors seem to carry into punishment; assigning Scriptural reasons for it. Here is a text for stripes.

> "I have said my master found religious sanction for his cruelty. As an example, I will state one of many facts going to prove the charge. I have seen him tie up a lame young woman, and whip her with a heavy cowskin upon her naked shoulders, causing the warm red blood to drip; and, in justification of the bloody deed, he would quote this passage of Scripture—'He that knoweth his master's will, and doeth it not, shall be beaten with many stripes.' " [41]

If this narrative is really true in its basis, and untouched by any one save Douglass himself, it is a singular book, and he is a more singular man. Even if it is of the nature of the true stories of De Foe,[1] it is curious as a picture of slavery, and worth reading.

A. C. C. THOMPSON

[Letter from a Former Slaveholder]

[As pointed out in the article by Peter Ripley (below, pp. 135–46), A. C. C. Thompson was a neighbor of Thomas Auld, who was one of Douglass's owners. Following the publication of the *Narrative of the Life of Frederick Douglass*, Thompson challenged its veracity in the Wilmington *Delaware Republican*. The item was reprinted in the *Liberator* on December 12, 1845.]

It is with considerable regret that I find myself measurably compelled to appear before the public; but my attention has lately been arrested by a pamphlet which has been freely circulated in Wilmington and elsewhere, with the following superscription:—*Extract from a Narrative of Frederick Douglass, on American Slave, written by himself.*

And although I am aware that no sensible, unprejudiced person will credit such a ridiculous publication, which bears the glaring impress of falsehood on every page, yet I deem it expedient that I should give the public some information respecting the validity of this narrative, because I was for many years a citizen of the section of country where the scenes of the above mentioned narrative are laid; and am intimately acquainted with most of the gentlemen whose characters are so shamefully traduced, and I am also aware, that the Narrative was not written by the professed author; but from statements of this runaway slave, some evil designed person or persons have composed this catalogue of lies to excite the indignation of the public opinion against the slaveholders of the South; and have even attempted to plunge their venomous fangs in the vitals of the church.

I shall, therefore, briefly notice some of the most glaring falsehoods contained in the aforesaid Narrative, and give a true representation of the character of those gentlemen, who have been censured in such an uncharitable manner, as murderers, hypocrites, and everything else that is vile.

I indulge no animosity against the fabricators and circulators of the

---

1. Daniel Defoe (1661?–1731), British journalist and novelist, most famous for his fictitious work *The Life and Adventures of Robinson Crusoe.* In his writing, Defoe would oftentimes "stretch the truth" or exaggerate to get his point across. By making a somewhat sarcastic reference to Defoe, the review implies that Douglass's story is embellished or even ghost-written [*Editors*].

Narrative, neither do I know them; but I positively declare the whole to be a budget of falsehoods, from beginning to end.

1st. The identity of the author. About eight years ago, I knew this recreant slave by the name of Frederick Bailey, (instead of Douglass.) He then lived with Mr. Edward Covy, and was an unlearned, and rather an ordinary negro, and am confident he was not capable of writing the Narrative alluded to; for none but an educated man, and one who had some knowledge of the rules of grammar, could write so correctly. Although, to make the imposition at all creditable, the composer has labored to write it in as plain a style as possible: consequently, the detection of this first falsehood proves the whole production to be notoriously untrue.

Again. 'It is a common custom in the part of Maryland from which I ran away, to separate children from their mothers at a very early age.'

This also I know to be false. There is no such custom prevalent in that section of the country; but, on the contrary, the children are raised with their mothers, and generally live with them in the same house, except in some few instances where the mother is hired out as a cook or laborer in some other family.

The gentlemen whose names are so prominently set forth in the said Narrative are Col. Edward Lloyd, Capt. Anthony, Austin Gore, Thomas Lamdin, (not Lanman,) Giles Hicks, Thomas Auld, and Edward Covy. Most of these persons I am intimately acquainted with, and shall give a brief sketch of their *characters as follows:*

Col. Edward Lloyd was one of the most wealthy and respectable planters in the State of Maryland. He was at one time the Governor of the State, and for several years, a member of the Legislature. He owned several thousand acres of land, and between 4 and 500 slaves. He died before I had much knowledge of him: but I know that he was a kind and charitable man, and in every respect an honorable and worthy citizen.

Most of the same slaves are now owned by his three sons, and they manage their servants in the same manner as did their father; and I know there are no such barbarities committed on their plantations.

Could it be possible that charitable feeling men could murder human beings, with as little remorse of conscience, as the narrative of this infamous libel wishes to make us believe; and that the laws of Maryland, which operate *alike upon black and white,* bond or free, could permit such foul murders to pass unnoticed? No! it is impossible; and every sensible man knows that these false accusations are the ebullition of an unchristian prejudice.

Captain Anthony and Giles Hicks, I know but little of. The accused murderer, Mr. Gore, is a respectable citizen, living near St. Michaels, and I believe a worthy member of the Methodist Episcopal Church; he was formerly an overseer for Col. Lloyd, and at this time, all who know him, think him anything but a murderer.

Thomas Lamdin, who, it is said, (in the Narrative,) boasted so frequently of his murders, is at this time an honest school teacher in the District where I formerly lived; and all the harm that can be said of him is, that he is too good-natured and harmless to injure any person but himself.

Capt. Thomas Auld, whose hypocritical meanness is so strongly depicted in the aforesaid Narrative, was for many years a respectable merchant in the town of St. Michaels, and an honorable and worthy member of the Methodist E. Church, and only notable for his integrity and irreproachable Christian character. He is now retired from the turmoil of a mercantile life, and engaged in the worthy occupation of tilling the soil, little dreaming of the foul accusations that are circulated against him.

Edward Covy, the renowned 'negro breaker,'[1] is also a plain, honest farmer, and a tried and faithful member of the Methodist E. Church. Mr. Covy lived for several years on a farm adjoining my father's, at which time this runaway negro lived with him, and I am well aware that no such bloody tragedy as is recorded in that lying Narrative ever occurred on Mr. Covy's farm: All that can be said of Mr. Covy is that he is a good Christian, and a hard working man, and makes every one around him work and treats them well. By his honest industry, he has purchased a fine farm, and is now reaping the reward of his labor.

Such are the characters of the men whom the imposers of this dirty Narrative have so uncharitably traduced, and by blending these false accusations with the Methodist religion of the South, they wish to lacerate her already bleeding wounds.

I was raised among slaves, and have also owned them, and am well aware that the slaves live better and fare better in many respects than the free blacks.

Yet, I am positively opposed to slavery, for I know it is a great evil; but *the evil falls not upon the slave*, but on the owner.

Intrigue and false accusations will never liberate the slave of the South; but, on the contrary, every such attempt will only forge for them new and stronger fetters.

Let the tender-hearted philanthropists of the North speak truth and love towards their southern brethren, and make a liberal application of their gold for the removing the blacks from the country, and their chance of success will be more flattering.

I have given a true representation of the persons connected with the

---

1. Douglass refers not to a formal profession, but to a man known for his ability to break the will of a slave [*Editors*].

aforesaid Narrative, and I respectfully submit the facts to the judgment of an impartial public.

A. C. C. THOMPSON.

No. 101 Market-st. Wilmington, Del.

FREDERICK DOUGLASS

Reply to Thompson's Letter

[Shortly after the appearance of A. C. C. Thompson's critique of the *Narrative of the Life of Frederick Douglass*, Douglass replied in the *Liberator*. His letter ran on February 27, 1846.]

To the Editor of the Liberator:

DEAR FRIEND—For the sake of our righteous cause, I was delighted to see, by an extract copied into the Liberator of 12th Dec. 1845, from the Delaware Republican, that Mr. A. C. C. Thompson, No. 101, Market-street, Wilmington, has undertaken to invalidate my testimony against the slaveholders, whose names I have made prominent in the narrative of my experience while in slavery.

Slaveholders and slave-traders never betray greater indiscretion, than when they venture to defend themselves, or their system of plunder, in any other community than a slaveholding one. Slavery has its own standard of morality, humanity, justice, and Christianity. Tried by that standard, it is a system of the greatest kindness to the slave—sanctioned by the purest morality—in perfect agreement with justice—and, of course, not inconsistent with Christianity. But, tried, by any other, it is doomed to condemnation. The naked relation of master and slave is one of those monsters of darkness, to whom the light of truth is death! The wise ones among the slaveholders know this, and they studiously avoid doing any thing, which, in their judgment, tends to elicit truth. They seem fully to understand, that their safety is in their silence. They may have learned this wisdom from Junius, who counselled his opponent, Sir William Draper, when defending Lord Granby, never to attract attention to a character, which would only pass without condemnation, when it passed without observation.[1]

1. Junius (Sir William Draper) and Lord Granby are key figures in a 1769 British media controversy. John Manners, the marquis of Granby (1721–1770) and a skilled tactician and combat-seasoned lieutenant-general, was attacked in the press by the anonymous "Junius." "Junius" claimed that as commander-in-chief, Granby had (among other things) degraded the office to that of a "broker of commissions," awarding other officers higher status on the basis of favoritism rather than merit. Sir William Draper (1721–1787), a colonel and lieutenant governor, defended Granby against the aspersions of his unknown assailant. A bitter series of letters traveled back and forth in the press between "Junius" and Draper, debating the merits of Granby's adminstrative qualities [Editors].

I am now almost too far away to answer this attempted refutation by Mr. Thompson. I fear his article will be forgotten, before you get my reply. I, however, think the whole thing worth reviving, as it is seldom we have so good a case for dissection. In any country but the United States, I might hope to get a hearing through the columns of the paper in which I was attacked. But this would be inconsistent with American usage and magnanimity. It would be folly to expect such a hearing. They might possibly advertise me as a runaway slave, and share the reward of my apprehension; but on no other condition would they allow my reply a place in their columns.

In this, however, I may judge the 'Republican' harshly. It may be that, having admitted Mr. Thompson's article, the editor will think it but fair—negro though I am—to allow my reply an insertion.

In replying to Mr. Thompson, I shall proceed as I usually do in preaching the slaveholder's sermon,—dividing the subject under two general heads, as follows:—

1st. The statement of Mr. Thompson, in confirmation of the truth of my narrative.

2ndly. His denials of its truthfulness.

Under the first, I beg Mr. Thompson to accept my thanks for his full, free and unsolicited testimony, in regard to my identity. There now need be no doubt on that point, however much there might have been before. Your testimony, Mr. Thompson, has settled the question forever. I give you the fullest credit for the deed, saying nothing of the motive. But for you, sir, the pro-slavery people in the North might have persisted, with some show of reason, in representing me as being an imposter—a free negro who had never been south of Mason & Dixon's line—one whom the abolitionists, acting on the jesuitical principle, that the end justifies the means, had educated and sent forth to attract attention to their faltering cause. I am greatly indebted to you, sir, for silencing those truly prejudicial insinuations. I wish I could make you understand the amount of service you have done me. You have completely tripped up the heels of your pro-slavery friends, and laid them flat at my feet. You have done a piece of anti-slavery work, which no anti-slavery man could do. Our cautious and truth-loving people in New-England would never have believed this testimony, in proof of my identity, had it been borne by an abolitionist. Not that they really think an abolitionist capable of bearing false witness intentionally; but such persons are thought fanatical, and to look at every thing through a distorted medium. They will believe you—they will believe a slaveholder. They have, some how or other, imbibed (and I confess strangely enough) the idea that persons such as yourself are dispassionate, impartial and disinterested, and therefore capable of giving a fair representation of things connected with slavery. Now, under these circumstances, your testimony is of the utmost importance. It will serve to give effect to my exposures of slavery, both at home and abroad. I hope I shall not administer to your vanity when I tell you that you seem to have been raised up for this purpose! I came to this land with the highest testimonials from some of the most intelligent and distinguished abolitionists in the United States; yet some here have entertained and expressed doubt as to whether I have ever been a slave. You may easily imagine the perplexing and embarrassing nature of my situation, and how anxious I must have been to be relieved from it. You, sir, have relieved me. I now stand before both the American and British public, endorsed by you as being just what I have ever represented myself to be—to wit, an *American slave.*

You say, 'I knew this recreant slave by the name of Frederick Bailey' (instead of Douglass.) Yes, that was my name; and, leaving out the term recreant, which savors a little of bitterness, your testimony is direct and perfect—just what I have long wanted. But you are not yet satisfied. You seem determined to bear the most ample testimony in my favor. You say you knew me when I lived with Mr. Covey.—'And with most of the persons' mentioned in my narrative, 'you are intimately acquainted.' This is excellent. Then Mr. Edward Covey is not a creature of my imagination, but really did, and may yet exist.

You thus brush away the miserable insinuation of my northern pro-slavery enemies, that I have used fictitious not real names. You say— 'Col. Lloyd was a wealthy planter. Mr. Gore was once an overseer for Col. Lloyd, but is now living near St. Michael's, is respected, and [you] believe he is a member of the Methodist Episcopal Church. Mr. Thomas Auld is an honorable and worthy member of the Methodist Episcopal Church. Mr. Covey, too, is a member of the Methodist church, and all that can be said of him is, that he is a good Christian,' & c. &c. Do allow me, once more, to thank you for this triumphant vindication of the truth of my statements; and to show you how highly I value your testimony, I will inform you that I am now publishing a second edition of my narrative in this country, having already disposed of the first. I will insert your article with my reply as an appendix to the edition now in progress. If you find any fault with my frequent thanks, you may find some excuse for me in the fact, that I have serious fears that you will be but poorly thanked by those whose characters you have felt it your duty to defend. I am almost certain they will regard you as running before you were sent, and as having spoken when you should have been silent. Under these trying circumstances, it is evidently the duty of those interested in your welfare to extend to you such words of consolation as may ease, if not remove, the pain of your sad disappointment! But enough of this.

Now, then, to the second part—or your denials. You are confident I did not write the book; and the reason of your confidence is, that when you knew me, I was an unlearned and rather an ordinary negro. Well, I have to admit I was rather an ordinary negro when you knew me, and I do not claim to be a very extraordinary one now. But you knew me under very unfavorable circumstances. It was when I lived with Mr. Covey, the negro-breaker, *and member of the Methodist Church*. I had just been living with master Thomas Auld, where I had been reduced by hunger. Master Thomas did not allow me enough to eat. Well, when I lived with Mr. Covey, I was driven so hard, and whipt so often, that my soul was crushed and my spirits broken. I was a mere wreck. The degradation to which I was then subjected, as I now look back to it, seems more like a dream than a horrible reality. I can scarcely realize how I ever passed through it, without quite losing all my moral and intellectual energies. I can easily understand that you sincerely doubt if I wrote the narrative; for if any one had told me, seven years ago, I should ever be able to write such an one, I should have doubted as strongly as you now do. You must not judge me now by what I then was—a change of circumstances, has made a surprising change in me. Frederick Douglass, the *freeman*, is a very different person from Frederick Bailey, the *slave*. I feel myself almost a new man—freedom has given me new life. I fancy you would scarcely know me. I think I have altered very much in my general appearance, and know I have in my manners. You remember when I used to meet you on the road to St. Michael's, or near Mr. Covey's lane gate, I hardly dared to lift my head, and look up at you. If I should meet you now, amid the free hills of old Scotland, where the ancient 'black Douglass'[2] once met his foes, I presume I might summon sufficient fortitude to look you full in the face; and were you to attempt to make a slave of me, it is possible you might find me almost as disagreeable a subject, as was the Douglass to whom I have just referred. Of one thing, I am certain—you would see *a great change* in me!

I trust I have now explained away your reason for thinking I did not write the narrative in question.

You next deny the existence of such cruelty in Maryland as I reveal in my narrative; and ask, with truly marvellous simplicity, 'could it be possible that charitable, feeling men could murder human beings with as little remorse as the narrative of this infamous libeller would make us believe; and that the laws of Maryland, which operate alike upon black and white, bond and free, could permit such foul murders to pass unnoticed?' 'No,' you say, 'it is impossible.' I am not to determine what charitable, feeling men can do; but, to show what Maryland slaveholders actually do, their charitable feeling is to be determined by their deeds, and not their deeds by their charitable feelings. The cowskin makes as

---

2. A character, perhaps of African descent, in Walter Scott, *The Fair Maid of Perth* [Editors].

deep a gash in my flesh, when wielded by a professed saint, as it does when wielded by an open sinner. The deadly musket does as fatal execution when its trigger is pulled by Austin Gore, the Christian, as when the same is done by Beal Bondly, the infidel. The best way to ascertain what those charitable, feeling men can do, will be to point you to the laws made by them, and which you say operate alike upon the white and the black, the bond and the free. By consulting the statute laws of Maryland, you will find the following:—☞'Any slave for rambling in the night, or riding horses in the day time without leave, or running away, may be punished by whipping, cropping branding in the cheek, or otherwise—not rendering him unfit for labor.'—p. 337.☜

Then another:—☞'Any slave convicted of petty treason, murder, or wilful burning of dwelling-houses, may be sentenced to have the right hand cut off, to be hanged in the usual way—his head severed from his body—the body divided into four quarters, and the head and quarters set up in the most public place where such act was committed.'—Page 190.☜

Now, Mr. Thompson, when you consider with what ease a slave may be convicted of any one or all of these crimes, how bloody and atrocious do those laws appear! Yet, sir, they are but the breath of those pious and charitable feeling men, whom you would defend. I am sure I have recorded in my narrative, nothing so revoltingly cruel, murderous, and infernal, as may be found in your own statute book.

You say that the laws of Maryland operate alike upon the white and black, the bond and free. If you mean by this, that the parties named are all equally protected by law, you perpetrate a falsehood as big as that told by President Polk in his inaugural address.[3] It is a notorious fact, even on this side the Atlantic, that a black man cannot testify against a white in any court in Maryland, or any other slave State. If you do not know this, you are more than ordinarily ignorant, and are to be pitied rather than censured. I will not say 'that the detection of this falsehood proves all you have said to be false'—for I wish to avail myself of your testimony, in regard to my identity,—but I will say, you have made yourself very liable to suspicion.

I will close these remarks by saying, your positive opposition to slavery is fully explained, and will be well understood by anti-slavery men, when you say the evil of the system does not fall upon the slave, but the

---

3. In his March 1845 inaugural address, Polk made a statement similar to A. C. C. Thompson's when he claimed that the federal government "leaves individuals over whom it casts its protecting influence entirely free to improve their own condition by the legitimate exercise of all their mental and physical powers. It is a common protector . . . of every man who lives upon our soil, whether of native or foreign birth; . . . of every shade of opinion, and the most free inquiry." Polk then went on to laud the Constitution, stating that its "one great object" was to "restrain majorities from oppressing minorities, or encroaching upon their just rights. Minorities have a right to appeal to the Constitution, as a shield against such oppression"; qtd. in John S. Jenkins, *James Knox Polk* (Auburn: John E. Beardsley, 1850) 148–49 [*Editors*].

slaveholder. This is like saying that the evil of being burnt is not felt by the person burnt, but by him who kindles up the fire about him.

FREDERICK DOUGLASS.

Perth, (Scotland,) 27th Jan. 1846.

FREDERICK DOUGLASS

Preface to the Second Dublin Edition of the *Narrative of the Life of Frederick Douglass*

[Following the excellent reception of the *Narrative of the Life of Frederick Douglass*, published in 1845 in America and shortly thereafter in Ireland, Douglass arranged with his Irish publisher to issue a second Dublin edition. The following is a new Preface that he wrote to accompany the text. Also added was an Appendix consisting of the letter of A. C. C. Thompson and Douglass's rebuttal (pp. 88–96).]

In May last,[1] the present Narrative was published in Boston, Massachusetts, and when I sailed for England in September, about 4,500 copies had been sold. I have lately heard that a fifth edition has been called for. This rapid sale may be accounted for by the fact of my being a fugitive slave, and from the circumstance that for the last four years I have been engaged in travelling as a lecturing agent of the American Anti-slavery Society, by which means I became extensively known in the United States.

My visit to Great Britain had a threefold object. I wished to be out of the way during the excitement consequent on the publication of my book; lest the information I had there given as to my identity and place of abode, should induce my *owner* to take measures for my restoration to his 'patriarchal care.' For it may not be generally known in Europe, that a slave who escapes from his master is liable, by the Constitution of the United States, to be dragged back into bondage, no matter in what part of the vast extent of the States and their territories he may have taken refuge.

My next inducement was a desire to increase my stock of information, and my opportunities of self-improvement, by a visit to the land of my *paternal* ancestors.

My third and chief object was, by the public exposition of the contaminating and degrading influences of Slavery upon the slaveholder and his abettors, as well as the slave, to excite such an intelligent interest on the subject of American Slavery, as may react upon my own country,

1. 1845 [*Editors*].

and may tend to shame her out of her adhesion to a system so abhorrent to Christianity and to her republican institutions.

My last object is, I am happy to say, in a fair way of being accomplished. I have held public meetings in Dublin, Wexford, Waterford, Cork, Youghal, Limerick, Belfast, Glasgow, Aberdeen, Perth, and Dundee, within the five months which have elapsed since I landed in England. An edition of 2000 copies of my Narrative has been exhausted, and I am in great hopes that before my visit to Great Britain shall be completed, thousands and tens of thousands of the intelligent and philanthropic will be induced to co-operate with the noble band of American abolitionists, for the overthrow of the meanest, hugest, and most dastardly system of iniquity that ever disgraced any country laying claim to the benefits of religion and civilization.

I beg to refer my reader to the Preface to the First edition, and the Letter which follows it; to some notices of my Narrative from various sources, which will be found at the end of the book;[2] and to the following notice of a public meeting held the evening previous to my departure from home, in the town of Lynn, Massachusetts, where I have resided for the last two years:—

"Last Friday evening a meeting was held in Lyceum Hall, for the purpose of exchanging farewells with Frederick Douglass and James N. Buffum,[3] prior to their departure, on the ensuing day, for the Old World. The spacious hall was crowded to its utmost capacity—hundreds of men and women being obliged to stand all the evening. This was a most gratifying fact, and spoke volumes for the onward progress of the anti-slavery movement—since but six or seven years back, the people, instead of meeting with two such anti-slavery men for the interchange of kindly feelings, would have been more likely to meet them for the purpose of inflicting some summary punishment. Hundreds of persons enjoyed on this occasion the first good opportunity they have had to judge of Frederick Douglass's ability as a speaker and a reasoner; and unless I am much mistaken, their judgment was such as not only to increase their respect for him, but for his race, and the great movement now on foot to release it from thraldom. He spoke twice, and both times with great power. His second effort sparkled with wit from beginning to end.

"The following resolutions were adopted, *nem. con.*

"RESOLVED—As the sense of this great gathering of the inhabitants of Lynn and vicinity, that we extend to our esteemed fellow citizens Frederick Douglass and James N. Buffum, whose proposed

2. Douglass refers to excerpts from reviews of the *Narrative* published in U.S. and British newspapers [*Editors*].
3. James Needham Buffum (1807–1887), businessman, Massachusetts politician, and civil rights activist [*Editors*].

departure for England has brought this multitude together, our heartiest good wishes for a successful issue of their journey.

"RESOLVED—That we are especially desirous that Frederick Douglass, who came to this town a fugitive from slavery, should bear with him to the shores of the Old World, our unanimous testimony to the fidelity with which he has sustained the various relations of life, and to the deep respect with which he is now regarded by every friend of liberty throughout our borders."

It gives me great pleasure to be able to add, in an Appendix to the present edition, an attempted Refutation of my Narrative, lately published in the "Delaware Republican" by Mr. A. C. C. Thompson.[4] My reply will be found along with Mr. Thompson's letter. I have thanked him there; but I cannot refrain from repeating my acknowledgments for the testimony he bears to the substantial truth of my story. We differ in our details, to be sure. But this was to be expected. He is the friend of slave-holders; he resides in a slave state, and is probably a slave-holder himself. He dares not speak the whole truth, if he would. I am an American slave, who have given my tyrant the slip. I am in a land of liberty, with no man to make me afraid. He agrees with me at least in the important fact, that I am what I proclaim myself to be, an ungrateful fugitive from the 'patriarchal institutions' of the Slave States; and he certifies that many of the heroes of my Narrative are still living and doing well, as "honored and worthy members of the Methodist Episcopal Church."

FREDERICK DOUGLASS.

Glasgow, Feb. 6th, 1846.

Douglass on His Mother and His Father

[No aspect of the *Narrative* has proved more troubling to readers than Douglass's compelling references to his mother and father. It is clear, in fact, that his relationships to the two were deeply troubling to Douglass as well. He describes them differently in his three autobiographies, *Narrative of the Life of Frederick Douglass* (1845), *My Bondage and My Freedom* (1855), and *Life and Times of Frederick Douglass* (1892).]

From *Narrative of the Life of Frederick Douglass* (1845)

* * *

My mother was named Harriet Bailey. She was the daughter of Isaac and Betsey Bailey, both colored, and quite dark. My mother was of a darker complexion than either my grandmother or grandfather.

---

4. See the exchange between Douglass and Thompson, pp. 88–96 [*Editors*].

*   *   * My mother and I were separated when I was but an infant—before I knew her as my mother. It is a common custom, in the part of Maryland from which I ran away, to part children from their mothers at a very early age. Frequently, before the child has reached its twelfth month, its mother is taken from it, and hired out on some farm a considerable distance off, and the child is placed under the care of an old woman, too old for field labor. For what this separation is done, I do not know, unless it be to hinder the development of the child's affection toward its mother, and to blunt and destroy the natural affection of the mother for the child. This is the inevitable result.

I never saw my mother, to know her as such, more than four or five times in my life; and each of those times was very short in duration, and at night. She was hired by a Mr. Stewart, who lived about twelve miles from my home. She made her journeys to see me in the night, travelling the whole distance on foot, after the performance of her day's work. She was a field hand, and a whipping is the penalty of not being in the field at sunrise, unless a slave has special permission from his or her master to the contrary—a permission which they seldom get, and one that gives to him that gives it the proud name of being a kind master. I do not recollect of ever seeing my mother by the light of day. She was with me in the night. She would lie down with me, and get me to sleep, but long before I waked she was gone. Very little communication ever took place between us. Death soon ended what little we could have while she lived, and with it her hardships and suffering. She died when I was about seven years old, on one of my master's farms, near Lee's Mill. I was not allowed to be present during her illness, at her death, or burial. She was gone long before I knew any thing about it. Never having enjoyed, to any considerable extent, her soothing presence, her tender and watchful care, I received the tidings of her death with much the same emotions I should have probably felt at the death of a stranger.

*   *   *

My father was a white man. He was admitted to be such by all I ever heard speak of my parentage. The opinion was also whispered that my master was my father; but of the correctness of this opinion, I know nothing; the means of knowing was withheld from me.

*   *   *

From *My Bondage and My Freedom* (1855)

*   *   *

But to return, or rather, to begin. My knowledge of my mother is very scanty, but very distinct. Her personal appearance and bearing are ineffaceably stamped upon my memory. She was tall, and finely proportioned; of deep black, glossy complexion; had regular features, and, among the other slaves, was remarkably sedate in her manners. There is in "*Prichard's Natural History of Man,*" the head of a figure[1]—on page 157—the features of which so resemble those of my mother, that I often recur to it with something of the feeling which I suppose others experience when looking upon the pictures of dear departed ones.

Yet I cannot say that I was very deeply attached to my mother; certainly not so deeply as I should have been had our relations in childhood been different. We were separated, according to the common custom, when I was but an infant, and, of course, before I knew my mother from any one else.

The germs of affection with which the Almighty, in his wisdom and mercy, arms the helpless infant against the ills and vicissitudes of his lot, had been directed in their growth toward that loving old grandmother, whose gentle hand and kind deportment it was the first effort of my infantile understanding to comprehend and appreciate. Accordingly, the tenderest affection which a beneficent Father allows, as a partial compensation to the mother for the pains and lacerations of her heart, incident to the maternal relation, was, in my case, diverted from its true and natural object, by the envious, greedy, and treacherous hand of slavery. The slave-mother can be spared long enough from the field to endure all the bitterness of a mother's anguish, when it adds another name to a master's ledger, but *not* long enough to receive the joyous reward afforded by the intelligent smiles of her child. I never think of this terrible interference of slavery with my infantile affections, and its diverting them from their natural course, without feelings to which I can give no adequate expression.

I do not remember to have seen my mother at my grandmother's at any time. I remember her only in her visits to me at Col. Lloyd's plantation, and in the kitchen of my old master. Her visits to me there were few in number, brief in duration, and mostly made in the night. The pains she took, and the toil she endured, to see me, tells me that a true mother's heart was hers, and that slavery had difficulty in paralyzing it with unmotherly indifference.

My mother was hired out to a Mr. Stewart, who lived about twelve miles from old master's, and, being a field hand, she seldom had leisure, by day, for the performance of the journey. The nights and the distance were both obstacles to her visits. She was obliged to walk, unless chance flung into her way an opportunity to ride; and the latter was sometimes her good luck. But she always had to walk one way or the other. It was a greater luxury than slavery could afford, to allow a black slave-mother a horse or a mule, upon which to travel twenty-four miles, when she could walk the distance. Besides, it is deemed a foolish whim for a slave-mother to manifest concern to see her children, and, in one point of

1. An ancient sculpture of an Egyptian male [*Editors*].

view, the case is made out—she can do nothing for them. She has no control over them; the master is even more than the mother, in all matters touching the fate of her child. Why, then, should she give herself any concern? She has no responsibility. Such is the reasoning, and such the practice. The iron rule of the plantation, always passionately and violently enforced in that neighborhood, makes flogging the penalty of failing to be in the field before sunrise in the morning, unless special permission be given to the absenting slave. "I went to see my child," is no excuse to the ear or heart of the overseer.

One of the visits of my mother to me, while at Col. Lloyd's, I remember very vividly, as affording a bright gleam of a mother's love, and the earnestness of a mother's care.

I had on that day offended "Aunt Katy," (called "Aunt" by way of respect,) the cook of old master's establishment. I do not now remember the nature of my offense in this instance, for my offenses were numerous in that quarter, greatly depending, however, upon the mood of Aunt Katy, as to their heinousness; but she had adopted, that day, her favorite mode of punishing me, namely, making me go without food all day— that is, from after breakfast. The first hour or two after dinner, I succeeded pretty well in keeping up my spirits; but though I made an excellent stand against the foe, and fought bravely during the afternoon, I knew I must be conquered at last, unless I got the accustomed reënforcement of a slice of corn bread, at sundown. Sundown came, but *no bread*, and, in its stead, their came the threat, with a scowl well suited to its terrible import, that she "meant to *starve the life out of me!*" Brandishing her knife, she chopped off the heavy slices for the other children, and put the loaf away, muttering, all the while, her savage designs upon myself. Against this disappointment, for I was expecting that her heart would relent at last, I made an extra effort to maintain my dignity; but when I saw all the other children around me with merry and satisfied faces, I could stand it no longer. I went out behind the house, and cried like a fine fellow! When tired of this, I returned to the kitchen, sat by the fire, and brooded over my hard lot. I was too hungry to sleep. While I sat in the corner, I caught sight of an ear of Indian corn on an upper shelf of the kitchen. I watched my chance, and got it, and, shelling off a few grains, I put it back again. The grains in my hand, I quickly put in some ashes, and covered them with embers, to roast them. All this I did at the risk of getting a brutal thumping, for Aunt Katy could beat, as well as starve me. My corn was not long in roasting, and, with my keen appetite, it did not matter even if the grains were not exactly done. I eagerly pulled them out, and placed them on my stool, in a clever little pile. Just as I began to help myself to my very dry meal, in came my dear mother. And now, dear reader, a scene occurred which was altogether worth beholding, and to me it was instructive as well as interesting. The friendless and hungry boy, in his extremest need—and when he did not dare to look for succor—found himself in the strong, protecting arms of a mother; a mother who was, at the moment (being endowed with high powers of manner as well as matter) more than a match for all his enemies. I shall never forget the indescribable expression of her countenance, when I told her that I had had no food since morning; and that Aunt Katy said she "meant to starve the life out of me." There was pity in her glance at me, and a fiery indignation at Aunt Katy at the same time; and, while she took the corn from me, and gave me a large ginger cake, in its stead, she read Aunt Katy a lecture which she never forgot. My mother threatened her with complaining to old master in my behalf; for the latter, though harsh and cruel himself, at times, did not sanction the meanness, injustice, partiality and oppressions enacted by Aunt Katy in the kitchen. That night I learned the fact, that I was not only a child, but *somebody's* child. The "sweet cake" my mother gave me was in the shape of a heart, with a rich, dark ring glazed upon the edge of it. I was victorious, and well off for the moment; prouder, on my mother's knee, than a king upon his throne. But my triumph was short. I dropped off to sleep, and waked in the morning only to find my mother gone, and myself left at the mercy of the sable virago, dominant in my old master's kitchen, whose fiery wrath was my constant dread.

I do not remember to have seen my mother after this occurrence. Death soon ended the little communication that had existed between us; and with it, I believe, a life—judging from her weary, sad, downcast countenance and mute demeanor—full of heartfelt sorrow. I was not allowed to visit her during any part of her long illness; nor did I see her for a long time before she was taken ill and died. The heartless and ghastly form of *slavery* rises between mother and child, even at the bed of death. The mother, at the verge of the grave, may not gather her children, to impart to them her holy admonitions, and invoke for them her dying benediction. The bondwoman lives as a slave, and is left to die as a beast; often with fewer attentions than are paid to a favorite horse. Scenes of sacred tenderness, around the deathbed, never forgotten, and which often arrest the vicious and confirm the virtuous during life, must be looked for among the free, though they sometimes occur among the slaves. It has been a life-long, standing grief to me, that I knew so little of my mother; and that I was so early separated from her. The counsels of her love must have been beneficial to me. The side view of her face is imaged on my memory, and I take few steps in life, without feeling her presence; but the image is mute, and I have no striking words of her's treasured up.

I learned, after my mother's death, that she could read, and that she was the *only* one of all the slaves and colored people in Tuckahoe who enjoyed that advantage. How she acquired this knowledge, I know not, for Tuckahoe is the last place in the world where she would be apt to

find facilities for learning. I can, therefore, fondly and proudly ascribe
to her an earnest love of knowledge. That a "field hand" should learn to
read, in any slave state, is remarkable; but the achievement of my
mother, considering the place, was very extraordinary; and, in view of
that fact, I am quite willing, and even happy, to attribute any love of
letters I possess, and for which I have got—despite of prejudices—only
too much credit, *not* to my admitted Anglo-Saxon paternity, but to the
native genius of my sable, unprotected, and uncultivated *mother*—a
woman, who belonged to a race whose mental endowments it is, at
present, fashionable to hold in disparagement and contempt.

*   *   *

I say nothing of *father*, for he is shrouded in a mystery I have never
been able to penetrate. Slavery does away with fathers, as it does away
with families. Slavery has no use for either fathers or families, and its
laws do not recognize their existence in the social arrangements of the
plantation. When they *do* exist, they are not the outgrowths of slavery,
but are antagonistic to that system. The order of civilization is reversed
here. The name of the child is not expected to be that of its father, and
his condition does not necessarily affect that of the child. He may be
the slave of Mr. Gross. He may be a *freeman*; and yet his child may be
a *chattel*. He may be white, glorying in the purity of his Anglo-Saxon
blood; and his child may be ranked with the blackest slaves. Indeed, he
may be, and often *is*, master and father to the same child. He can be
father without being a husband, and may sell his child without incurring reproach, if the child be by a woman in whose veins courses one
thirty-second part of African blood. My father was a white man, or nearly
white. It was sometimes whispered that my master was my father.

*   *   *

From Life and Times of Frederick Douglass (1892)

*   *   *

My grandmother's five daughters were hired out in this way, and my
only recollections of my own mother are of a few hasty visits made in
the night on foot, after the daily tasks were over, and when she was
under the necessity of returning in time to respond to the driver's call to
the field in the early morning. These little glimpses of my mother,
obtained under such circumstances and against such odds, meager as
they were, are ineffaceably stamped upon my memory. She was tall and
finely proportioned, of dark, glossy complexion, with regular features,
and amongst the slaves was remarkably sedate and dignified. There is,
in Prichard's *Natural History of Man*, the head of a figure, on page 157,
the features of which so resemble my mother that I often recur to it

with something of the feelings which I suppose others experience when looking upon the likenesses of their own dear departed ones.

Of my father I know nothing. Slavery had no recognition of fathers, as none of families. That the mother was a slave was enough for its deadly purpose. By its law the child followed the condition of its mother. The father might be a white man, glorying in the purity of his Anglo-Saxon blood, and the child ranked with the blackest slaves. Father he might be, and not be husband, and could sell his own child without incurring reproach, if in its veins coursed one drop of African blood.

Douglass on His Escape from Slavery †

[When Douglass wrote yet again of his life, long after slavery had ended, he responded to earlier readers' curiosity about how he escaped. In the first edition of the *Life and Times of Frederick Douglass* (1881, rev. 1882), he tells this story well, but he does not fully suggest how well the escape was orchestrated by devoted antislavery people operating in what was called the Underground Railroad. This careful coordination is in evidence from the moment the taxi driver got him to the train, only at the last minute, through to the two Quakers being on hand to get the Douglasses onto the stagecoach for the last leg of their trip. Only in New York City, where he had trouble finding David Ruggles's house, did the plan falter briefly.]

In the first narrative of my experience in slavery, written nearly forty years ago, and in various writings since, I have given the public what I considered very good reasons for withholding the manner of my escape. In substance these reasons were, first, that such publication at any time during the existence of slavery might be used by the master against the slave, and prevent the future escape of any who might adopt the same means that I did. The second reason was, if possible, still more binding to silence—for publication of details would certainly have put in peril the persons and property of those who assisted. Murder itself was not more sternly and certainly punished in the State of Maryland than that of aiding and abetting the escape of a slave. Many colored men, for no other crime than that of giving aid to a fugitive slave, have, like Charles T. Torrey,[1] perished in prison. The abolition of slavery in my native State and throughout the country, and the lapse of time, render the caution hitherto observed no longer necessary. But, even since the abolition of slavery, I have sometimes thought it well enough to baffle curiosity by saying that while slavery existed there were good reasons for not telling the manner of my escape, and since slavery had ceased to exist there was no reason for telling it. I shall now, however, cease to avail myself of this formula, and, as far as I can, endeavor to satisfy this very

---

† From *Life and Times of Frederick Douglass* (Hartford, Conn.: Park Publishing, 1882) 242–55.
1. Maryland antislavery reformer (1813–1846). In 1844 he was sentenced to prison for attempting to aid in the escape of several slaves [*Editors*].

natural curiosity. I should perhaps have yielded to that feeling sooner, had there been anything very heroic or thrilling in the incidents connected with my escape, for I am sorry to say I have nothing of that sort to tell; and yet the courage that could risk betrayal and the bravery which was ready to encounter death if need be, in pursuit of freedom, were essential features in the undertaking. My success was due to address rather than courage; to good luck rather than bravery. My means of escape were provided for me by the very men who were making laws to hold and bind me more securely in slavery. It was the custom in the State of Maryland to require of the free colored people to have what were called free papers. This instrument they were required to renew very often, and by charging a fee for this writing, considerable sums from time to time were collected by the State. In these papers the name, age, color, height, and form of the free man were described, together with any scars or other marks upon his person, which could assist in his identification. This device of slaveholding ingenuity, like other devices of wickedness, in some measure defeated itself—since more than one man could be found to answer the same general description. Hence many slaves could escape by personating the owner of one set of papers; and this was often done as follows: A slave nearly or sufficiently answering the description set forth in the papers, would borrow or hire them till he could by their means escape to a free state, and then, by mail or otherwise, return them to the owner. The operation was a hazardous one for the lender as well as the borrower. A failure on the part of the fugitive to send back the papers would imperil his benefactor, and the discovery of the papers in possession of the wrong man would imperil both the fugitive and his friend. It was therefore an act of supreme trust on the part of a freeman of color thus to put in jeopardy his own liberty that another might be free. It was, however, not unfrequently bravely done, and was seldom discovered. I was not so fortunate as to sufficiently resemble any of my free acquaintances as to answer the description of their papers. But I had one friend—a sailor—who owned a sailor's protection, which answered somewhat the purpose of free papers—describing his person, and certifying to the fact that he was a free American sailor. The instrument had at its head the American eagle, which gave it the appearance at once of an authorized document. This protection did not, when in my hands, describe its bearer very accurately. Indeed, it called for a man much darker than myself, and close examination of it would have caused my arrest at the start. In order to avoid this fatal scrutiny on the part of the railroad official, I had arranged with Isaac Rolls, a hackman, to bring my baggage to the train just on the moment of starting, and jumped upon the car myself when the train was already in motion. Had I gone into the station and offered to purchase a ticket, I should have been instantly and carefully examined, and undoubtedly arrested. In choosing this plan upon which to act, I considered the jostle of the train, and the natural haste of the conductor, in a train crowded with passengers, and relied upon my skill and address in playing the sailor as described in my protection, to do the rest. One element in my favor was the kind feeling which prevailed in Baltimore, and other seaports at the time, towards "those who go down to the sea in ships." "Free trade and sailors' rights" expressed the sentiment of the country just then. In my clothing I was rigged out in sailor style. I had on a red shirt and a tarpaulin hat and black cravat, tied in sailor fashion, carelessly and loosely about my neck. My knowledge of ships and sailor's talk came much to my assistance, for I knew a ship from stem to stern, and from keelson to cross-trees, and could talk sailor like an "old salt." On sped the train, and I was well on the way to Havre de Grace before the conductor came into the negro car to collect tickets and examine the papers of his black passengers. This was a critical moment in the drama. My whole future depended upon the decision of this conductor. Agitated I was while this ceremony was proceeding, but still externally, at least, I was apparently calm and self-possessed. He went on with his duty—examining several colored passengers before reaching me. He was somewhat harsh in tone, and peremptory in manner until he reached me, when, strangely enough, and to my surprise and relief, his whole manner changed. Seeing that I did not readily produce my free papers, as the other colored persons in the car had done, he said to me in a friendly contrast with that observed towards the others: "I suppose you have your free papers?" To which I answered: "No, sir; I never carry my free papers to sea with me." "But you have something to show that you are a free man, have you not?" "Yes, sir," I answered; "I have a paper with the American eagle on it, that will carry me round the world." With this I drew from my deep sailor's pocket my seaman's protection, as before described. The merest glance at the paper satisfied him, and he took my fare and went on about his business. This moment of time was one of the most anxious I ever experienced. Had the conductor looked closely at the paper, he could not have failed to discover that it called for a very different looking person from myself, and in that case it would have been his duty to arrest me on the instant, and send me back to Baltimore from the first station. When he left me with the assurance that I was all right, though much relieved, I realized that I was still in great danger: I was still in Maryland, and subject to arrest at any moment. I saw on the train several persons who would have known me in any other clothes, and I feared they might recognize me, even in my sailor "rig," and report me to the conductor, who would then subject me to a closer examination, which I knew well would be fatal to me.

Though I was not a murderer fleeing from justice, I felt, perhaps, quite as miserable as such a criminal. The train was moving at a very high rate of speed for that time of railroad travel, but to my anxious mind, it was moving far too slowly. Minutes were hours, and hours were days during this part of my flight. After Maryland I was to pass through Delaware—another slave State, where slave-catchers generally awaited their prey, for it was not in the interior of the State, but on its borders, that these human hounds were most vigilant and active. The border lines between slavery and freedom were the dangerous ones, for the fugitives. The heart of no fox or deer, with hungry hounds on his trail, in full chase, could have beaten more anxiously or noisily than did mine, from the time I left Baltimore till I reached Philadelphia. The passage of the Susquehanna river at Havre de Grace was made by ferry-boat at that time, on board of which I met a young colored man by the name of Nichols, who came very near betraying me. He was a "hand" on the boat, but instead of minding his business, he insisted upon know-ing me, and asking me dangerous questions as to where I was going, and when I was coming back, etc. I got away from my old and inconvenient acquaintance as soon as I could decently do so, and went to another part of the boat. Once across the river I encountered a new danger. Only a few days before I had been at work on a revenue cutter, in Mr. Price's ship-yard, under the care of Captain McGowan. On the meeting at this point of the two trains, the one going south stopped on the track just opposite to the one going north, and it so happened that this Cap-tain McGowan sat at a window where he could see me very distinctly, and would certainly have recognized me had he looked at me but for a second. Fortunately, in the hurry of the moment, he did not see me; and the trains soon passed each other on their respective ways. But this was not the only hair-breadth escape. A German blacksmith, whom I knew well, was on the train with me, and looked at me very intently, as if he thought he had seen me somewhere before in his travels. I really believe he knew me, but had no heart to betray me. At any rate he saw me escaping and held his peace.

The last point of imminent danger, and the one I dreaded most, was Wilmington. Here we left the train and took the steamboat for Philadel-phia. In making the change here I again apprehended arrest, but no one disturbed me, and I was soon on the broad and beautiful Delaware, speeding away to the Quaker City. On reaching Philadelphia in the afternoon I inquired of a colored man how I could get on to New York? He directed me to the Willow street depot, and thither I went, taking the train that night. I reached New York Tuesday morning, having com-pleted the journey in less than twenty-four hours. Such is briefly the manner of my escape from slavery—and the end of my experience as a slave. Other chapters will tell the story of my life as a freeman.

* * *

My free life began on the third of September, 1838. On the morning of the 4th of that month, after an anxious and most perilous but safe journey, I found myself in the big city of New York, a *free man*; one more added to the mighty throng which, like the confused waves of the troubled sea, surged to and fro between the lofty walls of Broadway. Though dazzled with the wonders which met me on every hand, my thoughts could not be much withdrawn from my strange situation. For the moment the dreams of my youth, and the hopes of my manhood, were completely fulfilled. The bonds that had held me to "old master" were broken. No man now had a right to call me his slave or assert mastery over me. I was in the rough and tumble of an outdoor world, to take my chance with the rest of its busy number. I have often been asked, how I felt when first I found myself on free soil. And my readers may share the same curiosity. There is scarcely anything in my experience about which I could not give a more satisfactory answer. A new world had opened upon me. If life is more than breath, and the "quick round of blood," I lived more in one day than in a year of my slave life. It was a time of joyous excitement which words can but tamely describe. In a letter written to a friend soon after reaching New York, I said: "I felt as one might feel upon escape from a den of hungry lions." Anguish and grief, like darkness and rain, may be depicted; but gladness and joy, like the rainbow, defy the skill of pen or pencil. During ten or fifteen years I had, as it were, been dragging a heavy chain, whieh no strength of mine could break; I was not only a slave, but a slave for life. I might become a husband, a father, an aged man, but through all, from the cradle to the grave, I had felt myself doomed. All efforts I had previously made to secure my freedom, had not only failed, but had seemed only to rivet my fetters the more firmly, and to render my escape more difficult. Baffled, entangled, and discouraged, I had at times asked myself the question, May not my condition after all be God's work, and ordered for a wise purpose, and if so, was not submission my duty? A contest had in fact been going on in my mind for a long time, between the clear consciousness of right, and the plausible make-shifts of theology and superstition. The one held me an abject slave—a prisoner for life, punished for some transgression in which I had no lot or part; and the other counseled me to manly endeavor to secure my freedom. This contest was now ended; my chains were broken, and the victory brought me unspeakable joy. But my gladness was short lived, for I was not yet out of the reach and power of the slaveholders. I soon found that New York was not quite so free, or so safe a refuge as I had supposed, and a sense of loneliness and insecurity again oppressed me most sadly. I chanced to meet on the street, a few hours after my landing, a fugitive slave whom I had once known well in slavery. The information received from him alarmed me. The fugitive in question was known in Baltimore as "Allender's Jake," but in New York he wore the more respectable name of "William Dixon." Jake in law was the property of Doctor Allender, and Tolly Allender, the son of the doctor, had once made an effort to recapture Mr. Dixon, but had failed for want of evidence to support his claim. Jake told me the circumstances of this attempt, and how narrowly he escaped being sent back to slavery and torture. He told me that New York was then full of southeners returning from the watering-places north; that the colored people of New York were not to be trusted; that there were hired men of my own color who would betray me for a few dollars; that there were hired men ever on the lookout for fugitives; that I must trust no man with my secret; that I must not think of going either upon the wharves, or into any colored boarding-house, for all such places were closely watched; that he was himself unable to help me; and, in fact, he seemed while speaking to me, to fear lest I myself might be a spy and a betrayer. Under this apprehension, as I suppose, he showed signs of wishing to be rid of me, and with whitewash brush in hand, in search of work, he soon disappeared. This picture, given by poor "Jake," of New York, was a damper to my enthusiasm. My little store of money would soon be exhausted, and since it would be unsafe for me to go on the wharves for work, and I had no introductions elsewhere, the prospect for me was far from cheerful. I saw the wisdom of keeping away from the ship-yards, for, if pursued, as I felt certain I would be, Mr. Auld would naturally seek me there among the calkers. Every door seemed closed against me. I was in the midst of an ocean of my fellow-men, and yet a perfect stranger to every one. I was without home, without acquaintance, without money, without credit, without work, and without any definite knowledge as to what course to take, or where to look for succor. In such an extremity, a man has something beside his new-born freedom to think of. While wandering about the streets of New York, and lodging at least one night among the barrels on one of the wharves, I was indeed free—from slavery, but free from food and shelter as well. I kept my secret to myself as long as I could, but was compelled at last to seek some one who should befriend me, without taking advantage of my destitution to betray me. Such an one I found in a sailor named Stuart, a warm-hearted and generous fellow, who from his humble home on Center street, saw me standing on the opposite sidewalk, near "The Tombs."[2] As he approached me I ventured a remark to him which at once enlisted his interest in me. He took me to his home to spend the night, and in the morning went with me to Mr. David Ruggles, the secretary of the New York vigilance committee, a co-worker with Isaac T. Hopper, Lewis and Arthur Tappan, Theodore S. Wright, Samuel Cornish, Thomas Downing, Philip A. Bell,[3] and other true men of their time. All these (save Mr. Bell, who still lives,

---

2. New York City prison finished in 1838 and built in the style of Ancient Egyptian architecture [Editors].

3. David Ruggles (1810–1849), see above, p. 70n; Isaac T. Hopper (1771–1852), white Quaker philanthropist; Arthur (1786–1865) and Lewis Tappan (1788–1873), brothers, wealthy white businessmen; Theodore Sedgwick Wright (1797–1847), prominent black clergyman; Samuel E. Cornish (1795–1858), black editor and clergyman; George Thomas Downing (1819–1903), black businessman; Philip A. Bell (1808–1889), black newspaper editor.

and is editor and publisher of a paper called the *Elevator*, in San Francisco) have finished their work on earth. Once in the hands of these brave and wise men, I felt comparatively safe. With Mr. Ruggles, on the corner of Lispenard and Church streets, I was hidden several days, during which time my intended wife came on from Baltimore at my call, to share the burdens of life with me. She was a free woman, and came at once on getting the good news of my safety. We were married by Rev. J. W. C. Pennington,[4] then a well-known and respected Presbyterian minister. I had no money with which to pay the marriage fee, but he seemed well pleased with our thanks.

Mr. Ruggles was the first officer on the underground railroad with whom I met after coming North; and was indeed the only one with whom I had anything to do, till I became *such* an officer myself. Learning that my trade was that of a calker, he promptly decided that the best place for me was in New Bedford, Mass. He told me that many ships for whaling voyages were fitted out there, and that I might there find work at my trade, and make a good living. So, on the day of the marriage ceremony, we took our little luggage to the steamer John W. Richmond, which at that time was one of the line running between New York and Newport, R. I. Forty-three years ago colored travelers were not permitted in the cabin, nor allowed abaft the paddle-wheels of a steam vessel. They were compelled, whatever the weather might be, whether cold or hot, wet or dry, to spend the night on deck. Unjust as this regulation was, it did not trouble us much. We had fared much harder before. We arrived at Newport the next morning, and soon after an old-fashioned stage-coach with "New Bedford" in large, yellow letters on its sides, came down to the wharf. I had not money enough to pay our fare, and stood hesitating to know what to do. Fortunately for us, there were two Quaker gentlemen who were about to take passage on the stage,— Friends William C. Taber and Joseph Ricketson,[5]—who at once discerned our true situation, and in a peculiarly quiet way, addressing me, Mr. Taber said: "Thee get in." I never obeyed an order with more alacrity, and we were soon on our way to our new home. When we reached "Stone Bridge" the passengers alighted for breakfast, and paid their fares to the driver. We took no breakfast, and when asked for our fares I told the driver I would make it right with him when we reached New Bedford. I expected some objection to this on his part, but he made none. When, however, we reached New Bedford he took our baggage, including three music books,—two of them collections by Dyer, and one by Shaw,—and held them until I was able to redeem them by paying to him the sums due for our rides. This was soon done, for Mr. Nathan

4. James W. C. Pennington (1807–1870), see above p. 70n [*Editors*].
5. Member of a prominent, wealthy Quaker family and friend of Henry David Thoreau; active in the antislavery movement. William C. Taber, Quaker proprietor of a New Bedford bookstore, also headed a large private library in that city [*Editors*].

Johnson[6] not only received me kindly and hospitably, but, on being informed about our baggage, at once loaned me the two dollars with which to square accounts with the stagedriver. Mr. and Mrs. Nathan Johnson reached a good old age, and now rest from their labors. I am under many grateful obligations to them. They not only "took me in when a stranger," and "fed me when hungry," but taught me how to make an honest living.

Thus, in a fortnight after my flight from Maryland, I was safe in New Bedford,—a citizen of the grand old commonwealth of Massachusetts.

* * *

FREDERICK DOUGLASS

I Am Here to Spread Light on American Slavery †

[In 1845, shortly after the publication of *Narrative of the Life of Frederick Douglass*, the American Anti-Slavery Society sent Douglass to Great Britain. Douglass and the society's objective was to further consolidate their alliance with the still active antislavery movement. (Parliament had emancipated slaves in the West Indian colonies in 1831.) Many of the leaders of the society, particularly William Lloyd Garrison and Wendell Phillips, were especially proud of Douglass and eager to have him known in Great Britain. They were certain that he would do credit to the movement. Others, such as Maria Weston Chapman, in charge of arranging speaking tours, were not sorry to have him out of the country for a time. Douglass had gained so much self-confidence as an orator and a writer that he seemed to them too big for any black man's britches. All white antislavery people, however dedicated to the cause, were not free of racist attitudes.

Douglass went first to Dublin, where Richard D. Webb published the first European edition of the *Narrative* (Webb & Chapman, 1845). Next he went south to Cork, which had an active antislavery society, to give one of the first of scores of successful lectures throughout Ireland, Scotland, and England. In all of his talks, he told stories about slavery similar to those told in the *Narrative*, but these stories often diverged as he reached to make rhetorical points.

As the editors of the *Douglass Papers* noted, "On the afternoon of 14 October 1845, approximately a week after arriving in Cork, Douglass delivered an antislavery lecture in the city courthouse. The *Southern Reporter* noted that long before the meeting was scheduled to begin, the building

6. Mr. and Mrs. Nathan Johnson were leaders of the substantial black community in New Bedford; the Johnsons were successful caterers; Nathan Johnson was the sole black member of Taber's private library [*Editors*].

† An address delivered in Cork, Ireland, on October 14, 1845. From the *Cork Southern Reporter*, October 16, 1845 (supplement). Cited in John W. Blassingame et al., eds., *The Frederick Douglass Papers* (New Haven: Yale UP, 1979–) vol. 1, pp. 39–45.

was 'densely crowded in every part.' The gallery was 'thronged with ladies' who seemed to 'take the liveliest interest in the proceedings.' The *Cork Examiner* (October 15, 1845) reported the presence of 'over one hundred ladies' and a 'large audience of respectable gentlemen and citizens.' Mayor Richard Dawden presided. After Cork resident and American abolitionist James Buffum introduced a series of antislavery resolutions, Douglass addressed the audience. According to the *Southern Reporter* Douglass's oratorical skills were a matter of 'admiration' and even 'astonishment.' The Maryland fugitive joined 'facility and power of expression' with 'a most impressive and energetic delivery.' It was, however, Douglass's extremely 'humorous method' of exposing the 'hypocrisy and duplicity' of American slaveholders which 'kept the meeting in a roar.' "]

* * *

Mr. Frederick Douglas[s] then came forward amid loud cheering. He said—Sir, I never more than at present lacked words to express my feelings. The cordial and manly reception I have met with, and the spirit of freedom that seems to animate the bosoms of the entire audience have filled my heart with feelings I am incapable of expressing. I stand before you in the most extraordinary position that one human being ever stood before his race—a slave. A slave not in the ordinary sense of the term, not in a political sense, but in its real and intrinsic meaning. I have not been stripped of one of my rights and privileges, but of all. By the laws of the country whence I came, I was deprived of myself—of my own body, soul, and spirit, and I am free only because I succeeded in escaping the clutches of the man who claimed me as his property. There are fourteen Slave States in America, and I was sold as a slave at a very early age, little more than seven years, in the southern part of Maryland. While there I conceived the idea of escaping into one of the Free States, which I eventually succeeded in accomplishing. On the 3rd Sept., 1838, I made my escape into Massachusetts, a free state, and it is a pleasing coincidence that just seven years after I stood up in the Royal Exchange in Dublin, to unfold to the people of that good City the wrongs and sufferings to which my race in America were exposed. (Applause.) On escaping into Massachusetts, I went to work on the quays, rolling oil casks,[1] to get a livelihood, and in about three years after having been induced to attend an anti-slavery meeting at Nantucket, it was there announced that I should go from town to town to expose their nefarious system. For four years I was then engaged in discussing the slavery question, and during that time I had opportunities of arranging my thoughts and language. It was at last doubted if I had ever been a slave, and this doubt being used to injure the anti-slavery cause, I was induced to set the matter at rest by publishing the narrative of my life. A person undertaking to write a book without learning will appear rather

---

1. The heavy physical labor Douglass did loading ships on New Bedford docks [*Editors*].

novel, but such as it was I gave it to the public. (Hear, hear.) The excitement at last increased so much that it was thought better for me to get out of the way lest my master might use some stratagem to get me back into his clutches. I am here then in order to avoid the scent of the blood hounds of America, and of spreading light on the subject of her slave system. There is nothing slavery dislikes half so much as the light. It is a gigantic system of iniquity, that feeds and lives in darkness, and, like a tree with its roots turned to the sun, it perishes when exposed to the light. (Loud cheering.) We want to arouse public indignation against the system of slavery and to bring the concentrated execrations of the civilized world to bear on it like a thunderbolt. (Loud cheering.) The relation of master and slave in America should be clearly understood. The master is allowed by law to hold his slave as his possession and property, which means the right of one man to hold property in his fellow. The master can buy, sell, bequeath his slave as well as any other property, nay, he shall decide what the poor slave is to eat, what he is to drink, where and when he shall speak. He also decides for his affections, when and whom he is to marry, and, what is more enormous, how long that marriage covenant is to endure. The slaveholder exercises the bloody power of tearing asunder those whom God had joined together—of separating husband from wife, parent from child, and of leaving the hut vacant, and the hearth desolate. (Sensation.) The slave holders of America resort to every species of cruelty, but they can never reduce the slave to a willing obedience. The natural elasticity of the human soul repels the slightest attempt to enslave it. The black slaves of America are not wholly without that elasticity; they are men, and, being so, they do not submit readily to the yoke. (Great cheering.) It is easy to keep a brute in the position of a brute, but when you undertake to place a man in the same state, believe me you must build your fences higher, and your doors firmer than before. A brute you may molest sometimes with impunity, but never a man. Men—the black slaves of America—are capable of resenting an insult, of revenging an outrage, and of looking defiance at their masters. (Applause.) Oftentimes, when the poor slave, after recovering from the application of the scourge and the branding iron, looks at his master with a face indicating dissatisfaction, he is subjected to fresh punishment. That cross look must be at once repulsed, and the master whips, as he says "the d—l out of him;" for when a slave looks dissatisfied with his condition, according to his cruel taskmaster's idea, it looks as if he had the devil in him, and it must be whipped out. (Oh, oh.) The state of slavery is one of perpetual cruelty. When very young, as I stated, I was sold into slavery, and was placed under the control of a little boy who had orders to kick me when he liked, whenever the little boy got cross, his mother used to say "Go and whip Freddy." I however, soon began to reason upon the matter, and found that I had as good a right to kick Tommy, as Tommy had me.

(Loud laughter and cheering.) My dissatisfaction with my condition soon appeared, and I was most brutally treated. I stand before you with the marks of the slave-driver's whip, that will go down with me to my grave; but, what is worse, I feel the scourge of slavery itself piercing into my heart, crushing my feelings, and sinking me into the depths of moral and intellectual degradation. (Loud cheering.) In the South, the laws are exceedingly cruel, more so than in the Northern States. The most cruel feature of the system in the Northern States is the slave Trade. The domestic slave trade of America is now in the height of its prosperity from the Annexation of Texas to our Union. In the Northern States they actually breed slaves, and rear them for the Southern markets; and the constant dread of being sold is often more terrible than the reality itself. Here the speaker proceeded to comment upon the law of America relative to the punishment of slaves, and read the following:—

"If more than seven slaves are found together in any road, without a white person—*twenty lashes* a piece. For visiting a plantation without a written pass—*ten lashes*. For letting loose a boat from where it is made fast—*thirty nine lashes*; and for the second offence, shall have his ear cut off. For having an article for sale without a ticket from his master—*ten lashes*. For being on horseback without the written permission of his master—*twenty five lashes*."

I saw one poor woman (continued the speaker) who had her ear nailed to a post, for attempting to run away, but the agony she endured was so great, that she tore away, and left her ear behind. (Great sensation.) This is the law of America after her Declaration of Independence—the land in which are millions of professed Christians, and which supports their religion at a cost of 20 million dollars annually, and yet she has three millions of human beings the subjects of the hellish laws I have read. We would not ask you to interfere with the politics of America, or invoke your military aid to put down American slavery. No, we only demand your moral and religious influence on the slave [holder] in question, and believe me the effects of that influence will be overwhelming. (Cheers.) We want to awaken the slave holder to a sense of the iniquity of his position, and to draw him from his nefarious habits. We want to encircle America with a girdle of Anti-slavery fire, that will reflect light upon the darkness of the slave institutions, and alarm their guilty upholders—(great applause). It must also be stated that the American pulpit is on the side of slavery, and the Bible is blasphemously quoted in support of it. The Ministers of religion actually quoted scripture in support of the most cruel and bloody outrages on the slaves. My own master was a Methodist class leader (Laughter, and "Oh"), and he bared the neck of a young woman, in my presence, and he cut her with a cow skin. He then went away, and when he returned to complete the castigation, he quoted the passage, "He that knoweth his master's will and doeth it not, shall be beaten with many stripes."[2] (Laughter.) The preachers say to the slaves they should obey their masters, because God commands it, and because their happiness depended on it. (A laugh.) Here the Speaker assumed the attitude and drawling manner so characteristic of the American preachers, amid the laughter of all present, and continued—Thus do these hypocrites cant. They also tell the slaves there is no happiness but in obedience, and wherever you see poverty and misery, be sure it results from disobedience. (Laughter.) In order to illustrate this they tell a story of a slave having been sent to work, and when his master came up, he found poor *Sambo* asleep. Picture the feelings, say they, of that pious master, his authority thrown off, and his work not done. The master then goes to the law and the testimony, and he there read the passage I have already quoted, and *Sambo* is lashed so that he cannot work for a week after. "You servants," continued the preacher, "To what was this whipping traceable, to disobedience, and if you would not be whipped, and if you would bask in the sunshine of your master's favour, let me exhort you to obedience. You should also be grateful that God in his mercy brought you from Africa to this Christian land." (Great laughter.) They also tell the wretched slaves that God made them to do the working, and the white men the thinking. And such is the ignorance in which the slaves are held that some of them go home and say, "Me hear a good sermon to day, de Minister make ebery thing so clear, white man above a Nigger any day." (Roars of laughter.) It is punishable with death for the second attempt to teach a slave his letters in America (Loud expression of disgust), and in that Protestant country the slave is denied the privilege of learning the name of the God that made him. Slavery with all its bloody paraphernalia is upheld by the church of the country. We want them to have the Methodists of Ireland speak to those of America, and say, "While your hands are red with blood, while the thumb screws and gags and whips are wrapped up in the pontifical robes of your Church, we will have no fellowship with you, or acknowledge you [as] Christians." (Great applause.) There are men who come here and preach, whose robes are yet red with blood, but these things should not be.—Let these American Christians know their hands are too red to be grasped by Irishmen. Presbyterians, Episcopalians, Congregationalists, and Roman Catholics, stand forth to the world and declare to the American Church, that until she puts away slavery, you can have no sympathy or fellowship with them—(Applause). For myself I believe in Christianity. I love it. I love that religion which is from above, without partiality or hypocrisy—that religion based upon that broad, that world-embracing principle, "That whatever you would that men should do to you, do ye

2. Paraphrase of Luke 12.47 [*Editors*].

even so to them." (Loud cheering.)—In America Bibles and slave-holders go hand in hand. The Church and the slave prison stand together, and while you hear the chanting of psalms in one, you hear the clanking of chains in the other. The man who wields the cow hide during the week, fills the pulpit on Sunday—here we have robbery and religion united—devils dressed in angels' garments. The man who whipped me in the week used to attend to show me the way of life on the Sabbath. I cannot proceed without alluding to a man who did much to abolish slavery, I mean Daniel O'Connell.[3] (Tremendous cheers.) I feel grateful to him, for his voice has made American slavery shake to its centre.—I am determined wherever I go, and whatever position I may fill, to speak with grateful emotions of Mr. O'Connell's labours. (Cheering.) I heard his denunciation of slavery, I heard my master curse him, and therefore I loved him. (Great cheering.) In London, Mr. O'Connell tore off the mask of hypocrisy from the slave-holders, and branded them as the vilest of the vile, and the most execrable of the execrable, for no man can put words together stronger than Mr. O'Connell. (Laughter and cheering.) The speaker proceeded at some length, and related amusing anecdotes connected with his history in the United States. In one instance he was travelling to Vermont, and having arrived at a stage, they took in five new passengers. It being dark at the time, they did not know the colour of his (the Speaker's) skin, and he was treated with all manner of respect. In fact he could not help thinking at the time that he would be a great man if perpetual darkness would only take the place of day. (Laughter.) Scarcely however had the light gilded the green mountains of Vermont than he saw one of the chaps in the coach take a sly peep at him, and whisper to another "Egad after all 'tis a nigger." (Great laughter.) He had black looks for the remainder of the way, and disrespect. That feeling of prejudice had now changed, and he could now walk through Boston in the most refined company. The speaker concluded by saying that he would again address them during his stay in Cork.

FREDERICK DOUGLASS

What to the Slave Is the Fourth of July? †

[Frederick Douglass's "5th of July" speech, as it has come to be called, is perhaps his most famous. He was asked by his Rochester neighbors to give the traditional Independence Day address in 1852. As it turned out, the

---

3. Daniel O'Connell (1775–1847), Irish patriot and opponent of slavery who rallied Irish support crucial to the passage of Britain's Emancipation Act of 1833 [Editors].
† An address delivered in Rochester, New York, on Monday, July 5, 1852. Cited in John W. Blassingame et al., eds., The Frederick Douglass Papers (New Haven: Yale UP, 1979–) vol. 2, pp. 359–88.

Fourth of July fell on a Sunday that year and celebrations of the holiday were, therefore, moved to the next day, July 5.

Douglass made this innocuous shift in dates into a powerful image of black protest. Other Americans could cheerfully celebrate their independence with a gala holiday year after year, but that independence, he pointed out, was denied black Americans. The Fugitive Slave Act, enacted as part of the Compromise of 1850, had greatly increased the fervor of northern white antislavery people, and Douglass took the occasion to thunder out his hatred not only of slavery but of the denial of rights to free African Americans as well.

This speech is a fine example of the scholarship which Douglass, who had no schooling, brought to his work. He gave his audience an elaborate discussion of the reach for independence by the patriots of 1776. Still more impressive are the rhetorical heights which he achieves.]

Mr. President, Friends and Fellow Citizens: He who could address this audience without a quailing sensation, has stronger nerves than I have. I do not remember ever to have appeared as a speaker before any assembly more shrinkingly, nor with greater distrust of my ability, than I do this day. A feeling has crept over me, quite unfavorable to the exercise of my limited powers of speech. The task before me is one which requires much previous thought and study for its proper performance. I know that apologies of this sort are generally considered flat and unmeaning. I trust, however, that mine will not be so considered. Should I seem at ease, my appearance would much misrepresent me. The little experience I have had in addressing public meetings, in country school houses, avails me nothing on the present occasion.

The papers and placards say, that I am to deliver a 4th [of] July oration. This certainly sounds large, and out of the common way, for me. It is true that I have often had the privilege to speak in this beautiful Hall, and to address many who now honor me with their presence. But neither their familiar faces, nor the perfect gage I think I have of Corinthian Hall, seems to free me from embarrassment.

The fact is, ladies and gentlemen, the distance between this platform and the slave plantation, from which I escaped, is considerable—and the difficulties to be overcome in getting from the latter to the former, are by no means slight. That I am here to-day is, to me, a matter of astonishment as well as of gratitude. You will not, therefore, be surprised, if in what I have to say, I evince no elaborate preparation, nor grace my speech with any high sounding exordium. With little experience and with less learning, I have been able to throw my thoughts hastily and imperfectly together; and trusting to your patient and generous indulgence, I will proceed to lay them before you.

This, for the purpose of this celebration, is the 4th of July. It is the birthday of your National Independence, and of your political freedom. This, to you, is what the Passover was to the emancipated people of

God. It carries your minds back to the day, and to the act of your great deliverance; and to the signs, and to the wonders, associated with that act, and that day. This celebration also marks the beginning of another year of your national life; and reminds you that the Republic of America is now 76 years old. I am glad, fellow-citizens, that your nation is so young. Seventy-six years, though a good old age for a man, is but a mere speck in the life of a nation. Three score years and ten is the allotted time for individual men; but nations number their years by thousands. According to this fact, you are, even now, only in the beginning of your national career, still lingering in the period of childhood. I repeat, I am glad this is so. There is hope in the thought, and hope is much needed, under the dark clouds which lower above the horizon. The eye of the reformer is met with angry flashes, portending disastrous times; but his heart may well beat lighter at the thought that America is young, and that she is still in the impressible stage of her existence. May he not hope that high lessons of wisdom, of justice and of truth, will yet give direction to her destiny? Were the nation older, the patriot's heart might be sadder, and the reformer's brow heavier. Its future might be shrouded in gloom, and the hope of its prophets go out in sorrow. There is consolation in the thought that America is young. Great streams are not easily turned from channels, worn deep in the course of ages. They may sometimes rise in quiet and stately majesty, and inundate the land, refreshing and fertilizing the earth with their mysterious properties. They may also rise in wrath and fury, and bear away, on their angry waves, the accumulated wealth of years of toil and hardship. They, however, gradually flow back to the same old channel, and flow on as serenely as ever. But, while the river may not be turned aside, it may dry up, and leave nothing behind but the withered branch, and the unsightly rock, to howl in the abyss-sweeping wind, the sad tale of departed glory. As with rivers so with nations.

Fellow-citizens, I shall not presume to dwell at length on the associations that cluster about this day. The simple story of it is that, 76 years ago, the people of this country were British subjects. The style and title of your "sovereign people" (in which you now glory) was not then born. You were under the British Crown. Your fathers esteemed the English Government as the home government; and England as the fatherland. This home government, you know, although a considerable distance from your home, did, in the exercise of its parental prerogatives, impose upon its colonial children, such restraints, burdens and limitations, as, in its mature judgement, it deemed wise, right and proper.

But, your fathers, who had not adopted the fashionable idea of this day, of the infallibility of government, and the absolute character of its acts, presumed to differ from the home government in respect to the wisdom and the justice of some of those burdens and restraints. They went so far in their excitement as to pronounce the measures of government unjust, unreasonable, and oppressive, and altogether such as ought not to be quietly submitted to. I scarcely need say, fellow-citizens, that my opinion of those measures fully accords with that of your fathers. Such a declaration of agreement on my part would not be worth much to anybody. It would, certainly, prove nothing, as to what part I might have taken, had I lived during the great controversy of 1776. To say *now* that America was right, and England wrong, is exceedingly easy. Everybody can say it; the dastard, not less than the noble brave, can flippantly discant on the tyranny of England towards the American Colonies. It is fashionable to do so; but there was a time when to pronounce against England, and in favor of the cause of the colonies, tried men's souls. They who did so were accounted in their day, plotters of mischief, agitators and rebels, dangerous men. To side with the right, against the wrong, with the weak against the strong, and with the oppressed against the oppressor! *here* lies the merit, and the one which, of all others, seems unfashionable in our day. The cause of liberty may be stabbed by the men who glory in the deeds of your fathers. But, to proceed.

Feeling themselves harshly and unjustly treated by the home government, your fathers, like men of honesty, and men of spirit, earnestly sought redress. They petitioned and remonstrated; they did so in a decorous, respectful, and loyal manner. Their conduct was wholly unexceptionable. This, however, did not answer the purpose. They saw themselves treated with sovereign indifference, coldness and scorn. Yet they persevered. They were not the men to look back.

As the sheet anchor takes a firmer hold, when the ship is tossed by the storm, so did the cause of your fathers grow stronger, as it breasted the chilling blasts of kingly displeasure. The greatest and best of British statesmen admitted its justice, and the loftiest eloquence of the British Senate came to its support. But, with that blindness which seems to be the unvarying characteristic of tyrants, since Pharoah and his hosts were drowned in the Red Sea, the British Government persisted in the exactions complained of:

The madness of this course, we believe, is admitted now, even by England; but we fear the lesson is wholly lost on our present rulers.

Oppression makes a wise man mad. Your fathers were wise men, and if they did not go mad, they became restive under this treatment. They felt themselves the victims of grievous wrongs, wholly incurable in their colonial capacity. With brave men there is always a remedy for oppression. Just here, the idea of a total separation of the colonies from the crown was born! It was a startling idea, much more so, than we, at this distance of time, regard it. The timid and the prudent (as has been intimated) of that day, were, of course, shocked and alarmed by it.

Such people lived then, had lived before, and will, probably, ever have a place on this planet; and their course, in respect to any great change, (no matter how great the good to be attained, or the wrong to be redressed by it), may be calculated with as much precision as can be the course of the stars. They hate all changes, but silver, gold and copper change! Of this sort of change they are always strongly in favor.

These people were called tories in the days of your fathers; and the appellation, probably, conveyed the same idea that is meant by a more modern, though a somewhat less euphonious term, which we often find in our papers, applied to some of our old politicians.

Their opposition to the then dangerous thought was earnest and powerful; but, amid all their terror and affrighted vociferations against it, the alarming and revolutionary idea moved on, and the country with it.

On the 2d of July, 1776, the old Continental Congress, to the dismay of the lovers of ease, and the worshippers of property, clothed that dreadful idea with all the authority of national sanction. They did so in the form of a resolution; and as we seldom hit upon resolutions, drawn up in our day, whose transparency is at all equal to this, it may refresh your minds and help my story if I read it.

> "Resolved, That these united colonies *are*, and of right, ought to be free and Independent States; that they are absolved from all allegiance to the British Crown; and that all political connection between them and the State of Great Britain *is*, and ought to be, dissolved."

Citizens, your fathers made good that resolution. They succeeded; and to-day you reap the fruits of their success. The freedom gained is yours; and you, therefore, may properly celebrate this anniversary. The 4th of July is the first great fact in your nation's history—the very ring-bolt in the chain of your yet undeveloped destiny.

Pride and patriotism, not less than gratitude, prompt you to celebrate and to hold it in perpetual remembrance. I have said that the Declaration of Independence is the RING-BOLT to the chain of your nation's destiny; so, indeed, I regard it. The principles contained in that instrument are saving principles. Stand by those principles, be true to them on all occasions, in all places, against all foes, and at whatever cost.

From the round top of your ship of state, dark and threatening clouds may be seen. Heavy billows, like mountains in the distance, disclose to the leeward huge forms of flinty rocks! That *bolt* drawn, that *chain* broken, and all is lost. *Cling to this day—cling to it*, and to its principles, with the grasp of a storm-tossed mariner to a spar at midnight.

The coming into being of a nation, in any circumstances, is an interesting event. But, besides general considerations, there were peculiar circumstances which make the advent of this republic an event of special attractiveness.

The whole scene, as I look back to it, was simple, dignified and sublime.

The population of the country, at the time, stood at the insignificant number of three millions. The country was poor in the munitions of war. The population was weak and scattered, and the country a wilderness unsubdued. There were then no means of concert and combination, such as exist now. Neither steam nor lightning had then been reduced to order and discipline. From the Potomac to the Delaware was a journey of many days. Under these, and innumerable other disadvantages, your fathers declared for liberty and independence and triumphed.

Fellow Citizens, I am not wanting in respect for the fathers of this republic. The signers of the Declaration of Independence were brave men. They were great men too—great enough to give fame to a great age. It does not often happen to a nation to raise, at one time, such a number of truly great men. The point from which I am compelled to view them is not, certainly, the most favorable; and yet I cannot contemplate their great deeds with less than admiration. They were statesmen, patriots and heroes, and for the good they did, and the principles they contended for, I will unite with you to honor their memory.

They loved their country better than their own private interests; and, though this is not the highest form of human excellence, all will concede that it is a rare virtue, and that when it is exhibited, it ought to command respect. He who will, intelligently, lay down his life for his country, is a man whom it is not in human nature to despise. Your fathers staked their lives, their fortunes, and their sacred honor, on the cause of their country. In their admiration of liberty, they lost sight of all other interests.

They were peace men; but they preferred revolution to peaceful submission to bondage. They were quiet men; but they did not shrink from agitating against oppression. They showed forbearance; but that they knew its limits. They believed in order; but not in the order of tyranny. With them, nothing was "settled" that was not right. With them, justice, liberty and humanity were "final;" not slavery and oppression. You may well cherish the memory of such men. They were great in their day and generation. Their solid manhood stands out the more as we contrast it with these degenerate times.

How circumspect, exact and proportionate were all their movements! How unlike the politicians of an hour! Their statesmanship looked beyond the passing moment, and stretched away in strength into the distant future. They seized upon eternal principles, and set a glorious example in their defence. Mark them!

Fully appreciating the hardship to be encountered, firmly believing in the right of their cause, honorably inviting the scrutiny of an onlooking world, reverently appealing to heaven to attest their sincerity, soundly comprehending the solemn responsibility they were about to assume, wisely measuring the terrible odds against them, your fathers, the fathers of this republic, did, most deliberately, under the inspiration of a glorious patriotism, and with a sublime faith in the great principles of justice and freedom, lay deep the corner-stone of the national super-structure, which has risen and still rises in grandeur around you. Of this fundamental work, this day is the anniversary. Our eyes are met with demonstrations of joyous enthusiasm. Banners and pennants wave exultingly on the breeze. The din of business, too, is hushed. Even Mammon[1] seems to have quitted his grasp on this day. The ear-piercing fife and the stirring drum unite their accents with the ascending peal of a thousand church bells. Prayers are made, hymns are sung, and ser-mons are preached in honor of this day; while the quick martial tramp of a great and multitudinous nation, echoed back by all the hills, valleys and mountains of a vast continent, bespeak the occasion one of thrilling and universal interest—a nation's jubilee.

Friends and citizens, I need not enter further into the causes which led to this anniversary. Many of you understand them better than I do. You could instruct me in regard to them. That is a branch of knowledge in which you feel, perhaps, a much deeper interest than your speaker. The causes which led to the separation of the colonies from the British crown have never lacked for a tongue. They have all been taught in your common schools, narrated at your firesides, unfolded from your pulpits, and thundered from your legislative halls, and are as familiar to you as household words. They form the staple of your national poetry and eloquence.

I remember, also, that, as a people, Americans are remarkably famil-iar with all facts which make in their own favor. This is esteemed by some as a national trait—perhaps a national weakness. It is a fact, that whatever makes for the wealth or for the reputation of Americans, and can be had *cheap!* will be found by Americans. I shall not be charged with slandering Americans, if I say I think the American side of any question may be safely left in American hands.

I leave, therefore, the great deeds of your fathers to other gentlemen whose claim to have been regularly descended will be less likely to be disputed than mine!

The Present

My business, if I have any here to-day, is with the present. The accepted time with God and his cause is the ever-living now.

> "Trust no future, however pleasant,
> Let the dead past bury its dead;
> Act, act in the living present,
> Heart within, and God overhead."[2]

1. Wealth worshipped as a false god [*Editors*].
2. Stanza quoted from Henry Wadsworth Longfellow's poem "A Psalm of Life."

We have to do with the past only as we can make it useful to the present and to the future. To all inspiring motives, to noble deeds which can be gained from the past, we are welcome. But now is the time, the important time. Your fathers have lived, died, and have done their work, and have done much of it well. You live and must die, and you must do your work. You have no right to enjoy a child's share in the labor of your fathers, unless your children are to be blest by your labors. You have no right to wear out and waste the hard-earned fame of your fathers to cover your indolence. Sydney Smith[3] tells us that men seldom eulogize the wisdom and virtues of their fathers, but to excuse some folly or wickedness of their own. This truth is not a doubtful one. There are illustrations of it near and remote, ancient and modern. It was fashionable, hundreds of years ago, for the children of Jacob to boast, we have "Abraham to our father," when they had long lost Abraham's faith and spirit. That people contented themselves under the shadow of Abraham's great name, while they repudiated the deeds which made his name great. Need I remind you that a similar thing is being done all over this country to-day? Need I tell you that the Jews are not the only people who built the tombs of the prophets, and garnished the sepulchres of the righteous? Washington could not die till he had broken the chains of his slaves. Yet his monument is built up by the price of human blood, and the traders in the bodies and souls of men, shout—"We have Washington to *our father*." Alas! that it should be so; yet so it is.

"The evil that men do, lives after them,
The good is oft' interred with their bones."[4]

Fellow-citizens, pardon me, allow me to ask, why am I called upon to speak here to-day? What have I, or those I represent, to do with your national independence? Are the great principles of political freedom and of natural justice, embodied in that Declaration of Independence, extended to us? and am I, therefore, called upon to bring our humble offering to the national altar, and to confess the benefits and express devout gratitude for the blessings resulting from your independence to us?

Would to God, both for your sakes and ours, that an affirmative answer could be truthfully returned to these questions! Then would my task be light, and my burden easy and delightful. For *who* is there so cold, that a nation's sympathy could not warm him? Who so obdurate and dead to the claims of gratitude, that would not thankfully acknowledge such priceless benefits? Who so stolid and selfish, that would not give his voice to swell the hallelujahs of a nation's jubilee, when the chains of servitude had been torn from his limbs? I am not that man. In

3. Anglican minister and master essayist and lecturer (1771–1845), whose skills were employed in the causes of Catholic emancipation and parliamentary reform [*Editors*].
4. Shakespeare, *Julius Caesar* 3.2 76–77 [*Editors*].

a case like that, the dumb might eloquently speak, and the "lame man leap as an hart."[5]

But, such is not the state of the case. I say it with a sad sense of the disparity between us. I am not included within the pale of this glorious anniversary! Your high independence only reveals the immeasurable distance between us. The blessings in which you, this day, rejoice, are not enjoyed in common. The rich inheritance of justice, liberty, prosperity and independence, bequeathed by your fathers, is shared by you, not by me. The sunlight that brought life and healing to you, has brought stripes and death to me. This Fourth [of] July is *yours*, not *mine*. *You* may rejoice, *I* must mourn. To drag a man in fetters into the grand illuminated temple of liberty, and call upon him to join you in joyous anthems, were inhuman mockery and sacrilegious irony. Do you mean, citizens, to mock me, by asking me to speak to-day? If so, there is a parallel to your conduct. And let me warn you that it is dangerous to copy the example of a nation whose crimes, towering up to heaven, were thrown down by the breath of the Almighty, burying that nation in irrecoverable ruin! I can to-day take up the plaintive lament of a peeled and woe-smitten people!

"By the rivers of Babylon, there we sat down. Yea! we wept when we remembered Zion. We hanged our harps upon the willows in the midst thereof. For there, they that carried us away captive, required of us a song; and they who wasted us required of us mirth, saying, Sing us one of the songs of Zion. How can we sing the Lord's song in a strange land? If I forget thee, O Jerusalem, let my right hand forget her cunning. If I do not remember thee, let my tongue cleave to the roof of my mouth."[6]

Fellow-citizens; above your national, tumultous joy, I hear the mournful wail of millions! whose chains, heavy and grievous yesterday, are, to-day, rendered more intolerable by the jubilee shouts that reach them. If I do forget, if I do not faithfully remember those bleeding children of sorrow this day, "may my right hand forget her cunning, and may my tongue cleave to the roof of my mouth!" To forget them, to pass lightly over their wrongs, and to chime in with the popular theme, would be treason most scandalous and shocking, and would make me a reproach before God and the world. My subject, then fellow-citizens, is American Slavery. I shall see, this day, and its popular characteristics, from the slave's point of view. Standing, there, identified with the American bondman, making his wrongs mine, I do not hesitate to declare, with all my soul, that the character and conduct of this nation never looked blacker to me than on this 4th of July! Whether we turn to the declarations of the past, or to the professions of the present, the conduct of the

5. Isaiah 35.6 [*Editors*].
6. This and the first quotation in the paragraph below are from Psalms 137.1–6 [*Editors*].

nation seems equally hideous and revolting. America is false to the past, false to the present, and solemnly binds herself to be false to the future. Standing with God and the crushed and bleeding slave on this occasion, I will, in the name of humanity which is outraged, in the name of liberty which is fettered, in the name of the constitution and the Bible, which are disregarded and trampled upon, dare to call in question and to denounce, with all the emphasis I can command, everything that serves to perpetuate slavery—the great sin and shame of America! "I will not equivocate; I will not excuse;"[7] I will use the severest language I can command; and yet not one word shall escape me that any man, whose judgement is not blinded by prejudice, or who is not at heart a slave-holder, shall not confess to be right and just.

But I fancy I hear some one of my audience say, it is just in this circumstance that you and your brother abolitionists fail to make a favorable impression on the public mind. Would you argue more, and denounce less, would you persuade more, and rebuke less, your cause would be much more likely to succeed. But, I submit, where all is plain there is nothing to be argued. What point in the anti-slavery creed would you have me argue? On what branch of the subject do the people of this country need light? Must I undertake to prove that the slave is a man? That point is conceded already. Nobody doubts it. The slaveholders themselves acknowledge it in the enactment of laws for their government. They acknowledge it when they punish disobedience on the part of the slave. There are seventy-two crimes in the State of Virginia, which, if committed by a black man, (no matter how ignorant he be), subject him to the punishment of death; while only two of the same crimes will subject a white man to the like punishment. What is this but the acknowledgement that the slave is a moral, intellectual and responsible being? The manhood of the slave is conceded. It is admitted in the fact that Southern statute books are covered with enactments forbidding, under severe fines and penalties, the teaching of the slave to read or to write. When you can point to any such laws, in reference to the beasts of the field, then I may consent to argue the manhood of the slave. When the dogs in your streets, when the fowls of the air, when the cattle on your hills, when the fish of the sea, and the reptiles that crawl, shall be unable to distinguish the slave from a brute, *then* will I argue with you that the slave is a man!

For the present, it is enough to affirm the equal manhood of the negro race. It is not astonishing that, while we are ploughing, planting and reaping, using all kinds of mechanical tools, erecting houses, constructing bridges, building ships, working in metals of brass, iron, cop-

7. From the first issue of the *Liberator* (January 1, 1831), in which William Lloyd Garrison promised, "I am in earnest—I will not equivocate—I will not excuse—I will not retreat a single inch—and I will be heard" [*Editors*].

per, silver and gold; that, while we are reading, writing and cyphering, acting as clerks, merchants and secretaries, having among us lawyers, doctors, ministers, poets, authors, editors, orators and teachers; that, while we are engaged in all manner of enterprises common to other men, digging gold in California, capturing the whale in the Pacific, feeding sheep and cattle on the hill-side, living, moving, acting, thinking, planning, living in families as husbands, wives and children, and, above all, confessing and worshipping the Christian's God, and looking hopefully for life and immortality beyond the grave, we are called upon to prove that we are men!

Would you have me argue that man is entitled to liberty? that he is the rightful owner of his own body? You have already declared it. Must I argue the wrongfulness of slavery? Is that a question for Republicans? Is it to be settled by the rules of logic and argumentation, as a matter beset with great difficulty, involving a doubtful application of the principle of justice, hard to be understood? How should I look to-day, in the presence of Americans, dividing, and subdividing a discourse, to show that men have a natural right to freedom? speaking of it relatively, and positively, negatively, and affirmatively. To do so, would be to make myself ridiculous, and to offer an insult to your understanding. There is not a man beneath the canopy of heaven, that does not know that slavery is wrong *for him*.

What, am I to argue that it is wrong to make men brutes, to rob them of their liberty, to work them without wages, to keep them ignorant of their relations to their fellow men, to beat them with sticks, to flay their flesh with the lash, to load their limbs with irons, to hunt them with dogs, to sell them at auction, to sunder their families, to knock out their teeth, to burn their flesh, to starve them into obedience and submission to their masters? Must I argue that a system thus marked with blood, and stained with pollution, is *wrong*? No! I will not. I have better employments for my time and strength, than such arguments would imply.

What, then, remains to be argued? Is it that slavery is not divine; that God did not establish it; that our doctors of divinity are mistaken? There is blasphemy in the thought. That which is inhuman, cannot be divine! *Who* can reason on such a proposition? They that can, may; I cannot. The time for such argument is past.

At a time like this, scorching irony, not convincing argument, is needed. O! had I the ability, and could I reach the nation's ear, I would, to-day, pour out a fiery stream of biting ridicule, blasting reproach, withering sarcasm, and stern rebuke. For it is not light that is needed, but fire; it is not the gentle shower, but thunder. We need the storm, the whirlwind, and the earthquake. The feeling of the nation must be quickened; the conscience of the nation must be roused; the propriety of the nation must be startled; the hypocrisy of the nation must be exposed;

and its crimes against God and man must be proclaimed and denounced.

What, to the American slave, is your 4th of July? I answer: a day that reveals to him, more than all other days in the year, the gross injustice and cruelty to which he is the constant victim. To him, your celebration is a sham; your boasted liberty, an unholy license; your national greatness, swelling vanity; your sounds of rejoicing are empty and heartless; your denunciations of tyrants, brass fronted impudence; your shouts of liberty and equality, hollow mockery; your prayers and hymns, your sermons and thanksgivings, with all your religious parade, and solemnity, are, to him, mere bombast, fraud, deception, impiety, and hypocrisy—a thin veil to cover up crimes which would disgrace a nation of savages. There is not a nation on the earth guilty of practices, more shocking and bloody, than are the people of these United States, at this very hour.

Go where you may, search where you will, roam through all the monarchies and despotisms of the old world, travel through South America, search out every abuse, and when you have found the last, lay your facts by the side of the everyday practices of this nation, and you will say with me, that, for revolting barbarity and shameless hypocrisy, America reigns without a rival.

* * *

JAMES MONROE GREGORY

From Frederick Douglass, the Orator †

[In 1893, Professor James Monroe Gregory, a professor of Latin at Howard University, wrote *Frederick Douglass, the Orator.* (When Douglass died in 1895, a revised edition was printed with additional chapters on Douglass's death, his funeral services, and his obituary tributes.) As a student of the classics, Gregory was well-equipped to analyze Douglass's oratory, although he had not heard him in his prime.]

* * *

By whatever standard judged Mr. Douglass will take high rank as orator and writer. It may be truly said of him that he was born an orator; and, though he is a man of superior intellectual faculties, he has not relied on his natural powers alone for success in this his chosen vocation. He is called a self-made man, but few college bred men have been more diligent students of logic, of rhetoric, of politics, of history, and

† From *Frederick Douglass, the Orator* (New York: Thomas Y. Cromwell, 1893) 89–92.

general literature than he. He belongs to that class of orators of which Fox of England and Henry and Clay[1] in our own country are the most illustrious representatives. His style, however, is peculiarly his own. Cicero says, "The best orator is he that so speaks as to instruct, to delight, and to move the mind of his hearers." Mr. Douglass is a striking example of this definition. Few men equal him in his power over an audience. He possesses wit and pathos, two qualities which character- ized Cicero and which, in the opinion of the rhetorician Quintilian, gave the Roman orator great advantage over Demosthenes.[2] Judge Ruf- fin of Boston,[3] in his introduction to Mr. Douglass' autobiography, says: "Douglass is brimful of humor,—at times of the driest kind; it is of a quaint kind; you can see it coming a long way off in a peculiar twitch of his mouth; it increases and broadens gradually until it becomes irre- sistible and all-pervading with his audience." The humor of Mr. Doug- lass is much like that of Mr. Joseph Jefferson,[4] the great actor, who never makes an effort to be funny, but his humor is of the quiet, suppressed type. Like Mr. Jefferson, now he excites those emotions which cause tears, and now he stirs up those which produce laughter. Grief and mirth may be said to reside in adjoining apartments in the same edifice, and the passing from one apartment to the other is not a difficult thing to do.

The biographer of Webster[5] gives the following amusing anecdote to show the simplicity of expressing thought for which that Colossus of American intellect is distinguished in his speeches: "On the arrival of that singular genius, David Crockett,[6] at Washington, he had an oppor- tunity of hearing Mr. Webster. A short time afterwards he met him and abruptly accosted him as follows: 'Is this Mr. Webster?' 'Yes, sir.' 'The great Mr. Webster of Massachusetts?' continued he, with a significant tone. 'I am Mr. Webster of Massachusetts,' was the calm reply. 'Well, sir,' continued the eccentric Crockett, 'I had heard that you were a great

1. Henry Clay (1777–1852), Whig senator from Kentucky; in the decades before the Civil War, Clay became famous as an orator and compromiser in such legislative events as the Missouri Compromise. Charles James Fox (1749–1806), English statesman, politician, and renowned orator. Patrick Henry (1736–1799), Virginia statesman and orator; one of the most influential politicians of the Revolutionary era. His most famous words to the Continental Congress in March of 1775: "Give me liberty, or give me death" [Editors].
2. Celebrated Athenian orator (383 B.C.–322 B.C.) whom Cicero admired. Cicero (106 B.C.–43 B.C.), the greatest of the Roman orators. Marcus Fabius Quintilianus (A.D. 35?–A.D. 97?), cele- brated Roman rhetorician in the style of Cicero [Editors].
3. George Lewis Ruffin (1834–1886); born of African descent but of free parentage, Ruffin stud- ied law, graduated from Harvard and in 1883 was appointed judge of a Boston municipal court, the only black justice to hold office in New England at that time [Editors].
4. Famous American actor (1829–1905) who brilliantly played a number of roles for over seventy years in theater companies in the United States, England, and Australia [Editors].
5. Daniel Webster (1782–1852), Whig senator from Massachusetts; famous orator, though not in the cause of antislavery [Editors].
6. Famous frontiersman from Tennessee (1786–1836); Crockett represented Tennessee in the state legislature and in the U.S. Congress; he later became a legend after his heroic death at the Alamo in Texas [Editors].

man, but I don't think so; I heard your speech and *understood every word you said.*' "

President Lincoln gave this reply to the question asked, to what secret he owed his success in public debate: "I always assume that my audiences are in many things wiser than I am, and I say the most sensible things I can to them. I never found that they did not understand me."

The power of simple statement is one of the chief characteristics of Mr. Douglass' style of speaking, and in this respect he resembles Fox, the great British statesman, who, above all his countrymen, was distinguished on account of plainness, and, as I may express it, homeliness of thought which gave him great power in persuading and moving his audience.

Mr. Douglass' influence in public speaking is due largely to the fact that he touches the hearts of his hearers—that he impresses them with the belief of his sincerity and earnestness. His heart is in what he says. "Clearness, force, and earnestness," says Webster, "are the qualities which produce conviction. True eloquence, indeed, does not consist in speech; it cannot be brought from far; labor and learning may toil for it, but they will toil for it in vain. Words and phrases may be marshaled in every way, but they cannot compass it; it must exist in the man, in the subject, and in the occasion."

There have been those of brilliant minds who have gained some reputation as speakers; they have been successful in pleasing and amusing those they addressed, but their success stopped here. They could not reach the depths of the heart, because their own hearts were not touched. The poet Horace[7] admirably enforces this thought when he says: "If you wish me to weep, you must first yourself be deeply grieved."

But to be fully appreciated, Mr. Douglass must be seen and heard. This was also true of Henry Clay. One could form but a faint conception of his eloquence and grandeur by reading his speeches, and yet, as reported, they were both logical and argumentative. The fire and action of the man could not be transferred to paper. Mr. Douglass in speaking does not make many gestures, but those he uses are natural and spontaneous. His manner is simple and graceful, and there is nothing about his style artificial or declamatory.

☆   ☆   ☆

---

7. Quintus Horatius Flaccus (65 B.C.–8 B.C.), celebrated Roman poet [*Editors*].

ELIZABETH CADY STANTON

[Diary Entry on Douglass's Death] †

[Of the many tributes paid Frederick Douglass on his death, perhaps the one that best captured the essence of the public man was what his old friend and fellow human rights reformer Elizabeth Cady Stanton (1815–1902) wrote in her diary the day after his death. She had known Douglass since the 1840s, the decade of the *Narrative* and the time of the speech that she recalls.]

NEW YORK, *February 21* [1895].
Taking up the papers to-day, the first word that caught my eye thrilled my very soul. Frederick Douglass is dead! What memories of the long years since he and I first met chased each other, thick and fast, through my mind and held me spellbound. A graduate from the "Southern Institution," he was well fitted to stand before a Boston audience and, with his burning eloquence, portray his sufferings in the land of bondage. He stood there like an African prince, majestic in his wrath, as with wit, satire, and indignation he graphically described the bitterness of slavery and the humiliation of subjection to those who, in all human virtues and powers, were inferior to himself. Thus it was that I first saw Frederick Douglass, and wondered that any mortal man should have ever tried to subjugate a being with such talents, intensified with the love of liberty. Around him sat the great antislavery orators of the day, earnestly watching the effect of his eloquence on that immense audience, that laughed and wept by turns, completely carried away by the wondrous gifts of his pathos and humor. On this occasion, all the other speakers seemed tame after Frederick Douglass. In imitation of the Methodist preachers of the South, he used to deliver a sermon from the text, "Servants, obey your masters," which some of our literary critics pronounced the finest piece of satire in the English language. The last time I visited his home at Anacosta [*sic*], near Washington, I asked him if he had the written text of that sermon. He answered, "No, not even notes of it." "Could you give it again?" I asked. "No," he replied; "or at least I could not bring back the old feelings even if I tried, the blessing of liberty I have so long enjoyed having almost obliterated the painful memories of my sad early days."

† From Theodore Stanton and Harriet Stanton Blach, eds., *Elizabeth Cady Stanton*, 2 vols. (New York: Harper & Brothers, 1922), vol. 2, pp. 311–12.

CRITICISM

WILLIAM S. McFEELY

[The Writing of the *Narrative*]†

[How the *Narrative* came to be is told in a recent biography of Douglass. No account is known to exist that describes exactly where he wrote the book, how many drafts he prepared, and other details that would illuminate the inception of this remarkable work.]

* * *

He was, in fact, determined to be something far beyond a curiosity when in 1844 he began to write a story of his life that would make the world pay him true attention. His book, he and his friends felt sure, not only would reach readers who had not heard him, but would also rein- force the picture in the mind's eye, the sonorous sound still in the ear, of those who had. Wendell Phillips, in particular, urged him to write his story, and in the spring of 1845 was telling his audiences to be on the lookout for it. The *Narrative of the Life of Frederick Douglass* would be a powerful antislavery tract, but it would also be far more than that.

In his writing, Douglass outran being a runaway. Never satisfied with the degree to which a nineteenth-century white world took the ex-slave seriously as an intellectual, he would have been profoundly gratified by the attention paid his work in the twentieth century. Read now only secondarily for what they tell us about slavery, his *Narrative* (1845) and *My Bondage and My Freedom* (1855) have earned the regard of critics, such as William L. Andrews, who see them as two in the series of great "I" narratives of that most remarkable of all decades of American letters. The *Narrative* carries none of the poetry of Whitman's first edition of *Leaves of Grass* (1855), but it too is a song of myself. There is not the epic tragedy of Melville's *Moby-Dick* (1851), and yet it is a story—not wholly unlike Ishmael's—of survival in a world at sea with evil. On the other hand, with its message of growing self-confidence, of self-reliance, the *Narrative* is kin to Emerson's essays. But perhaps Douglass's telling of his odyssey is closest cousin to Thoreau's account of his altogether safe escape to Walden Pond. That quietly contained, subversive tale has reverberated ever since its telling with a message of radical repudiation of corrupt society. Thoreau heard a Wendell Phillips lecture describing Douglass's exodus—and reporting that a written account was on its way—in the spring of 1845 as he was planning his sojourn outside Con- cord. Robert D. Richardson, Jr., who wrote Thoreau's intellectual biog- raphy, has said that it is not "an accident that the earliest stages of

† From William S. McFeely, *Frederick Douglass* (New York: W. W. Norton, 1991) 114–17. Copyright © 1991 by William S. McFeely. Reprinted by permission.

Thoreau's move to Walden coincide with . . . the publication of Douglass's narrative of how he gained his freedom. *Walden* is about self-emancipation."

In all three of his autobiographies, Douglass tantalizes us with the many things he leaves out; not the least of these is discussion of why and how he wrote them. His correspondence is equally void of references to what must have been a compelling exercise for him. We know that Phillips and others in the Anti-Slavery Society urged him to put his story into print, but whom did he talk to about the project, who helped, who was its editor? His later quarrels with his British publisher make it clear that he cared not only about the content—he resisted any censoring of material thought to be offensive to Christians—but also about the appearance of the front matter and the cover. Such concerns must have been with Douglass even at the time of the first printing of the first book.

But perhaps not. To a remarkable degree *Narrative of the Life of Frederick Douglass* does seem to have simply sprung from a man who had been telling the same story in much the same language from the anti-slavery platform for four years. And once he had created, with his voice and then his pencil, the Frederick Douglass of the *Narrative*, the author never altered either the character or the plot significantly. This, more than the fact that speaking came easier than writing for Douglass, explains why he wrote no books other than the autobiographies. He had but one character to craft, one story to tell. The two later books, *My Bondage and My Freedom* and *Life and Times of Frederick Douglass*, reveal important shifts in approach and detail, but the Frederick Douglass of the *Narrative* remains inviolate.

The *Narrative* is short and direct, from the "I was born" of its first line to its closing account of the Nantucket speech, describing how Douglass "felt strongly moved to speak" and was urged to do so as well: "It was a severe cross, and I took it up reluctantly. The truth was, I felt myself a slave, and the idea of speaking to white people weighed me down. I spoke but a few moments, when I felt a degree of freedom." The person we come to know in these brief pages is unforgettable. From the *Narrative* and the many other accounts of runaways published in Douglass's day, right down to Toni Morrison's *Beloved* in ours, there has been no escape from the slave in American letters. And for the fifty years following publication of the *Narrative* in 1845, there was no escape for the author from the runaway he had created.

It is easy when reading the *Narrative* to misjudge the reason for the author's many omissions—the nature of his relationships with his brothers and sisters, for example. His focused concentration on himself does invite the charge of insensitivity to others. But there were other, deeper reasons for such voids. We get a hint of them when he tells of slaves on a Wye House farm singing "most exultingly" when "leaving home: . . .

they would sing, as a chorus, to words which to many would seem unmeaning jargon, but which, nevertheless, were full of meaning to themselves." There were some sounds of slavery that Douglass could not render in words that his readers would hear, private torments and horrors too deep in the well to be drawn up.

The book was published by the "Anti-Slavery Office" in Boston in June 1845 and priced at fifty cents. The *Liberator* had announced its publication in May, and Phillips and his allies in the literary world saw to it that reviews appeared promptly. By fall, 4,500 copies had been sold in the United States; soon there were three European editions, and within five years 30,000 copies were in the hands of readers. The inevitable charge appeared that a slave boy could not have written the book—Lydia Maria Child[1] (also falsely credited with having written Harriet Jacobs's *Incidents in the Life of a Slave Girl*) was one of many suspected of having been the ghost writer. But anyone who had heard Douglass—and by 1845 thousands of people had—knew that the language of the *Narrative* was the same as that of the man who so passionately told his tale from the platform.

PETER RIPLEY

The Autobiographical Writings of Frederick Douglass†

[Historian Peter Ripley, a distinguished authority on abolitionism, has written of doubts which both Frederick Douglass and some of his fellow abolitionists had about the publication of the *Narrative*. One concern was that Douglass, so recently a slave and without a formal education, would not be believed to be the true author of the book. They expected challenges from proponents of slavery and they got them. One of these challenges, by A. C. C. Thompson, discussed by Ripley, appears above, on pp. 88–91. Douglass's rebuttal is above, on pp. 91–96.]

* * *

The Narrative signaled Douglass's emergence as a committed abolitionist and suggests his developing intellectual skills during those early years of freedom. His first abolitionist speech, given in Massachusetts in the summer of 1841, when he was just three years out of Maryland slavery, was remembered by William Lloyd Garrison as an awkward affair. Called forth to address an antislavery gathering, Douglass took

---

1. White New England abolitionist and author (1802–1880); between 1833 and 1860 she wrote, edited, and published many books, journals, and magazines on the abolition of slavery [*Editors*].

† From *Southern Studies* 24.1 (Spring 1985): 5–29. Reprinted by permission. Bracketed page numbers refer to this Norton Critical Edition.

the stage with "hesitancy and embarrassment. . . . After apologizing for his ignorance, and reminding the audience that slavery was a poor school for the human intellect and heart, he proceeded to narrate some of the facts in his own history as a slave. . . ."[1] Douglass's presentation the following day in a neighboring town prompted the Massachusetts Anti-Slavery Society to enlist him as a lecturer. For the next four years, he crisscrossed New England and the Northwest stumping against slavery, increasing both his oratorical skills and his knowledge of reform issues. Ambitious and intellectually curious, Douglass educated himself by reading reform literature, by participating in discussions, and by absorbing the lectures of his associates on the tour.

Douglass's role and position in the antislavery movement changed significantly during those early years. Initially recruited as a lecturer because he possessed two particularly appealing qualities—he was a fugitive slave and a capable speaker—Douglass typified the "awfull example" not long out of slavery, visible on the platform and effective at the lectern. He related his experiences in a clear, narrative style and in a manner not yet free of "plantation dialect." But Douglass showed signs of discontent at simply discussing his personal experiences as a slave. His lectures soon included interpretation and analysis of slavery, abolition, and other reform movements. Douglass would not long remain the "awfull example." His growth was too rapid for that.[2]

Friends cautioned that an articulate, responsive, reasoning lecturer, who claimed to be a fugitive slave, would be unconvincing to the general public and counterproductive to the crusade. Their fears were justified. Public skepticism kept pace with Douglass's rising reputation. His reluctance to disclose specific information about his slavery past as a means of confirming his fugitive status encouraged the skeptics, many of whom claimed he had never been inside the peculiar institution. Douglass, who had changed his name from Frederick Bailey, worried about revealing his slave name, or the name of his master, or the scene of his bondage for fear it would result in his arrest and reenslavement. Technically, he was still a slave and subject to capture as the property of his last owner. The issue was persistent and important enough for Douglass to give, at one point (probably 1841 to 1842), the essential facts to the officers of the Massachusetts Anti-Slavery Society.

The combined issues of Douglass's slave past and his antislavery skills were more important than simply certifying yet another antislavery lecturer. Douglass came upon the scene at a time when he—or someone like him—was needed by the movement, perhaps for the well-being and continuation of the crusade. Proslavery apologists insisted that slavery was a positive good for its civilizing and christianizing influence, and

1. Douglass, *Narrative*, v1. [4]
2. See *The Papers of Frederick Douglass:* Series I, Volume I, Speeches, Debates and Interviews, 1841–1846, John W. Blassingame, ed. (New Haven, 1979).

they charged that few, if any, abolitionists had experienced the institution from any dimension.[3] Those arguments were heard regularly and were gaining authority in the North as well as the South when Douglass took the lectern, and with his own experiences and whip-scarred back, challenged them in ways that no white or free black abolitionist could. Yet he could do that effectively only if he was believed.

Convincing his friends was one thing; persuading the public was another. Douglass was troubled. He knew that doubts about him were, in his words, "being used to injure the antislavery cause." He could backslide and return to relating personal stories and anecdotes; or he could continue as a lecturer of superior quality but increasingly low credibility; or he could make public the facts of his past and risk being returned to the Eastern Shore of Maryland in chains. Rejecting the first alternative as personally unacceptable and refusing to compromise his usefulness, Douglass chose instead to write and publish his slave experiences, "giving names . . . and places and dates."[4] He devoted the winter of 1844-45 to that enterprise.

Friends shared Douglass's concern. Abolitionist Wendell Phillips recalled that, early in their association, he stopped Douglass from revealing his slave name and birthplace—"[I] preferred to remain ignorant of it all," wrote Phillips. He was equally uneasy about *The Narrative* in 1845. When Douglass read it to his friend before having it printed, Phillips proposed that Douglass "throw the manuscript into the fire" because northern law would not protect his freedom.[5]

The preface of *The Narrative*, made up of statements by William Lloyd Garrison and Wendell Phillips, touches on the issue of Douglass's credentials and hints at yet another potential problem—if Douglass was doubted as a lecturer, why should he be believed as an author? Phillips assured readers that those who knew Douglass had "the most entire confidence in his truth, candor, and sincerity," and he promised that the book would give readers "a fair specimen of the whole truth." Accompanying Phillips's testimonial on *The Narrative*'s truthfulness and fairness was Garrison's assurances that the book was entirely Douglass's "own production." Douglass had "very properly chosen to write his own narrative, in his own style, and according to his best abilities, rather than to employ some one else."[6]

The prospects of William Lloyd Garrison and Wendell Phillips's confirming the truthfulness and honesty of Frederick Douglass irritated some skeptics. Mr. A. C. C. Thompson was one of the more active

3. Philip S. Foner, *The Life and Times of Frederick Douglass* (New York, 1950), I, 45–46.
4. Frederick May Holland, *Frederick Douglass, the Colored Orator* (New York, 1891), 102. Holland had access to Douglass's private papers and interviewed him while writing the biography; Washington, *Frederick Douglass*, 99; Charles W. Chestnut, *Frederick Douglass* (Boston, 1899), 46; *Supplement to the [Cork] Southern Reporter*, 16 October 1845.
5. Frederick Douglass, *Narrative*, xvii; London *Inquirer*, 17 January 1846.
6. Frederick Douglass, *Narrative*, xvi, ix.

critics, but his skepticism provided Douglass with the foil he sought to validate his credentials—to still the debate over his slavery past and his fugitive status.

Thompson had lived on Maryland's Eastern Shore (where Douglass was held bondage) and was a neighbor and acquaintance of Thomas Auld (Douglass's owner). For reasons that are uncertain, Thompson challenged The Narrative with a letter to a local newspaper, the Wilmington Delaware Republican, which was widely reprinted, particularly by the antislavery press.

Thompson offered the standard proslavery challenge: Douglass was not the author. The Narrative, proposed Thompson, was written by some "evil designed person or persons . . . from the statements of this runaway slave." His proof? "About eight years ago" he had known "the recent slave by the name of Frederick Bailey. . . ." Thompson described that slave as an "unlearned and rather ordinary negro . . . not capable of writing The Narrative. . . ." And although the major figures mentioned in The Narrative were indeed residents of the area, and they did have the professions and occupations attributed to them by the author, and they did live where the author put them, they were not the sort of folks Douglass claimed they were, wrote Thompson. These people, he continued, were not slave-killing, family-separating, Negro-breaking barbarians but were "good natured and harmless" and "honorable and worthy" citizens; they were Christian farmers, teachers, planters, and politicians. Thompson concluded that he was willing to "submit the facts to the judgment of an impartial public."[7]

Douglass was delighted. He seized the opportunity the Thompson letter presented and responded with a long, public reply.[8] Douglass began philosophically with a general statement about slavery and antislavery tactics that is vintage Douglass for its insights and clarity and for its unstated comment on the folly of Thompson's offer to let an impartial public judge the issue: "Slaveholders and slave-traders never betray greater indiscretion than when they venture to defend themselves . . . in any community than a slaveholding one. Slavery has its own standard. . . . Tried by that standard, it is a system of the greatest kindness to the slave. . . . But, tried by any other, it is doomed to condemnation." Douglass knew that the Thompson challenge would have little effect on him (or The Narrative) in a debate outside the slaveholding South.

With a touch of irony that characterized so much of Douglass's writings, he thanked Thompson for the "full, free, and unsolicited testimony, in regard to [his] identity." A grateful Douglass wrote that Thompson had settled the "question forever" by acknowledging that

7. Delaware Republican in The Liberator, 12 December 1845; see also The Liberator, 20 February 1846, for a reprint from the Albany Patriot of another Thompson effort accompanied by short statements by other Maryland citizens.
8. The Liberator, 27 February 1846.

Douglass was what he had claimed all along; Douglass had worried that northern defenders of slavery "might have persisted . . . in representing [him] as . . . an imposter—a free Negro," who had never seen slavery and was but an antislavery creation sent out to revive the cause. Douglass knew that Thompson, who was associated with slaveholders, would be believed as he, Douglass, never would be, and he was thankful: "You, sir, have relieved me. I now stand before both the American and British public, endorsed by you as being just what I have represented myself to be—to wit, an *American slave.*" Douglass was equally cheered that Thompson confirmed the identity of the Maryland whites in *The Narrative*—"You thus brush away the miserable insinuations of my Northern pro-slavery enemies, that I have used fictitious, not real names."

Douglass proposed that "Thompson's letter had done what *The Narrative* never could have done as well alone"—it established Douglass as a genuine fugitive slave.

Douglass turned to the second essential issue raised by Thompson—authorship of *The Narrative*. Thompson had dismissed the bondsman "Frederick Bailey" as "uneducated and rather ordinary" and incapable of writing anything like *The Narrative*. Douglass agreed. The slave that had bowed his head when last seen by Thompson on a dirt road in Maryland was then in the hands of a Negro-breaker, who, wrote Douglass, had worked him so hard, beaten him so often, fed him so little, and had so broken his spirit that he could not have written *The Narrative*. Douglass understood Thompson's doubt: "If anyone had told me, seven years ago, I should ever be able to write such a one, I should have doubted as strongly as you now do." He continued, "Frederick Douglass the *freeman*, is a very different person from Frederick Bailey. . . ." Douglass disarmed the charge that he had not written *The Narrative* and, in so doing, suggested the debilitating qualities of slavery and the rejuvenation that accompanied liberation.

The exchange verified Douglass's past. It identified the author as an exslave and a fugitive; it confirmed the authenticity of the names, occupations, and residences—if not the disposition—of masters, mistresses, overseers, Negro-breakers, and assorted whites that parade through *The Narrative*. The Wilmington letter made the primary objective of *The Narrative*—establishing Douglass's identity and past—an easy one and quickly ended a debate that might have dragged on endlessly and without resolution.

The Narrative, in its way, sent Douglass on a tour of the British Isles while doing service at home. A number of Douglass's abolitionist associates encouraged the trip, for they feared that, once *The Narrative* identified Douglass as a fugitive, it would be unsafe for him to remain in the states. Douglass appeared amenable; after all, a British visit was a signpost of success among abolitionists. Douglass welcomed the idea of a rest after finishing his first major writing chore. He jokingly spoke of visiting the land of his "paternal ancestors"—a reference to his alleged (but unidentified) white father. But Douglass, normally alert to the threat of slavecatchers, seemed reluctant to leave even though the notoriety generated by *The Narrative* should have sent him on his way. Not until his good friend and abolitionist colleague James Buffum suggested they take the voyage together did Douglass make arrangements.[9]

Douglass landed in England without specific plans except to elude American slave-catchers. Yet, on his arrival in August 1845, he found that *The Narrative* and his reputation had preceded him. Sales in the United States and England for those first five months numbered in the thousands; Bristol, England, alone accounted for 150 copies even before a visit by the author.[1] There, as in city after city, he lodged in the best homes and stepped to the lectern after introductions by local dignitaries and municipal officials. Reform-minded England turned out to greet fugitive slave author and lecturer of skill and ability. "I find I am hardly black enough for British taste . . ." he wrote in early 1846.

The Narrative blended with the tour, one contributing to the success of the other. By providing advance publicity, the book helped launch Douglass's tour of the British Isles, and its sales sustained him while there "I realize enough from it to meet my expenses . . .").[2] Strong sales prompted an enthusiastic Douglass to write from Belfast, Ireland, in December 1845, ". . . all my Books went last night at one blow—I want more[,] I want more." When successful Dublin businessman and Garrisonian abolitionist Richard D. Webb, who printed the Irish edition of *The Narrative*, offered to send fifty copies, Douglass responded that they would sell easily at the next lecture. The first Irish printing sold out before the end of 1845, leaving an axcious author waiting for copies of the second. Webb, "purging" sections he considered offensive to Victorian tastes, was apparently responsible for the delay. In early March 1846 Douglass requested all the books ready for shipping, up to five hundred, in anticipation of good sales during an upcoming visit to Glasgow, Scotland. On occasion, Douglass had to shape his traveling and speaking schedule to fit the sometimes idiosyncratic publishing routing of *The Narrative*. "Our [Dublin] stay is protracted in consequence of the publication here of my narrative."[3]

The scenario of the writing and the publication of *The Narrative* is the stuff of good antislavery speeches, and Douglass had an eye for such materials. "It was . . . doubted I had ever been a slave," he told an eager

9. Arna Bontemps, *Free at Last*, 101–2; Benjamin Quarles, (New York, 1969), *Frederick Douglass*, 35.
1. Booker T. Washington, *Frederick Douglass*, 101; Quarles, *Frederick Douglass*, 55–56.
2. Frederick Douglass to Frances Jackson, 29 January 1846, William Lloyd Garrison MSS, Boston Public Library, hereinafter cited at BPL.
3. Frederick Douglass to Richard D. Webb, 6 December 1845, [7 December 1845], 2 March 1846, all Garrison MSS BPL; *Jane H. Pease and William H. Pease and William H. Pease, They Who Would Be Free: Blacks' Search for Freedom, 1830–1861* (New York, 1974), 41; Frederick Douglass to William L. Garrison, 9 September 1845, Frederick Douglass MSS, LC.

audience packed into the Cork Ireland, city hall the fall of 1845, "and this doubt being used to injure the antislavery cause, I . . . set the matter to rest by publishing the narrative of my life." After apologizing for the idea of a person "without learning" writing a book, Douglass acknowledged the "excitement" it produced in American, and, he continued, "the excitement . . . increased so much that it was better for me to get out of the way lest my master might use some stratagem to get me back into his clutches." "I am here," he concluded, "in order to avoid the scent of the blood hounds of America. . . ." The crowd loved it, and Douglass often returned to this theme during his tour.

Douglass shared genuine anxieties with his audiences over the consequences of publishing *The Narrative*. Many British reformers saw the situation as a mixed blessing, hoping to convince Douglass to stay in England and to continue his work with them. There was even an effort to raise money to bring Douglass's family over, but Douglass did not want to abandon his work in the United States unless necessary. He was cautious, convinced that the old master wanted "to feed his revenge" by capturing his now-famous escaped slave. "I know he feels keenly about my exposures [in *The Narrative*], and nothing would afford him more pleasure than to have me in his power," confided a worried Douglass in the spring of 1846.[4]

While Douglass riled old enemies on Maryland's East Shore and made new friends in the British Isles, he also alienated many of his Garrisonian coworkers.[5] The success of *The Narrative* and the tour were irritants.

Some Garrisonians seemed uncomfortable with Douglass's increasingly independent posture, a change that accompanied with his personal growth and was accelerated by *The Narrative* and the tour. Garrison wrote an introduction to *The Narrative*, and he reviewed it in the *Liberator*, but the review was perhaps symptomatic of things to come, for it is a rehash of his own introductory remarks in *The Narrative* more than it is a review of the book.[6] While in England, Douglass admirers and supporters raised money to purchase his freedom (to end the threat of reenslavement). At first ambivalent about tacitly acknowledging the right to hold property in man, Douglass eventually embraced the project, which was successfully concluded, Douglass believed he could be a more effective abolitionist if free. Many Garrisonians opposed the common practice of purchasing runaways' freedom and made no exception in doctrinal purity in Douglass's case. Garrison himself supported the enterprise and contributed to the Douglass fund.

4. Frederick Douglass to William Lloyd Garrison, 16 April 1846, Frederick Douglass MSS, LC.
5. See William H. Pease and Jane H. Pease, "Boston Garrisonians and the Problem of Frederick Douglass," *Canadian Journal of History*, II (September 1967), 29–48 for the best statement on the split.
6. *The Liberator*, 9 May 1845.

Other incidents on the tour irritated some Garrisonians and hinted that Douglass was slipping from the fold. Rumors circulated in England and the United States that *The Narrative* made him money "hand over hand," a prospect that troubled many of his spartan abolitionist colleagues. The rumors were kept current by Webb, although he knew that sales met Douglass's expenses and allowed him occasionally to send money to his family, but little else. Webb reacted strongly to the blossoming Douglass, who regularly disregarded the Irishman's advice, and Webb made his feelings known in Boston. Friction between author Douglass and publisher Webb turned to hostility over several rather minor disputes concerning *The Narrative* and over a larger crisis that Douglass puffed up by demanding from Webb a full statement of accounts for his handling of the publication and sales of the Irish edition.[7]

Douglass knew of some of the rumors and suspicions—he made money; he cultivated a personal following on the tour; he consorted with anti-Garrisonians; he had lapses in philosophical purity. When criticized for accepting a lecture fee from a London antislavery group that the Garrisonians found ideologically objectionable, Douglass responded that he was "not yet brought up," and he sought to reassure his friends that he was a Garrisonian abolitionist and probably would remain one—"at any rate poverty shall not drive me[,] nor money allure me[,] from my present position."[8]

In August 1846 Garrison joined Douglass in London. The two men toured the British Isles, devoting particular attention to Scotland, where they joined in the "Send Back the Money" controversy—an international dispute involving the Free Church of Scotland's acceptance of funds from the American slave South. Garrison returned to America after three months of lecturing and organizing with Douglass. As a parting gift, the antislavery women of Edinburgh gave Garrison a silver tea service.[9] The following month, money was raised to purchase Douglass's freedom; and four months after that, as Douglass prepared to return home, his British friends raised a testimonial fund approaching two thousand dollars—a heady contrast to a silver tea service.

The final break between Douglass and Garrison came some months later. The precipitant was the *North Star*, the newspaper Douglass established in Rochester, New York, in 1847 (with the two-thousand-dollar fund) despite Garrison's opposition to the enterprise. The newspaper dispute was only the most recent of many irritants. As Jane and William Pease note in an enduring article, the breach was in the making from

7. Pease and Pease, *Blacks' Search*, 61; Frederick Douglass to Richard D. Webb [16 April 1846, 20 April 1846], 26 April 1846, all Garrison MSS, BPL.
8. Frederick Douglass to Chapman [18 August 1846], Anti-Slavery MSS; Frederick Douglass to Richard D. Webb, 29 March 1845, Garrison MSS, both BPL.
9. Wendell Phillips Garrison,*William Lloyd Garrison: The Story of His Life Told By His Children* (New York, 1969), III, 150–54; Quarles, *Frederick Douglass*, 50, 57.

the time Douglass joined the movement—many in the Boston clique had problems dealing with blacks as equals, particularly a black as assertive and independent as Douglass, who was strong willed and combative at times.

Back in 1845, when *The Narrative* was first published, the *Herald of Freedom*, an abolitionist newspaper hostile to the Garrisonian wing of the movement, offered a prophetic, if fratricidal review. At first ready to put *The Narrative* aside untouched, but finally reading it with pleasure and approval, the reviewer hoped for Douglass's sake that "it will yield him a competent means of living"—something that he advised Douglass "to take prompt means to secure." "He may," warned the reviewer, "by and by feel the instability of patronage." [1]

While the break was probably inevitable and due to any number of causes, *The Narrative* played a major role. Douglass's refusal to compromise the quality of his lectures forced him to reveal his background. He did that with *The Narrative*, which sent him into triumphant exile and made him the best known black abolitionist on two continents. The resulting attention and prestige eventually separated him from his friends and mentors.

The Narrative is an important indicator of Douglass's growth and maturity. It is a personal statement with many implications. To Garrisonians such as Webb it suggested that Douglass could not be managed. For Douglass personally, it had cathartic qualities of putting slavery as an individual experience behind him. In a very real way, this, the first of his autobiographical statements, represents Douglass as of 1845, when he was moving beyond the intellectual and social posture of "exslave" Garrisonian lecturer and was maturing into a capable, independent, and strong-willed reformer. The debate generated by *The Narrative*, such as the Thompson letter, established Douglass as an exslave abolitionist who could speak with conviction born of experience. After 1846 Douglass had his antislavery credentials, and energy previously spent on fending off skeptics was then spent on antislavery.

The Narrative—perhaps the most influential and best received exslave autobiography of the antebellum era —attracted the widest critical attention of Douglass's three autobiographies. Except for an occasional dissent, such as the one from Wilmington, there was no prolonged debate over its truthfulness. Reviews and critics one after another echoed a Quaker journal, the *British Friend*, that "truth seems stamped on every page. . . ." [2] The *Boston Transcript* gave it equally high marks—"this little book bears throughout the indelible marks of truths." [3] A general consensus emerged, except in the South, that Doug-

1. Pease and Pease, "Boston Garrisonians and the Problem of Frederick Douglass," 29–48; *Herald of Freedom*, 30 May 1845.
2. *The British Friend*, 3 (29 November 1845), 174.
3. *Boston Transcript* in *The Liberator*, 6 June 1845.

lass portrayed slavery honestly and fairly. The *Boston Courier* concluded that Douglass offered "abundant and incontrovertible evidence of the misery which the mere condition of slavery . . . entails upon its victim."[4] Wilson Amisted, author of *A Tribute for the Negro*, felt no need to resort to hyperbole: The *Narrative* "presents no exaggerated picture of slavery."[5]

Even reviewers unsympathetic to antislavery acknowledged The *Narrative's* persuasiveness. *Littel's Living Age* proposed that no less than a million people in England and Ireland were "excited by the book."[6] A British upper-class organ, the *London League*, although not enthusiastic about Douglass's treatment of some individuals and institutions, nonetheless found the book persuasive. The reviewer concluded that The *Narrative* would convince "any impartial reader that the argument . . . which would uphold slavery on the grounds of the slaves' natural inferiority, has no foundation as regards such men as the writer, and therefore, totally fails in its general application."[7]

Not surprisingly, the *National Anti-Slavery Standard*, official organ of the American Anti-Slavery Society, held high expectations for The *Narrative* as a didactic piece: it would "convince" all proslavery men, "confirm" all abolitionists, and "amply satisfy" those who were indifferent.[8] The *Lynn Pioneer* surpassed the *Anti-Slavery Standard* in praising the potential influence of The *Narrative*. Published in the Massachusetts town where Douglass lived when he wrote The *Narrative*, the *Pioneer* blessed it with magical persuasive qualities: "It is a most thrilling work which the American press issued—*and the most important*. If it does not open the eyes of this people, they must be petrified into eternal sleep."[9]

Many reviewers saw The *Narrative* as an achievement for either human nature, for Douglass personally, for black people, or for all three. An Irish newspaper reported that a reading of The *Narrative* "deepened [our] conviction of the power which true men everywhere possess for triumphing over the most formidable obstacles—."[1] A Quaker reviewer regarded The *Narrative* as a personal victory for Douglass, a man born, raised, and trained as "chattle" [sic].[2]

The nonpartisan northern response (if there was such a thing in 1845 regarding a book about slavery) came from the *New York Tribune*. Not an active abolitionist paper, nevertheless it liked Douglass and his narrative. Having the courage "to name the persons, times and places" and,

4. Wilson Amisted, *A Tribute to the Negro* (Manchester, 1848), 454.
5. *Boston Courier* in The *Liberator*, 6 June 1845.
6. *Littel's Living Age*, 9 (14 April 1846).
7. *London League* in The *Liberator*, 28 November 1845.
8. NASS, 12 June 1845.
9. *Lynn Pioneer* in The *Liberator*, 30 May 1845.
1. *Cork Southern Reporter* in The *Liberator*, 29 November 1845.
2. *The British Friend*, III, 29 November 1845.

by so doing, making himself vulnerable to slave-catchers earned Douglass high praise and generated a "deep conviction" that he related the "whole truth." Douglass's work, described as "simple, true, coherent, and warm with genuine feeling," was prized as "a specimen of the powers of the Black Race. . . ." Generally favorable comparisons were made to the work of two French authors, Dumas and Soulie, but Douglass's writings were more impressive because his life, "being one of action and resistance," was less conducive to literary training.[3]

The *Tribune* reviewer spoke for others who felt an uneasy need to separate Douglass from his Garrisonian associates. Garrison's introduction—written "in his usual over emphatic style"—was unacceptable, while Phillips' was only a bit less offensive. Yet Douglass's prose passed muster as "just and temporate." "We feel that [Douglass's] view, even of those who have injured him, may be relied upon."[4]

Ephraim Peabody, pastor of Boston's Christ Church and author of a review essay on five exslave autobiographies for the *Christian Examiner*, shared some of the *Tribune*'s misgivings. Peabody's observations were a bit more thoughtful. "America has the mournful honor of adding a new department to the literature of civilization—the autobiographies of escaped slaves," he wrote in 1849. Peabody was not an abolitionist, although his wife gave Douglass his first job as a free person,[5] and the pastor knew Josiah Henson, another fugitive slave author. Peabody assured his readers that those exslaves did their own writing, and he found the works truthful and factual but cautioned that the five did "not give a full and complete view of the whole subject." He worried particularly about the overwhelmingly negative picture of the South and slavery that emerged from a collective reading of the autobiographies.[6]

Peabody wrote that Douglass's *Narrative* "contains the life of a superior man"—eloquent, perceptive and intelligent—particularly "when we consider that it is but a few years since he was a slave." Waffling back and forth, Peabody assured Douglass of his sympathies but chastised him for the "mode of address in which he sometimes indulges. . . ," not wanting to condemn an exslave "for seeing only the evils of slavery," the pastor was nevertheless troubled by Douglass's lack of "natural magnanimity." Peabody feared, even more than the *Tribune*'s reviewer, that the "extravagant" writing style of Douglass's abolitionist friends had already corrupted the exslave author. Not particularly antiblack or anti-Douglass (he offered Douglass an apology of sorts in a footnote), Peabody's concern centered on Garrisonian zealousness, but even his partially critical review faults Douglass only for an incomplete portrayal of southern life and an aggressive style and tone.[7]

3. *New York Tribune*, 12 June 1845.
4. Ibid.
5. Frederick Douglass, *Narrative*.
6. Ephraim Peabody, "Narratives of Fugitive Slaves," *Christian Examiner*, 47 (July 1849), 61, 64.
7. Ibid.; Pease and Pease, *Blacks' Search*, 41.

The Belfast *Northern Whig* perhaps best expressed those feelings of cautious admiration that characterized many reviews: "if *The Narrative* is really true . . . and untouched by any one save Douglass himself, it is a singular book and he is a most singular man." Similarly, the review in the *Herald of Freedom* is one of the most interesting when considered alongside the reasons Douglass felt compelled to write *The Narrative*. Douglass's skills as a lecturer—characterized by "able reasoning, genius wit and bold and stirring appeals"—were so impressive that the conviction rose that no exslave could be so talented, and that skepticism was responsible for the book. Yet the *Herald* assured its readers that it had no reservations about Douglass's ability to write such a book, for any reservations were easily pushed aside by Douglass's ability as a speaker. For Douglass, the book validated the speeches; for the *Herald of Freedom*, the speeches validated the book.[8]

The Narrative is a classic statement on slavery. It underscored Douglass's increasing intellectual skills as well as his independence and self-confidence; it forced him into temporary exile, and it accelerated a process that eventually caused a breach with his Garrisonian friends. *The Narrative* is Douglass's first important writing and, in many ways, his most significant.

* * *

ROBERT B. STEPTO

Narration, Authentication, and Authorial Control in Frederick Douglass' *Narrative* of 1845 †

The strident, moral voice of the former slave recounting, exposing, appealing, apostrophizing, and above all, *remembering* his ordeal in bondage is the single most impressive feature of a slave narrative. This voice is striking not only because of what it relates but because the slave's acquisition of that voice is quite possibly his only permanent achievement once he escapes and casts himself upon a new and larger landscape. In their most elementary form, slave narratives are, however, full of other voices that are frequently just as responsible for articulating a narrative's tale and strategy. These other voices may be those of various "characters" in the "story," but mainly they are those found in the

---

8. Belfast *Northern Whig*, 4 December 1845; *Herald of Freedom*, 1 August 1845.
 † Reprinted by permission of the Modern Language Association from Dexter Fisher and Robert B. Stepto, eds., *Afro-American Literature: The Reconstruction of Instruction* (New York: Modern Language Association, 1979) 178–91. Bracketed page numbers refer to this Norton Critical Edition.

appended documents written by slaveholders and abolitionists alike. These documents—and voices—may not always be smoothly integrated with the former slave's tale, but they are nevertheless parts of the narrative. Their primary function is, of course, to authenticate the former slave's account; in doing so, they are at least partially responsible for the narratives being accepted as historical evidence. However, in literary terms, the documents collectively create something close to a dialogue—of forms as well as of voices—which suggests that in its primal state or first phase the slave narrative is an eclectic narrative form.

When the various forms (letters, prefaces, guarantees, tales) and their accompanying voices become integrated in the slave narrative text, we are presented with another type of basic narrative which I call an integrated narrative. This type of narrative represents the second phase of narration in the slave narrative and usually yields a more sophisticated text, wherein most of the literary and rhetorical functions previously performed by several texts and voices (the appended prefaces, letters, and documents as well as the tale) are now rendered by a loosely unified single text and voice. In this second phase, the authenticating documents "come alive" in the former slave's tale as speech and even action; and the former slave—often while assuming a deferential posture toward his white friends, editors, and guarantors—carries much of the burden of introducing and authenticating his own tale. In short, a second-phase narrative is a more sophisticated narrative because the former slave's voice assumes many more responsibilities than that of recounting the tale.

Because an integrated or second-phase narrative is less a collection of texts and more a unified narrative, we may say that, in terms of narration, the integrated narrative is in the process of becoming—irrespective of authorial intent—a generic narrative, by which I mean a narrative of discernible genre such as history, fiction, essay, or autobiography. This process is no simple "gourd vine" activity: An integrated narrative does not become a generic narrative "overnight," and, indeed, there are no assurances that in becoming a new type of narrative it is transformed automatically into a distinctive generic text. What we discover, then, is a third phase to slave narrative narration wherein two developments may occur: The integrated narrative (Phase II) is dominated either by its tale or by its authenticating strategies. In the first instance, the narrative and moral energies of the former slave's voice and tale so resolutely dominate those of the narrative's authenticating machinery (voices, documents, rhetorical strategies) that the narrative becomes in thrust and purpose far more metaphorical than rhetorical. When the integrated narrative becomes in this way a figurative account of action, landscape, and heroic self-transformation, it is so close generically to history, fiction, and autobiography that I term it a generic narrative.

In the second instance, the authenticating machinery either remains as important as the tale or actually becomes, usually for some purpose residing outside the text, the dominant and motivating feature of the narrative. Since this is also a sophisticated narrative phase, figurative presentations of action, landscape, and self may also occur, but such developments are rare and always ancillary to the central thrust of the text. When the authenticating machinery is dominant in this fashion, the integrated narrative becomes an authenticating narrative.

As these remarks suggest, one reason for investigating the phases of slave narrative narration is to gain a clearer view of how some slave narrative types become generic narratives and how, in turn, generic narratives—once formed, shaped, and set in motion by certain distinctly Afro-American cultural imperatives—have roots in the slave narratives. This bears as well on our ability to distinguish between narrative modes and forms and to describe what we see. When, for example, a historian or literary critic calls a slave narrative an autobiography, what he *sees* is, most likely, a narrative told in the first person that possesses literary features distinguishing it from the ordinary documents providing historical and sociological data. But a slave narrative is not necessarily an autobiography. We need to know the finer shades between the more easily discernible categories of narration, and we must discover whether these stops arrange themselves in progressive, contrapuntal, or dialectic fashion—or whether they possess any arrangement at all. As the scheme described above and diagrammed below suggests, I believe there are at least four identifiable modes of narration within the slave narrative, all of which have a direct bearing on the development of subsequent Afro-American narrative forms.

Phase   I: basic narrative (a): "eclectic narrative"—authenticating documents and strategies (sometimes including one by the author of the tale) *appended* to the tale

Phase   II: basic narrative (b): "integrated narrative"—authenticating documents and strategies integrated into the tale and formally becoming voices and / or characters in the tale

Phase III:

(a) "generic narrative"—authenticating documents and strategies are totally subsumed by the tale; the slave narrative becomes an identifiable generic text, e.g., autobiography, etc.

(b) "authenticating narrative"—the tale is subsumed by the authenticating strategy; the slave narrative becomes an authenticating document for other, usually generic, texts, e.g., novel, history

II

What we observe in the first two phases of slave narrative narration is the former slave's ultimate lack of control over his own narrative occasioned primarily by the demands of audience and authentication. This dilemma is not unique to the authors of these narratives; indeed, many modern black writers still do not control their personal history once it assumes literary form. For this reason, Frederick Douglass' *Narrative of the Life of Frederick Douglass an American Slave Written by Himself* (1845) seems all the more a remarkable literary achievement. Because it contains several segregated narrative texts—a preface, a prefatory letter, the tale, an appendix—it appears to be, in terms of the narrative phases, a rather primitive slave narrative. But each of the ancillary texts seems to be drawn to the tale by some sort of extraordinary gravitational pull or magnetic attraction. There is, in short, a dynamic energy between the tale and each supporting text; the Douglass narrative is an integrated narrative of a very special order. While the integrating process does, in a small way, pursue the conventional path of creating characters out of authenticating texts (Wm. Lloyd Garrison silently enters Douglass' tale at the very end), its new and major thrust is the creation of that aforementioned energy that binds the supporting texts to the tale while at the same time removing them from participation in the narrative's rhetorical and authenticating strategies. In short, Douglass' tale dominates the narrative and does so because it alone authenticates the narrative.

The introductory texts to the tale are two in number: a Preface by Wm. Lloyd Garrison, the famous abolitionist and editor of *The Liberator*; and a "Letter from Wendell Phillips, Esq.," who was equally renowned as an abolitionist, a crusading lawyer, and a judge. In theory, each of these introductory documents should be a classic guarantee written almost exclusively to a white reading public, concerned primarily and ritualistically with the white validation of a newfound black voice, and removed from the tale in such ways that the guarantee and tale vie silently and surreptitiously for control of the narrative as a whole. But these entries simply are not fashioned that way. To be sure, Garrison offers a conventional guarantee when he writes:

Mr. DOUGLASS has very properly chosen to write his own Narrative, in his own style, and according to the best of his ability, rather
than to employ some one else. It is, therefore, entirely his own
production; and . . . it is, in my judgment, highly creditable to his
head and heart. [6]

And Phillips, while addressing Douglass, most certainly offers a guarantee to "another" audience as well:

Every one who has heard you speak has felt, and, I am confident,
every one who reads your book will feel, persuaded that you give
them a fair specimen of the whole truth. No one-sided portrait,—
no wholesale complaints,—but strict justice done, whenever individual kindliness has neutralized, for a moment, the deadly system
with which it was strangely allied. [11]

But these passages dominate neither the tone nor the substance of their
respective texts.

Garrison is far more interested in writing history (specifically that
of the 1841 Nantucket Anti-Slavery Convention and the launching of
Douglass' career as a lecture agent for various antislavery societies) and
recording his own place in it. His declaration, "I shall never forget his
[Douglass'] first speech at the convention," is followed shortly thereafter
by "*I rose,* and declared that Patrick Henry of revolutionary fame, never
made a speech more eloquent in the cause of liberty. . . . *I reminded* the
audience of the peril which surrounded this self-emancipated young
man. . . . *I appealed* to them, whether they would ever allow him to be
carried back into slavery,—law or no law, constitution or no constitution" (italics added) [4]. His Preface ends, not with a reference to Douglass or to his tale, but with an apostrophe very much like one he would
use to exhort and arouse an antislavery assembly. In short, with the following cry, Garrison hardly guarantees Douglass' tale but reenacts his
own abolitionist career instead:

Reader! are you with the man-stealers in sympathy and purpose, or
on the side of their down-trodden victims? If with the former, then
are you the foe of God and man. If with the latter, what are you
prepared to do and dare in their behalf? Be faithful, be vigilant, be
untiring in your efforts to break every yoke, and let the oppressed
go free. Come what may—cost what may—inscribe on the banner
which you unfurl to the breeze, as your religious and political
motto—NO COMPROMISE WITH SLAVERY! NO UNION
WITH SLAVEHOLDERS!" [9]

In the light of this closure and (no matter how hard we try to ignore
it) the friction that developed between Garrison and Douglass in later
years, we might be tempted to see Garrison's Preface at war with Douglass' tale for authorial control of the narrative as a whole. Certainly,

there is a tension, but that tension is stunted by Garrison's enthusiasm for Douglass' tale:

> This *Narrative* contains many affecting incidents, many *passages* of great eloquence and power; but I think the most thrilling one of them all is the *description* DOUGLASS gives of his feelings, as he stood soliloquizing respecting his fate, and the chances of his one day being a free man. . . . Who can read that *passage*, and be insensible to its pathos and sublimity? (italics added) [7]

What Garrison does, probably subconsciously, is an unusual and extraordinary thing—he becomes the first guarantor we have seen who not only directs the reader to the tale but also acknowledges the tale's singular rhetorical power. Thus, Garrison enters the tale by being at the Nantucket Convention with Douglass in 1841 and by authenticating the impact of the tale, not its facts. He fashions his own apostrophe, but finally he remains a member of Douglass' audience far more than he assumes the posture of a competing or superior voice. In this way, Garrison's Preface stands outside Douglass' tale but is steadfastly bound to it.

This is even more so the case for Wendell Phillips' "Letter." It contains passages that seem to be addressed to credulous readers in need of a "visible" authority's guarantee, but by and large the "Letter" is directed to Frederick Douglass alone. It opens with "My Dear Friend," and there are many extraliterary reasons for wondering initially if the friend is actually Frederick. Shortly thereafter, however, Phillips declares, "I am glad the time has come when the 'lions write history,' " and it becomes clear that he not only addresses Douglass but also writes in response to the tale. These features, plus Phillips' specific references to how Douglass acquired his "ABC" and learned of "where the 'white sails' of the Chesapeake were bound," serve to integrate Phillips' "Letter" into Douglass' tale. Above all, we must see in what terms the "Letter" is a cultural and linguistic event: Like the Garrison document, it presents its author as a member of Douglass' audience, but the act of letterwriting, of correspondence, implies a moral and linguistic parity between a white guarantor and black author that we have not seen before and that we do not always see in American literary history *after* 1845. In short, the tone and posture initiated in Garrison's Preface are completed and confirmed in Phillips' "Letter," and while these documents are integrated into Douglass' tale, they remain segregated outside the tale in the all-important sense that they yield Douglass sufficient narrative and rhetorical space in which to render personal history in—and as—a literary form.

What marks Douglass' narration and control of his tale is his extraordinary ability to pursue several types of writing with ease and with a degree of simultaneity. The principal types of writing we discover in the tale are syncretic phrasing, introspective analysis, internalized documentation, and participant-observation. Of course, each of these types has its accompanying authorial posture, the result being that even the telling of the tale (as distinct from the content of the tale) yields a portrait of a complex individual marvelously facile in the tones, shapes, and dimensions of his voice.

Douglass' syncretic [1] phrasing is often discussed, and the passage most widely quoted is probably "My feet have been so cracked with the frost, that the pen with which I am writing might be laid in the gashes" [26]. The remarkable clarity of this language needs no commentary, but what one admires as well is Douglass' ability to startlingly conjoin past and present and to do so with images that not only stand for different periods in his personal history but also, in their fusion, speak of his evolution from slavery to freedom. The pen, symbolizing the quest for literacy fulfilled, actually takes measure of the wounds of the past, and this measuring process becomes a metaphor in and of itself for the artful composition of travail transcended. While I admire this passage, the syncretic phrases I find even more intriguing are those that pursue a kind of acrid punning upon the names of Douglass' oppressors. A minor example appears early in the tale, when Douglass deftly sums up an overseer's character by writing, "Mr. Severe was rightly named: he was a cruel man." Here, Douglass is content with "glossing" the name; but late in the tale, just before attempting to escape in 1835, Douglass takes another oppressor's name and does not so much gloss it or play with it as *work upon* it to such an extent that, riddled with irony, it is devoid of its original meaning:

> At the close of the year 1834, Mr. Freeland again hired me of my master, for the year 1835. But, by this time, I began to want to live *upon free land* as well as *with Freeland;* and I was no longer content, therefore, to live with him or any other slaveholder. [56]

Of course, this is effective writing—far more effective than what is found in the average slave narrative—but the point I wish to make is that Douglass seems to fashion these passages for both his readership and himself. Each example of his wit and increasing facility with language charts his ever-shortening path to literacy; thus, in their way, Douglass' syncretic phrases reveal his emerging comprehension of freedom and literacy and are another introspective tool by which he may benchmark his personal history.

But the celebrated passages of introspective analysis are even more pithy and direct. In these, Douglass fashions language as finely honed and balanced as an aphorism or Popean couplet, and thereby orders his personal history with neat, distinct, and credible moments of transition.

1. Combining two or more differing concepts [*Editors*].

When Mr. Auld forbids Mrs. Auld to instruct Douglass in the ABC, for example, Douglass relates:

> From that moment, I understood the pathway from slavery to free-dom. . . . Whilst I was saddened by the thought of losing the aid of my kind mistress, I was gladdened by the invaluable instruction which, by the merest accident, I gained from my master. [29]

The clarity of Douglass' revelation is as unmistakable as it is remarkable. As rhetoric, the passage is successful because its nearly extravagant beginning is finally rendered quite acceptable by the masterly balance and internal rhyming of "saddened" and "gladdened," which is persuasive because it is pleasant and because it offers the illusion of a reasoned conclusion.

Balance is an important feature of two other equally celebrated passages that quite significantly open and close Douglass' telling of his relations with Mr. Covey, an odd (because he worked in the fields alongside the slaves) but vicious overseer. At the beginning of the episode, in which Douglass finally fights back and draws Covey's blood, he writes:

> You have seen how a man was made a slave; you shall see how a slave was made a man. [47]

And at the end of the episode, to bring matters linguistically and narratively full circle, Douglass declares:

> I now resolved that, however long I might remain a slave in form, the day has passed forever when I could be a slave in fact. I did not hesitate to let it be known of me, that the white man who expected to succeed in whipping, must also succeed in killing me. [50–51]

The sheer poetry of these statements is not lost on us, nor is the fact of why the poetry was created in the first place. One might suppose that in another age Douglass' determination and rage might take a more effusive expression, but I cannot imagine that to be the case. In the first place, his linguistic model is obviously scriptural; and in the second, his goal is the presentation of a historical self, not the record of temporary hysteria. This latter point persuades me that Douglass is about the business of discovering how personal history may be transformed into autobiography. Douglass' passages of introspective analysis almost singlehandedly create fresh space for themselves in the American literary canon.

Instead of reproducing letters and other documents written by white guarantors within the tale or transforming guarantors into characters, Douglass internalizes documents that, like the syncretic and introspective passages, order his personal history. For example, Douglass' discussion of slave songs begins with phrases such as "wild songs" and "unmeaning jargon" but concludes, quite typically for him, with a study of how he grew to "hear" the songs and how the hearing affords yet another illumination of his path from slavery to freedom:

> I did not, when a slave, understand the deep meaning of those rude and apparently incoherent songs. I was myself within the circle; so that I neither saw nor heard as those without might see and hear. They told a tale of woe which was then altogether beyond my feeble comprehension. . . . Every tone was a testimony against slavery, and a prayer to God for deliverance from chains. The hearing of those wild notes always depressed my spirit, and filled me with ineffable sadness. I have frequently found myself in tears while hearing them. The mere recurrence to those songs, even now, afflicts me; and while I am writing these lines, an expression of feeling has already found its way down my cheek. [19]

The tears of the past and present interflow, and Douglass not only documents his saga of enslavement but also, with typical recourse to syncretic phrasing and introspective analysis, advances his presentation of self.

Douglass' other internalized documents are employed with comparable efficiency as we see in the episode where he attempts an escape in 1835. In this episode, the document reproduced is the pass or "protection" Douglass wrote for himself and his compatriots in the escape plan:

> "This is to certify that I, the undersigned, have given the bearer, my servant, full liberty to go to Baltimore, and spend the Easter holidays. Written with mine own hand, &c., 1835.
>
> "WILLIAM HAMILTON,
> "Near St. Michael's, in Talbot county, Maryland." [58]

The protection exhibits Douglass' increasingly refined sense of how to manipulate language—he has indeed come a long way from that day Mr. Auld halted his ABC lessons—but even more impressive, I believe, is the act of reproducing the document itself. We know from the tale that when their scheme was thwarted, each slave managed to destroy his pass, so Douglass reproduces his language from memory, and there is no reason to doubt a single jot of his recollection. My point here is simply that Douglass can draw so easily from the wellsprings of memory because the protection is not a mere scrap of memorabilia but rather a veritable road sign on his path to freedom and literacy. In this sense, his protection assumes a place in Afro-American letters as a key antecedent to such documents as the fast-yellowing notes of James Weldon Johnson's Ex-Coloured Man [2] and "The Voodoo of Hell's Half Acre" in Richard Wright's Black Boy.

All of the types of narrative discourse discussed thus far reveal features of Douglass' particular posture as a participant-observer narrator. But the syncretic phrases, introspective studies, and internalized documents

---

2. The protagonist of James Weldon Johnson's novel The Autobiography of an Ex-Colored Man (1912) [Editors].

only exhibit Douglass as a teller and doer, and part of the great effect of his tale depends upon what Douglass does not tell, what he refuses to reenact in print. Late in the tale, at the beginning of Chapter xi, Douglass writes:

> I now come to that part of my life during which I planned, and finally succeeded in making, my escape from slavery. But before narrating any of the peculiar circumstances, I deem it proper to make known my intention not to state all the facts connected with the transaction. . . . I deeply regret the necessity that impels me to suppress any thing of importance connected with my experience in slavery. It would afford me great pleasure indeed, as well as materially add to the interest of my narrative, were I at liberty to gratify a curiosity, which I know exists. . . . But I must deprive myself of this pleasure, and the curious gratification which such a statement would afford. I would allow myself to suffer under the greatest imputations which evil-minded men might suggest, rather than exculpate myself, and thereby run the hazard of closing the slightest avenue by which a brother slave might clear himself of the chains and fetters of slavery. [65]

It has been argued that one way to test a slave narrative's authenticity is by gauging how much space the narrator gives to relating his escape as opposed to describing the conditions of his captivity. If the adventure, excitement, and perils of the escape seem to be the raison d'être for the narrative's composition, then the narrative is quite possibly an exceedingly adulterated slave's tale or a bald fiction. The theory does not always work perfectly: Henry "Box" Brown's narrative and that of William and Ellen Craft are predominantly recollections of extraordinary escapes,[3] and yet, as far as we can tell, these are authentic tales. But the theory nevertheless has great merit, and I have often wondered to what extent it derives from the example of Douglass' tale and emotionally, if not absolutely rationally, from his fulminations against those authors who unwittingly excavate the underground railroad and expose it to the morally thin mid-nineteenth-century American air. Douglass' tale is spectacularly free of suspicion, because he never tells a detail of his escape to New York, and it is this marvelously rhetorical omission or silence that both sophisticates and authenticates his posture as a participant-observer narrator. When a narrator wrests this kind of preeminent authorial control from the ancillary voices "circling" his narrative, we may say that he controls the presentation of his personal history and that his tale is becoming autobiographical. In this light the last few sentences of Douglass' tale take on special meaning:

---

3. Referred to here are two other slave narratives: *Narrative of Henry Box Brown, Who Escaped from Slavery Enclosed in a Box 3 Feet Long and 2 Wide* (1849), and William and Ellen Craft, *Running a Thousand Miles for Freedom* (1860) [*Editors*].

But, while attending an anti-slavery convention at Nantucket, on the 11th of August, 1841, I felt strongly moved to speak. . . . It was a severe cross, and I took it up reluctantly. The truth was, I felt myself a slave, and the idea of speaking to white people weighed me down. I spoke but a few moments, when I felt a degree of freedom, and said what I desired with considerable ease. From that time until now, I have been engaged in pleading the case of my brethren—with what success, and what devotion, I leave those acquainted with my labors to decide. [74–75]

With these words, the narrative, as many have remarked, comes full circle, taking us back, not to the beginning of the *tale*, but rather to Garrison's prefatory remarks on the Convention and Douglass' first public address. This return may be pleasing in terms of the sense of symmetry it affords, but it is also a remarkable feat of rhetorical strategy: Having traveled with Douglass through his account of his life, we arrive in Nantucket in 1841 to hear him speak and, in effect, to become, along with Mr. Garrison, his audience. The final effect is that Douglass reinforces his posture as an articulate hero while supplanting Garrison as the definitive historian of his past.

Even more important, I think, is the final image Douglass bestows of a slave shedding his last fetter and becoming a man by first finding his voice and then, as sure as light follows dawn, speaking "with considerable ease." In one brilliant stroke, the quest for freedom and literacy implied from the start even by the narrative's title is resolutely consummated.

The final text of the narrative, the Appendix, is a discourse by Douglass on his view of Christianity and Christian practice as opposed to what he exposed in his tale to be the bankrupt, immoral faith of slaveholders. As rhetorical strategy, the discourse is effective generally because it lends weight and substance to what passes for a conventional complaint of slave narrative narrators and because Douglass' exhibition of faith can only enhance his already considerable posture as an articulate hero. But more specifically, the discourse is most efficacious because at its heart lies a vitriolic poem written by a Northern Methodist minister, which Douglass introduces by writing

I conclude these remarks by copying the following portrait of the religion of the south, (which is, by communion and fellowship, the religion of the north,) which I soberly affirm is "true to life," and without caricature or the slightest exaggeration. [78]

The poem is strong and imbued with considerable irony, but what we must appreciate here is the effect of the white Northerner's poem conjoined with Douglass' authentication of the poem. The tables are clearly reversed. Douglass has controlled his personal history and at the same time fulfilled the prophecy suggested in his implicit authentication of

Garrison's Preface: He has explicitly authenticated what is convention-ally a white Northerner's validating text. Douglass' narrative thus offers what is unquestionably our best portrait in Afro-American letters of the requisite act of assuming authorial control. An author can go no further than Douglass did without writing all the texts constituting the narrative himself.

References

Blassingame, John W. *The Slave Community.* New York: Oxford Univ. Press, 1971.
Cox, James. "Autobiography and America." *Virginia Quarterly Review,* 47 (1971), 252–77.
Douglass, Frederick. *Narrative of the Life of Frederick Douglass an American Slave Written by Himself.* 1845; rpt. Cambridge: Belknap-Harvard Univ. Press, 1960.
Reed, Ishmael. *Mumbo Jumbo.* New York: Doubleday, 1972.
Stone, Albert E. "Identity and Art in Frederick Douglass' 'Narrative.' " *CLA Journal,* 17 (1973), 192–213.

WILLIAM L. ANDREWS

[Frederick Douglass and the American Jeremiad] †

* * *

When he wrote his *Narrative* in 1845, Frederick Douglass made a serious effort to appeal to white middle-class readers of the North by fashioning his autobiography into a kind of American jeremiad. This genre differs from that which Wilson J. Moses has labeled the black jeremiad in one crucial sense: while the latter was preoccupied with America's impending doom because of its racial injustices, the Ameri-can jeremiad foretold America's future hopefully, sustained by the con-viction of the nation's divinely appointed mission. The practitioners of both literary traditions tended to see themselves as outcasts, prophets crying in the wilderness of their own alienation from prevailing error and perversity. While the white Jeremiahs decry America's deviation from its original sacred mission in the New World, they usually cele-brate the national dream in the process of lamenting its decline. The American jeremiad affirms and sustains a middle-class consensus about America by both excoriating lapses from it and rhetorically coopting potential challenges (such as those offered by Frederick Douglass) to it.[1]
With Herman Melville and Henry David Thoreau,[2] contemporary

† From William L. Andrews, *To Tell a Free Story: The First Century of Afro-American Autobiog-raphy, 1760–1865* (Urbana: U of Illinois P, 1986) 123–132. Reprinted by permission of the University of Illinois Press. Bracketed page numbers refer to this Norton Critical Edition.
 1. Wilson J. Moses, *Black Messiahs and Uncle Toms* (University Park: Pennsylvania State Univer-sity Press, 1982), pp. 30–48, and Sacvan Bercovitch, *The American Jeremiad* (Madison: Univer-sity of Wisconsin Press, 1978), p. 180. My discussion of the American jeremiad as a genre is dependent on Bercovitch's excellent study and draws liberally from it.
 2. Melville (1819–1891) and Thoreau (1817–1862) were the authors of, respectively, *Moby-Dick* (1851) and *Walden* (1854) [*Editors*].

Jeremiahs who also addressed the national sin of slavery, Douglass confronted America with profoundly polarized emotions that produced in him a classic case of Du Boisian double consciousness.[3] As a fugitive slave orator in the early 1840s, he denounced the institutionalized racism that pervaded America and perverted its much-heralded blend of liberty, democracy, and Christianity. Following the Garrisonian line, his speeches poured contempt on the Constitution of the United States as a compact with slavery and condemned northern as well as southern Christians for being the slave's tyrants, "our enslavers."[4] The *Narrative*, however, goes to no such political or religious extremes. In that book, Douglass deploys the rhetoric of the jeremiad to distinguish between true and false Americanism and Christianity. He celebrates the national dream by concluding his story with a contrast between the thriving seacoast town of New Bedford, Massachusetts—where he was "surrounded with the strongest proofs of wealth" [72]—and the run-down Eastern Shore of Maryland, where "dilapidated houses, with poverty-stricken inmates," "half-naked children," and "barefooted women" testified to an unprogressive polity. Appended to Douglass's story is an apparent apology for his narrative's "tone and manner, respecting religion," but this quickly gives way to a final jeremiad against the pharisaical "hypocrites" of "the *slaveholding religion* of this land". [75] "I love the pure, peaceable, and impartial Christianity of Christ," Douglass proclaimed. All the more reason, therefore, for him to appropriate the language of Jeremiah 6:29 for his ultimate warning to corrupters of the faith: " 'Shall I not visit for these things? saith the Lord. Shall not my soul be avenged on such a nation as this?' " [78] . The *Narrative* builds a convincing case for Douglass's literary calling and his ultimate self-appointment as America's black Jeremiah.

Douglass's account of his rise from slavery to freedom fulfills certain features of the jeremiad's cultural myth of America. The *Narrative* dramatizes a "ritual of socialization" that Sacvan Bercovitch finds often in late eighteenth- and early nineteenth-century jeremiads: the rebellion of a fractious individual against instituted authority is translated into a heroic act of self-reliance, a reenactment of the national myth of regeneration and progress through revolution. The great rhetorical task of the jeremiad is to divest self-determinative individualism of its threatening associations with anarchy and antinomianism, the excesses of the unbridled self. In America the jeremiad made much of the distinction between rebellion and revolution. The rebel disobeys out of self-interest and defiance of the good of the community and the laws of Providence. His act parallels Lucifer's primal act of disobedience, which produced

---

3. In *The Souls of Black Folk* (1903), W. E. B. Du Bois (1868–1964) discusses the concept of African American "double-consciousness" [*Editors*].
4. See Douglass's address, "Southern Slavery and Northern Religion" (Feb. 11, 1844), in Blassingame, ed., *Douglass Papers*, 1:25.

only discord and a (temporary) thwarting of the divine plan. The revolutionary, on the other hand, promotes in the secular sphere the same sort of upward spiral toward perfection that God demanded of each individual soul in its private progress toward redemption. The American jeremiad obviated the distinction between secular and sacred revolution in order to endow the former with the sanction of the latter, the better to authorize the national myth of the American Revolution. America was a truly revolutionary society in the sense and to the extent that its people—that is to say, those who had been accorded the status of personhood in the Constitution—remained faithful to God's plan for the progressive conversion of their land into a new order. Americans were therefore called to be revolutionaries, but revolutionaries in the service of an evolving divine order within which Americans could achieve corporate self-realization as God's chosen people.

As several critics have noted, Douglass's Narrative seems to have been consciously drawn up along structural and metaphorical lines familiar to readers of spiritual autobiographies.[5] The young Frederick is initiated into a knowledge of the depravity of man when he witnesses the hideous flogging of his aunt Hester. "It was the blood-stained gate, the entrance to the hell of slavery, through which I was about to pass" [15]. Though seemingly damned to this southern hell, the eight-year-old boy is delivered by "a special interposition of divine Providence in my favor" from the plantation of Edward Lloyd in Talbot County to the Baltimore home of Hugh Auld. From that time forward, the boy is convinced that freedom—"this living word of faith and spirit of hope" [28]—would be his someday. The thought "remained like ministering angels to cheer me through the gloom." Douglass's faith in this intuitively felt heavenly promise of liberation undergoes a series of trials in his boyhood and early teens, when he is first led out of his "mental darkness" by Sophia Auld, who teaches him his letters, and then is thrust back into "the horrible pit" of enforced ignorance by her husband, who fears a mentally enlightened slave.

The middle chapters of the Narrative recount the slave youth's growing temptations to despair of deliverance from bondage. Returned to the rural region where he was born, Douglass discovers the hypocrisy of Christian slaveholders whose pretentions to piety mask their cruelty and licentiousness. He reaches a dark night of the soul in 1833, when the harsh regime of Edward Covey, "the snake," breaks him "in body, soul, and spirit." And yet, he undergoes "a glorious resurrection, from the tomb of slavery, to the heaven of freedom" [50] by violently resisting

5. G. Thomas Couser discusses the "analogy between the process of conversion and that of liberation" in the Narrative in his American Autobiography: The Prophetic Mode (Amherst: University of Massachusetts Press, 1979), p. 53. See also Houston Baker's observation in Long Black Song (Charlottesville: University Press of Virginia, 1972), p. 78: "Douglass's work is a spiritual autobiography akin to the writings of such noted white American authors as Cotton Mather, Benjamin Franklin, and Henry Adams."

Covey's attempt to apprehend him, one August morning, for another infraction of the rules. Thus, "resurrected," the sixteen-year-old youth, "a slave in form" but no longer "a slave in fact," begins to put his revived faith in freedom and his "self-confidence" into practice. Hired out in 1834 to William Freeland, he starts a "Sabbath school" in which to teach slaves how to read the Bible and "to imbue their minds with thoughts of freedom" [56]. "My tendency was upward," states Douglass, firmly committed to following the road to freedom analogized in the *Narrative* in imagery reminiscent of *Pilgrim's Progress*.[6] The first escape attempt, appropriately timed for Easter, is foiled, but his second, in September 1838, succeeds.

The last pages of the *Narrative* describe the new freeman's call to witness for the gospel of freedom that had preserved, regenerated, and pointed him northward. A subscription to the *Liberator* sets his "soul" on fire for "the cause" of abolitionism. At an antislavery meeting in Nantucket in August 1841, "I felt strongly moved to speak," but Douglass is restrained by a sense of unworthiness before white people. Still the promptings of the spirit cannot be resisted, even though it is "a severe cross" for the new convert to take up. "I spoke but a few moments, when I felt a degree of freedom, and said what I desired with considerable ease." This liberation of the tongue climaxes the life-long quest of Frederick Douglass toward his divinely appointed destiny in the antislavery ministry. The special plan of Providence is now fully revealed at the end of the *Narrative*. Frederick Douglass is a chosen man as well as a freeman. His trials of the spirit have been a test and a preparation for his ultimate mission as a black Jeremiah to a corrupt white Israel. This autobiography, as Robert G. O'Meally has emphasized, is a text meant to be preached.[7]

Like all American jeremiads, the *Narrative* is a political sermon. Douglass's self-realization as a freeman and a chosen man takes place via a process of outward and sometimes violent revolution as well as inner evolution of consciousness. The strategy of Douglass's jeremiad is to depict this revolution as a "process of Americanization," to use once again a key phrase in Bercovitch's analysis of the genre. As Bercovitch notes, the jeremiad was responsible for rationalizing and channeling the revolutionary individualistic impulse in America so as to reconcile it with the myth of America's corporate destiny as a chosen people. This meant distinguishing firmly between the truly American revolutionary individualism and the rebellious, un-American individualism of the

---

6. An English spiritual allegory published by John Bunyan in 1678 [*Editors*].
7. Robert G. O'Meally, "Frederick Douglass' 1845 *Narrative*: The Text Was Meant to Be Preached," in Dexter Fisher and Robert B. Stepto, eds., *Afro-American Literature: The Reconstruction of Instruction* (New York: Modern Language Association, 1978), pp. 192–211. O'Meally concentrates on the relationship of the *Narrative* to black sermonic traditions. For a discussion of Douglass's actual experience as a preacher, see William L. Andrews, "Frederick Douglass, Preacher," *American Literature* 54 (Dec. 1982), 592–97.

alien and seditious Indian, Negro, or feminist. Those marked by racial heritage as other had to *prove* that they were of "the people," the American chosen, by demonstrating in their own lives the rituals of Americanization that had converted them from non-persons, as it were, into members of the middle-class majority. "Blacks and Indians . . . could learn to be True Americans, when in the fullness of time they would adopt the tenets of black and red capitalism."[8] Douglass pledges allegiance to the economic tenets of the republic in his autobiography, entitled, appropriately enough, the narrative of *"An American Slave."* Douglass goes beyond his predecessors in the slave narrative, in using this orthodoxy to justify his revolution against slavery and its perverse, un-American profit motive.

John Seelye has pointed out some of the affinities between Douglass's *Narrative* and the cultural myth of America as dramatized in Franklin's memoir. Douglass is "Ben Franklin's specific shade," argues Seelye, though the ex-slave's story is "not a record of essays to do good but attempts to be bad, Douglass like Milton's Satan[9] inventing virtue from an evil necessity."[1] It is no small part of Douglass's rhetorical art, however, to translate his badness into revolutionary necessity of a kind his white reader could identify with. Douglass's life, like Franklin's, describes a rising arc from country to city; then it follows a downward curve of expectations when the town slave is returned to the plantation; but it revolves upward once more, after the fight with Covey, carrying the black youth from Talbot County to Baltimore and finally to New York and New Bedford. When given the opportunity for self-improvement in the city, young Fred is every bit as enterprising as Father Ben. As a boy he overcomes adversity to learn reading and writing on his own. Discovery of an eloquence handbook entitled *The Columbian Orator* foreshadows the day when he will become one. But first he must become a man. The battle with Covey halts his regression into the slave's "beast-like stupor" and "revived within me a sense of my own manhood." "Bold defiance" replaces "cowardice"; significantly, the spheres of this defiance are intellectual and economic. As a Sabbath school teacher at Freeland's, Douglass uses as his text the Bible, and his aim is consistent with America's middle-class civil religion. He encourages his slave pupils to behave "like intellectual, moral, and accountable beings" rather than "spending the Sabbath in wrestling, boxing, and drinking whisky" [55]. Douglass domesticates a greater gesture of defiance, his first escape attempt, by analogizing it to the hallowed decision of Patrick Henry (ironically, a slaveholder) for liberty or death. "We did

---

8. Bercovitch, *American Jeremiad,* p. 160.
9. The antagonist in John Milton's epic poem *Paradise Lost* (1667) [Editors].
1. John Seelye, "The Clay Foot of the Climber: Richard M. Nixon in Perspective," in William L. Andrews, ed., *Literary Romanticism in America* (Baton Rouge: Louisiana State University Press, 1981), p. 125.

more than Patrick Henry," the fugitive advances of himself and his fellow runaways, because their liberty was more dubious and their deaths more certain if they failed. By implication, then, these dauntless blacks were more heroically American in their struggle for independence than was one of the most prominent delegates of the convention of 1776.

After Douglass's return to Baltimore in the spring of 1835 to be hired out in various employments, the *Narrative* concentrates increasingly on the economic humiliations of an upwardly aspiring "slave in form but not in fact." While apprenticed as a ship's carpenter, the slave is attacked and beaten by four white workers who felt it "degrading to them to work with me." Manfully, Douglass returns the blows in kind despite the adverse odds. Taught the calking trade, he "was able to command the highest wages given to the most experienced calkers," $1.50 a day. The money "was rightfully my own," Douglass argues. "I contracted for it; I earned it; it was paid to me." Yet every week Hugh Auld took it. "And why? Not because he earned it,—not because he had any hand in earning it,—not because I owed it to him,—nor because he possessed the slightest shadow of a right to it; but solely because he had the power to compel me to give it up" [65]. With Grandy, Lane, and Henson,[2] Douglass appeals to his reader's respect for contract and resentment of arbitrary power as a way of preparing his case for the final break with slavery. The right at issue here is pragmatic and economic, not abstract or romantic. Douglass analogizes Auld to a "grim-visaged pirate" and a "robber"—an outlaw, in other words—to banish him from a consubstantial relationship with the northern reader. Meanwhile, Douglass qualifies himself for acceptance as an economic revolutionary in the best American tradition. He works his way up the economic ladder in the South from country slave to city apprentice to the quasi-free status of one who "hired his time."

Hiring his time required Douglass to meet all his living expenses out of the income that he could make for himself, while still paying his master a fixed return of $3 per week. This was "a hard bargain," but still "a step toward freedom to be allowed to bear the responsibilities of a freeman" [67]. Here again, Douglass stresses how he qualified himself, step by step, for freedom and its "responsibilities" as well as its "rights." "I bent myself to the work of making money," adds Douglass, by way of proving his dedication to the quintessential responsibilities of an American free man. "I was ready to work at night as well as day, and by the most untiring perseverance and industry, I made enough to meet my expenses, and lay up a little money every week" [67]. The savings were used, presumably, to help Douglass in his flight to freedom, for less than a month after Auld halted the slave's hiring out (fearing that too much

2. Moses Grandy, Lunsford Lane, and Josiah Henson were slave narrators featured in *Narrative of the Life of Moses Grandy* (1843), *The Narrative of Lunsford Lane* (1842), and *The Life of Josiah Henson* (1849) [*Editors*].

freedom would go to the black man's head), Douglass retaliated by taking the ultimate "step toward freedom."

One of the most unconventional features of the *Narrative* was Douglass's refusal to end his story with the stock-in-trade climax of the slave narrative. Watching the panting fugitive seize his freedom just ahead of snapping bloodhounds and clutching slavecatchers left white readers with a vicarious sense of the thrill of the chase as well as the relief of the successful escape. In the slave narrative a generation of readers found a factual parallel to the capture-flight-and-pursuit plots of their favorite romances by James Fenimore Cooper, William Gilmore Simms, and Robert Montgomery Bird.[3] Yet Douglass left only a hiatus in his story where the customary climax should have been, insisting, quite plausibly, that to recount his mode of escape would alert slaveholders to it and thus close it to others. The conclusion he chose for his *Narrative* indicates that in his mind the high point of a fugitive slave's career was not his arrival in the free states but his assumption of a new identity as a free man and his integration into the American mainstream.

Douglass notes graphically the initial terrors of the isolated fugitive in a strange and often hostile land, but his emphasis is on how quickly and happily he assimilated. He marries within two weeks of his arrival in New York. He and his wife Anna move immediately to New Bedford, where the morning after his arrival he receives from his Negro host a new name to denote his new identity in freedom. Two days later, he takes his first job stowing a sloop with a load of oil. "It was the first work, the reward of which was to be entirely my own." "It was to me the starting-point of a new existence" [74]. Everything falls into place for Douglass in New Bedford, where the American dream of "a new existence" is always possible for every man, black or white. New Bedford fulfills the ex-slave's socioeconomic quest; here every man pursues his work "with a sober, yet cheerful earnestness, which betokened the deep interest which he felt in what he was doing, as well as a sense of his own dignity as a man." Most marvelous of all, the black population of this paragon of industrial capitalism lives in "finer houses" and enjoys "more of the comforts of life, than the average of slaveholders in Maryland." True, Douglass admits, "prejudice against color" along the docks of New Bedford kept him from resuming his former trade as a calker. But a note to the text removes even this blemish from the image of the town as the epitome of progress and justice: "I am told that colored persons can now get employment at calking in New Bedford—a result of anti-slavery effort." Perhaps this is the reason for the mild manner and the absence of irony or bitterness with which Douglass brings up this lone instance of racism in the North. The refusal of New Bedford's calkers to work with him moves the narrator to none of the moral outrage that accompa-

3. Cooper, Simms, and Bird were popular nineteenth-century American novelists [*Editors*].

nies his recall of the same kind of treatment that he received from Balti-more's calkers. Now Douglass is more thick-skinned and matter-of-fact; his narrative business is not to complain about the barriers to his prog-ress but to show how he, like his adopted city, overcame them. Now is the time for understatement: "Finding my trade of no immediate bene-fit, I threw off my calking habiliments, and prepared myself to do any kind of work I could get to do" [74].

For the next three years, Douglass had to support his family via what-ever manual labor jobs he could find, including sawing wood, shoveling coal, sweeping chimneys, and rolling casks in an oil refinery. Yet the *Narrative* stresses only the bright side of this experience—Douglass's American ingenuity and industry—not the ugly side—New Bedford's economic repression of a trained black tradesman. Only in 1881, in his *Life and Times*, when Douglass no longer had the same rhetorical stake in a dramatic contrast between North and South, would he call the whole humiliating episode "the test of the real civilization of the com-munity" of New Bedford, which the town plainly failed.[4] In 1845 New Bedford had to serve as Douglass's standard of "real civilization," of true Americanism, so that he as a jeremiad writer could have something by which to measure the South's fall from national grace.

Like earlier popular literary genres from which Afro-American autobi-ography sought authentication and other rhetorical advantages, the American jeremiad provided a structure for Douglass's vision of America that was both empowering and limiting at the same time. The jeremiad gave the ex-slave literary license to excoriate the South pretty much as he pleased so long as the ideals and values by which he judged that region's transgressions remained American. Thus while bitterly evoking the nightmare of slavery, Douglass's example invoked just as reverently the dream of America as a land of freedom and opportunity. In a letter to Douglass several weeks before the *Narrative* was published, Wendell Phillips, one of the most forthright abolitionist critics of racism in the North as well as slavery in the South, urged the autobiographer to include a comparison of the status of blacks in both sections of the country. "Tell us whether, after all, the half-free colored man of Massa-chusetts is worse off than the pampered slave of the rice swamps!" [11], Phillips requested, with his usual penchant for irony. In Douglass's jere-miad, however, such a topic was not tellable. In the spiritual autobiogra-phy and the success story, of which Douglass's *Narrative* is an amalgam, doubts about the achievement or significance of salvation and success are clear evidence that they have not been attained. Douglass's story, by contrast, is determined to declare New Bedford as more than one slave's attainable secular salvation in America. Such a declarative act brought

---

4. *Life and Times of Frederick Douglass* (Hartford, Conn.: Park, 1881), p. 260.

into being New Bedford as Douglass needed it to be—a symbol of his belief in America as a free, prosperous, and progressive social order that thrived without caste distinctions or the exploitation of labor. For the sake of this symbol in his vision of America, Douglass could make his own exploitation in the New Bedford labor market seem like a useful lesson in the school of hard knocks, the sort of adversity that self-made men generally glory in. For the symbol's sake, Douglass would censor himself and say nothing of more humiliating Jim Crow experiences that he had been subjected to in the North, although he had been recounting such incidents from the abolitionist platform for the past three years.[5]

The American jeremiad structured Douglass into a fixed bipolar set of alternatives with which to define the experience and aspirations of "an American slave." That which was not American was conceived of as an absence, un-Americanism, false Americanism. America was constantly being analyzed and measured against its opposite, which was only the negative function of the interpretive possibilities of the symbol.[6] To get outside this self-enclosed dualism, one had to liberate oneself from the symbol of America as a self-valorizing plenitude and from the binary oppositions that maintained the symbol within a field of meanings of its own making. Henry Louis Gates, Jr., has argued convincingly that in the first chapter of the *Narrative*, the binary oppositions that inform and enforce the culture of the slavocracy are "mediated" by the narrator so as to "reverse the relations of the opposition" and reveal that "the oppositions, all along, were only arbitrary, not fixed."[7] For instance, as both the son and slave of his father-master, the mulatto Douglass deconstructs the fundamental opposition between white people and black animals on which much of the rationale for slavery was based. That separation between white and black cannot hold because it is culturally, not naturally, determined. By the time we finish the last chapter of the *Narrative*, however, it becomes evident that Douglass is not bent on the same kind of critique of the binary oppositions that govern and validate the symbol of America. The *Narrative* turns, structurally and thematically, on such dualities as southern slavery versus northern freedom, "slaveholding religion" versus "Christianity proper," Baltimore versus New Bedford, compulsion versus contract, stagnation versus progress, deprivation versus wealth, violence versus order, community versus caste system. And very little mediation takes place

5. For an example of Douglass's attacks on the racist Methodists of New Bedford, see his speech, "The Church Is the Bulwark of Slavery" (May 25, 1842), in Blassingame, ed., *Douglass Papers*, 1: 19.
6. Bercovitch, *American Jeremiad*, pp. 177–78.
7. Henry Louis Gates, Jr., "Binary Oppositions in Chapter One of *The Narrative of the Life of Frederick Douglass, an American Slave, Written by Himself*," in Fisher and Stepto, eds., *Afro-American Literature*, pp. 226–27.

between these fixed, shall we say "black-and-white," antitheses.[8] Indeed, Douglass suggests that the gap between these poles of true and false Americanism is growing wider, as New Bedford's progress against racial discrimination seems to testify.

Thus as an American jeremiad, Douglass's *Narrative* deconstructs binary oppositions that uphold slavery in the South while reconstructing the pattern of his life around other sets of oppositions whose support of the myth of America he might as readily have questioned, too. In 1845, however, Douglass was still exploring the rhetorical possibilities of binary oppositions as a means of establishing his own identity relative to America, South and North. It is through his own experiments with rhetoric that we see Douglass's particular brand of "opposing self" at work. As a jeremiadic autobiographer, he has more than his own story to tell. He must preach in such a way as to discredit the false oppositions and hierarchies of value that have arisen as a consequence of salvery's perversions of the true oppositions between good and evil, the natural and the unnatural.

*   *   *

HOUSTON A. BAKER, JR.

[The Economics of Douglass's *Narrative*]†

*   *   *

One of the most striking manifestations of the economic voice of Douglass's 1845 *Narrative* is the description of the wealthy slaveowner Colonel Lloyd's "finely cultivated garden, which afforded almost constant employment for four men, besides the chief gardener, (Mr. M'Durmond)" (p. 33) [20]. This garden, which is found at the outset of chapter 3,* * *is coded in a manner that makes it the most significant economic sign in the initial chapters of the *Narrative*. The entire store of the slaveholder's "Job-like" (p. 35) [21] riches is imaged by the garden, which was "probably the greatest attraction of the place [the Lloyd estate]" (p.33) [20]. Abounding in "fruit of every description," the gar-

---

8. Douglass's "Appendix" does question distinctions between Christianity in the South and the North through statements like "I can see no reason, but the most deceitful one, for calling the religion of this land Christianity." In this respect, Douglass was following the Garrisonian line of attacking all northern churches that maintained any sort of denominational "union with slaveholders." However, this hypocrisy of the northern church when linked with the corruption of the southern gave Douglass all the more reason to write as a Jeremiah lamenting the decline of present-day religion when contrasted to its opposite, "Christianity proper."

† From *Blues, Ideology, and Afro-American Literature* (Chicago: U of Chicago P, 1984) 44–50. Reprinted by permission of the University of Chicago Press. Bracketed page numbers refer to this Norton Critical Edition.

den is "quite a temptation to the hungry swarms of boys, as well as the older slaves . . . few of whom had the virtue or the vice to resist it" (p. 33) [20].

* * *

In the case of Colonel Lloyd's garden the fruits of slave labor are *all* retained by the master. And any attempts by slaves to share such fruits are not only dubbed stealing, but also severely punished. Even so, "the colonel had to resort to all kinds of stratagems [beyond mere flogging] to keep his slaves out of the garden" (p. 33) [20].

The image of vast abundance produced by slaves but denied them through the brutality of the owner of the means of production (i.e., the land) suggests a purely economic transformation of a traditional image of the biblical garden and its temptations. Douglass heightens the import of this economic coding through implicit and ironic detailings of the determination of general cultural consciousness *by commerce*. The folkloric aphorism that a single touch of the "tar brush" defiles the whole is invoked in the *Narrative* as a humorous analogue for Colonel Lloyd's ideological and mystifying designation of those who are denied the fruits of the garden as *unworthy*. The colonel *tars* the fence around his garden, and any slave "caught with tar upon his person . . . was severely whipped by the chief gardener" (p. 33) [20].

The promotion of *tar* (of a *blackness* so sticky and entangling for American conscience that the Tar Baby story[1] of African provenance has been an enduring cultural transplant) to a mark of low status, deprivation, and unworthiness is commented upon by the narrator as follows: "The slaves became as fearful of tar as of the lash. They seemed to realize the impossibility of touching *tar* without being defiled" (p. 33) [20]. Blacks, through the *genetic* touch of the tar brush that makes them people of color, are automatically guilty of the paradoxically labeled "crime" of seeking to enjoy the fruits of their own labor.

The "increase in store" of a traditional American history takes on quite other dimensions in light of Douglass's account of the garden in chapter 3. Later in the *Narrative*, he writes of the life of slaves on Thomas Auld's farm: "A great many times have we poor creatures been nearly perishing with hunger, when food in abundance lay mouldering in the safe and smoke-house, and our pious mistress was aware of the fact; and yet mistress and her husband would kneel every morning, and pray that God would bless them in basket and store!" (p. 66) [39]. The keenly literate and secular autobiographical self that so capably figures the economics of Lloyd's garden—summing in the process both the nil financial gain of blacks, and their placement in the left-hand, or debit, column of the ledgers of American status—is the same self encountered

1. The best known of the southern African American animal fables first popularized by Joel Chandler Harris in *Uncle Remus: His Songs and His Sayings* (1881) [*Editors*].

when the narrator returns as a teenager to southern, agrarian slavery. At the farm of Mr. Edward Covey, where he has been hired out for "breaking," the *Narrative* pictures four enslaved black men fanning wheat. Douglass comprises one of their number, "carrying wheat to the fan" (p. 77) [47]. The sun proves too much for the unacclimatized Douglass, and he collapses, only to be beaten by Mr. Covey for his failure to serve effectively as a mindless ("the work was simple requiring strength rather than intellect") cog in the machine of slave production. Seeking redress from his master (Mr. Thomas Auld) who hired him to Covey, Douglass finds that the profit motive drives all before it: "Master Thomas . . . said . . . that he could not think of taking me from . . . [Mr. Covey]; that should he do so, he would lose the whole year's wages" (p. 79) [48].

The most bizarre profit accruing to the owners in the Covey episode, however, is not slave wages, but slave offspring. If Colonel Lloyd would take the fruit of the slave's labor, Mr. Covey would take the very fruit of the slave's womb. He puts a black man "to stud" with one of his slave women and proclaims the children of this compelled union his property. This is a confiscation of surplus value with a vengeance. It manifests the supreme aberrancy of relationships conditioned by the southern traffic in human "chattel." At Covey's farm, produce, labor, wages, and profit create a crisis that Douglass must negotiate in the best available fashion. He resolves physically to combat Mr. Covey, the "man in the middle."

In contrast to a resolved young Douglass in Chapter 10 of the *Narrative* stands Sandy Jenkins, the slave mentioned earlier in this discussion who has a free wife. Sandy offers Douglass a folk means of negotiating his crisis at Covey's, providing him with "a certain *root*," which, carried "*always on* . . . [the] *right side*, would render it impossible for Mr. Covey or any other white man" to whip the slave (p. 80) [49]. What is represented by the introduction of Sandy Jenkins is a displacement of Christian metaphysics by Afro-American "superstition." Ultimately, this displacement reveals the inefficacy of trusting solely to any form of extra-secular aid for relief (or release) from slavery.

The root does not work. The physical confrontation does. Through physical battle, Douglass gains a measure of relief from Covey's harassments. Jenkins's mode of negotiating the economics of slavery, the *Narrative* implies, is not *a man's way*, since the narrator claims that his combat with Covey converted him, ipso facto, into *a man*. In the same chapter in which the inefficacy of Jenkins's way is implied, the text also suggests that Jenkins is the traitor who reveals the planned escape of Douglass and fellow slaves to their master Mr. Freeland. Sandy seems to represent the inescapable limiting conditions of Afro-American slavery in the South; he is the pure, negative product of an economics of slavery. Standing in clear and monumentally *present* (even to the extent of a foregrounding footnote) contrast to the Douglass of chapter 10,

Sandy represents the virtual impossibility of an escape from bondage on the terms implied by the attempted escape from Freeland's.

At its most developed, *southern* extension, the literate abolitionist self of the *Narrative* engages in an act of physical revolt, forms a Christian brotherhood of fellow slaves through a Sabbath school, and formulates a plan for a *collective* escape from bondage. But this progress toward liberation in the agrarian South is foiled by one whose mind is so "tarred" by the economics of slavery that he betrays the collective. The possibility of collective freedom is thus foreclosed by treachery within the slave community. A communally dedicated Douglass ("The work of instructing my dear fellow-slaves was the sweetest engagement with which I was ever blessed," p. 90 [55]) finds that revolt, religion, and literacy *all* fail. The slave does, indeed, *write* his "own pass" and the passes of his fellows, but the Sabbath school assembled group is no match for the enemy within.

What recourse, then, is available for the black man of talent who would be free? The *Narrative* answers in an economic voice similar to that found in *The Life of Olaudah Equiano*.[2] Returned to Baltimore and the home of Mr. Hugh Auld after a three-year absence, the teenaged slave is hired out to "Mr. William Gardner, an extensive shipbuilder in Fell's Point. I was put there to learn how to calk" (p. 99) [61]. In short space, Douglass is able "to command the highest wages given to the most experienced calkers" (p. 103) [64]. In lines that echo Vassa with resonant effect, he writes: "I was now of some importance to my master. I was bringing him from six to seven dollars per week. I sometimes brought him nine dollars per week: my wages were a dollar and a half a day" (p. 103) [64]. Having entered a world of real *wages*, Douglass is equivalent to the Vassa who realized what a small "venture" could produce. And like Vassa, the nineteenth-century slave recognizes that the surplus value his master receives is but stolen profit: "I was compelled to deliver every cent of that [money contracted for, earned, and paid for calking] to Master Auld. And why? Not because he earned it . . . but solely because he had the power to compel me to give it up" (p. 104) [65].

Like Vassa, Douglass has arrived at a fully commercial view of his situation. He, too, enters an agreement with his master that results in freedom. Having gained the right to hire his own time and to keep a portion of his wages, Douglass eventually converts property, through property, into humanity. Impelled by his commercial endeavors and the opportunities resulting from his free commerce, he takes leave of Mr. Auld. He thus removes (in his own person) the master's property and places it in the ranks of a northern humanity. "According to my resolution, on the third day of September, 1838, I left my chains and suc-

---

2. *The Interesting Narrative of the Life of Olaudah Equiano, or Gustavus Vassa, the African* (1798) [*Editors*].

ceeded in reaching New York" (p. 111) [69]. By "stealing away," Douglass not only steals the fruits of his own labor (not unlike the produce of Colonel Lloyd's garden), but also liberates the laborer—the chattel who works profitlessly in the garden.

The necessity for Douglass to effect his liberation through flight results from the complete intransigence to change of southern patriarchs. Mr. Auld, as the young slave knows all too well, cannot possibly conceive of the child of his "family," of the "nigger" fitted out to work only for his profit, as simply an economic investment. Instead of exchanging capital, therefore, Douglass appropriates his own labor and flees to the camp of those who will ultimately be Auld's adversaries in civil war.

The inscribed document that effectively marks Douglass's liberation in the *Narrative* is, I think, no less an economic sign than Vassa's certificate of manumission:

> This may certify, that I joined together in holy matrimony Frederick Johnson and Anna Murray, as man and wife, in the presence of Mr. David Ruggles and Mrs. Michaels.
>
> James W. C. Pennington
> *New York, Sept.* 15, 1838.

What Douglass's certificate of marriage, which is transcribed in full in chapter 11, signifies is that the black man has *repossessed* himself in a manner that enables him to enter the kind of relationship disrupted, or foreclosed, by the economics of slavery.

Unlike Sandy Jenkins—doomed forever to passive acquiescence and weekend visitation—Douglass enters a productive relationship promising a new bonding of Afro-American humanity. As a married man, who understands the necessity for *individual* wage earning (i.e., a mastery of the incumbencies of the economics of slavery), Douglass makes his way in the company of his new bride to a "New England factory village" where he quickly becomes a laborer at "the first work, the reward of which was to be entirely my own" (p. 116) [74].

The representation of New Bedford that the *Narrative* provides—with Douglass as wage-earning laborer—seems closely akin to the economic, utopian vision that closes Vassa's account: "Everything looked clean, new, and beautiful. I saw few or no dilapidated houses, with poverty-stricken inmates, no half-naked children and bare-footed women, such as I had been accustomed to see in . . . [Maryland]" (p. 116) [73]. Ships of the best order and finest size, warehouses stowed to their utmost capacity, and ex-slaves "living in finer houses, and evidently enjoying more of the comforts of life, than the average slaveholders in Maryland" complete the splendid panorama. Such a landscape is gained by free, dignified, and individualistic labor—the New England ideal so frequently appearing in Afro-American narratives. (One thinks, for example, of the DuBoisian vision in *The Souls of Black Folk* or of Ralph Ellison's Mr. Norton.[3])* * *And presiding over the concluding vision in both narratives is the figure of the black, abolitionist spokesman—the man who has arisen, found his "voice," and secured the confidence to address a "general public."

What one experiences in the conclusions of Vassa's and Douglass's narratives, however, is identity with a difference. For the expressive, married, economically astute self at the close of Douglass's work represents a convergence of the voices that mark the various autobiographical postures of the *Narrative* as a whole. The orator whom we see standing at a Nantucket convention at the close of Douglass's work is immediately to become a *salaried* spokesman, combining literacy, Christianity, and revolutionary zeal in an individual and economically profitable job of work. Douglass's authorship, oratory, and economics converge in the history of the *Narrative*'s publication and the course of action its appearance mandated in the life of the author.

Since his identity and place of residence were revealed in the *Narrative*, Douglass, who was still a fugitive when his work appeared, was forced to flee to England. In the United Kingdom, he sold copies of his book for profit, earned lecture fees, and aroused sufficient sympathy and financial support to purchase his freedom with solid currency. While his Garrisonian, abolitionist contemporaries were displeased by Douglass's commercial traffic with slaveholders, the act of purchase was simply the logical (and "traditionally" predictable) end of his negotiation of the economics of slavery.

What is intriguing for a present-day reading of the *Narrative*'s history is the manner in which ideological analysis reveals the black spokesperson's economic conditioning—that is, his necessary encounter with economics signaled by a commercial voice and the implications of this encounter in the domain of narrative transaction. The nineteenth-century slave, in effect, *publicly* sells his voice in order to secure *private* ownership of his voice-person. The ultimate convergence of the *Narrative*'s history is between money and the narrative sign. Exchanging words becomes both a function of commerce and a commercial function. Ideological analysis made available by the archaeology of knowledge, thus, reveals intriguingly commercial dimensions of Afro-American discourse.

---

3. A wealthy New Englander in Ralph Ellison's novel *Invisible Man* (1952) [*Editors*].

DEBORAH E. McDOWELL

In the First Place: Making Frederick Douglass and the Afro-American Narrative Tradition†

* * *

> This man shall be remembered . . . with lives grown out of his life, the
> lives fleshing his dream of the needful, beautiful thing.
> —Robert Hayden, "Frederick Douglass"

Students of the 1845 *Narrative* commonly designate the following as its key sentence: "You have seen how a man was made a slave, you shall see how a slave was made a man."[1] The clause that follows that pivotal comma—"you shall see how a slave was made a man"—captures with great prescience the focus of much contemporary scholarship on slavery. That focus is studiously on making the slave a man, according to cultural norms of masculinity. This accounts in part, as I will show below, for why Douglass is so pivotal, so mythological a figure. I am not out to argue for any distinction between Douglass "the myth" and Douglass "the man," but rather and simply to view him as a product of history, a construction of a specific time and place, developed in response to a variety of social contingencies and individual desires.

The process and production in literary studies of Douglass as "the first" have paralleled and perhaps been partly fueled by what revisionist historians have made of him. We might go even further to argue that "history" has operated as narrative, in the making of Douglass and his *Narrative*. And so we face constructions upon constructions. While the mythologization of Douglass and this text well antedates the 1960s, 1970s, and 1980s, these decades are especially crucial in efforts to understand this process.

These years were characterized by revisionist mythmaking, much of it prompted by Stanley Elkins's controversial book *Slavery: A Problem in American Institutional and Intellectual Life* (1959). I need not rehearse in detail Elkins's now-familiar Sambo thesis emphasizing the effects of black male emasculation in slavery.[2] Historians, armed with a

---

† From William L. Andrews, ed., *Critical Essays on Frederick Douglass* (Boston: G. K. Hall, 1991) 195–97, 201–8. Reprinted by permission of the author. Bracketed page numbers refer to this Norton Critical Edition.
1. Frederick Douglass, *Narrative of the Life of Frederick Douglass, An American Slave Written by Himself* (New York: Signet/New American Library, 1968), 47. Subsequent references are to this edition and will be indicated in parentheses in the text. I will also make reference to *My Bondage and My Freedom* (New York: Dover, 1969) and *Life and Times of Frederick Douglass, Written by Himself* (New York: Pathway Press, 1941).
2. Perhaps as influential as the Elkins book in sparking revisionist histories of slavery was Daniel P. Moynihan's federally commissioned *Moynihan Report: The Case for National Action* (1965). While Elkins virtually ignored black women in his study, attributing the failure of black males to achieve "manhood" to a paternalistic slave system that infantilized them, Moynihan assigns blame to black women for being the predominant heads of household.

172

mountain of supporting data, came forth to refute Elkins's data and his thesis. Among the most prominent of these revisionists was John Blassingame, whose *The Slave Community* was rightly celebrated for its attempt to write history from the perspective of slaves, not planters. Blassingame rejects Elkins's Sambo thesis as "intimately related to the planters's projections, desires, and biases,"[3] particularly their desire to be relieved of the "anxiety of thinking about slaves as men."[4]

Blassingame sets out to correct the record to show that the slave was not "half-man," "half-child,"[5] as the Elkins thesis tried to show, but a whole man. Blassingame doesn't simply lapse into the reflexive use of the generic "he," but throughout his study assumes the slave to be literally male, an assumption seen especially in his chapter titled "The Slave Family." There he opens with the straightforward observation: "The Southern plantation was unique in the New World because it permitted the development of a monogamous slave family," which was "one of the most important survival mechanisms for the slave." He continues, "the slave faced almost insurmountable odds in his efforts to build a strong stable family . . . his authority was restricted by his master . . . The master determined when both he and his wife would go to work [and] when or whether his wife cooked his meals." "When the slave lived on the same plantation with his mate he could rarely escape frequent demonstrations of his powerlessness." "Under such a regime," Blassingame adds, "slave fathers often had little or no authority." Despite that, the slave system "recognized the male as the head of the family."[6]

Blassingame is clearly not alone in revising the history of slavery to demonstrate the propensities of slaves toward shaping their lives according to "normative" cultural patterns of marriage and family life. But *The Slave Community* must be seen as a study of the institution that reflects and reproduces the assumptions of a much wider discursive network—scholarly and political—within which the black male is the racial subject.

There have been few challenges to this two-decade-long focus on the personality of the male slave. In her book *Ar'n't I a Woman?* (which might have been more aptly titled, "Can a slave be a woman; can a woman be a slave?"), Deborah White critiques the emphasis on negating Samboism, which characterizes so much recent literature on slavery. She argues that "the male slave's 'masculinity' was restored by putting black women in their proper 'feminine' place."[7] bell hooks offers an even stronger critique of this literature, noting eloquently its underlying assumption that "the most cruel and dehumanizing impact of slavery

3. John Blassingame, *The Slave Community* (New York: Oxford University Press, 1979), xi.
4. Blassingame, *The Slave*, 230.
5. Blassingame, *The Slave*, xi.
6. Blassingame, *The Slave*, 172, 152.
7. Deborah Gray White. *Ar'n't I a Woman* (New York: W. W. Norton, 1985), 22.

on the lives of black people was that black men were stripped of their masculinity." hooks continues, "To suggest that black men were dehumanized solely as a result of not being able to be patriarchs implies that the subjugation of black women was essential to the black male's development of a positive self-concept, an ideal that only served to support a sexist social order."[8]

While I would not argue that students of Afro-American literature have consciously joined revisionist historians in their efforts to debunk the Elkins thesis, their work can certainly be said to participate in and reinforce these revisionist histories. And what better way to do this than to replace the Sambo myth of childlike passivity with an example of public derring-do, with the myth of the male slave as militant, masculine, dominant, and triumphant in both private and public spheres?[9]

But the Elkins thesis, and the revisionist histories it engendered, are only part of a larger chain of interlocking events that have worked to mythologize Frederick Douglass. These include the demand for African and African-American Studies courses in universities, the publishers who capitalized on that demand, and the academic scholars who completed the chain. A series of individual slave narratives has appeared, along with anthologies and collections of less-popular narratives. The more popular the narrative, the more frequent the editions, and Douglass's 1845 *Narrative* has headed the list since 1960. Scholarly interest in African-American literature has accelerated correspondingly and, again, the 1845 *Narrative* has been premier. Although in his 1977 essay, "Animal Farm Unbound," H. Bruce Franklin could list in a fairly short paragraph critical articles on the 1845 *Narrative*, scarcely more than a decade later the book had stimulated a small industry of scholarship on its own.[1] Thus Douglass's assumed genius as a literary figure is the work of a diverse and interactive collective that includes publishers, editors, and literary critics who have helped to construct his reputation and to make it primary in Afro-American literature.

A major diachronic study of the production, reception, and circulation history of Douglass's 1845 *Narrative* is urgently needed; but even

---

8. bell hooks. *Ain't I a Woman* (Boston: South End Press, 1981), 20–21.
9. Ronald Takaki's interpretation is an example of making Douglass a militant. In "Not Afraid to Die: Frederick Douglass and Violence," in *Violence and the Black Imagination* (New York: Capricorn, 1972), Takaki traces Douglass's rise to a political activist who advocated killing for freedom. In a forthcoming essay, "Race, Violence, and Manhood: The Masculine Ideal in Frederick Douglass's 'The Heroic Slave,'" Richard Yarborough discusses Douglass's obsession with manhood in his novella "The Heroic Slave." There manhood was virtually synonymous with militant slave resistance. In the popular realm, Spike Lee's controversial film *Do the Right Thing* is structured according to this ideology of masculinity, which ranks black leaders (assumed to be male) according to their propensities for advocating violence.
1. For a bibliographic essay on the various editions of the Douglass narrative as compared to other slave narratives, see Ruth Miller and Peter J. Katopes, "Slave Narratives" and W. Burghardt Turner, "The Polemicists: David Walker, Frederick Douglass, Booker T. Washington, and W. E. B. DuBois," in M. Thomas Inge, Maurice Duke, and Jackson R. Bryer, *Black American Writers: Bibliographical Essays, Vol. 1* (New York: St. Martin's Press, 1978).

more urgent is the need for a thoroughgoing analysis of the politics of gender at work in that process. One could argue that the politics of gender have been obscured both by the predominance of nonfeminist interpretations of the *Narrative* and by the text itself. In other words, those who have examined it have tended, with few exceptions, to mimic the work of Douglass himself on the question of the feminine and its relation to the masculine in culture.

For example, in his most recent reading of the 1845 *Narrative*, Houston Baker assimilates the text to Marxist language and rhetoric, but a more conventional rhetoric of family resounds. Baker's reading foregrounds the disruption of the slave family and offers the terms of its reunion: economic solvency. "The successful negotiation of such economics," says Baker, "is, paradoxically, the *only* course that provides conditions for a reunification of woman and sable man."[2] He continues, "the African who successfully negotiates his way through the dread exchanges of bondage to the type of expressive posture characterizing *The Life's* conclusion is surely a man who has repossessed himself and, thus, achieved the ability to reunite a severed African humanity."[3] A sign of that self-repossession, Baker argues, is Douglass's "certificate of marriage." "As a married man," he concludes, Douglass "understands the necessity for *individual* wage earning."[4] "In the company of his new bride," he goes to a New England factory village where he participates "creatively in the liberation of his people."[5] This reading's implication in an old patriarchal script requires not a glossing, but an insertion and a backward tracking. However important Douglass's wage-earning capacities as a freeman are, one could say that the prior wage, if you will, was Anna Murray's, Douglass's "new bride." A freedwoman, Anna "helped to defray the costs for [Douglass's] runaway scheme by borrowing from her savings and by selling one of her feather beds."[6]

Mary Helen Washington is one of the few critics to insert Anna Murray Douglass into a discussion of the 1845 *Narrative*. She asks, "While our daring Douglass . . . was heroically ascending freedom's arc . . . who . . . was at home taking care of the children?"[7] But such questions are all too rare in discussions of the *Narrative*. Because critical commentary

2. Houston Baker, *Blues, Ideology, and Afro-American Literature*, (Chicago: University of Chicago Press, 1984), 38.
3. Baker, *Blues*, 38.
4. Baker, *Blues*, 48.
5. Baker, *Blues*, 49.
6. Waldo E. Martin. *The Mind of Frederick Douglass* (Chapel Hill: University of North Carolina Press, 1984), 15.
7. Mary Helen Washington, "These Self-Invented Women: A Theoretical Framework for a Literary History of Black Women," *Radical Teacher* (1980), 4. In a recent study David Leverenz also notes that "Douglass's whole sense of latter-day self, in both the *Narrative* and its revision, focuses on manhood; his wife seems an afterthought. He introduces her to his readers as a rather startling appendage to his escape and marries her almost in the same breath." See Frederick "Douglass's Self-Fashioning," in *Manhood and the American Renaissance* (Ithaca: Cornell University Press, 1989), 128.

has mainly repeated the text's elision of women, I would like to restore them for the moment, to change the subject of the text from man to woman.

* * *

> For heart of man though mainly right
> Hides many things from mortal sight
> Which seldom ever come to light
> except upon compulsion.
> —Frederick Douglass,
> "What Am I to You"

Frances Foster is one of the few critics to describe the construction in the popular imagination of the slave woman as sexual victim, a pattern she sees in full evidence in male slave narratives. Foster observes a markedly different pattern in slave narratives written by women. Unlike the male narratives, which portray graphically the sexual abuse of slave women by white men, female narratives "barely mention sexual experiences and never present rape or seduction as the most profound aspect of their existence."[8]

The pattern that Foster describes is abundantly evident in all three of Douglass's autobiographies. One can easily argue that, with perhaps the exception of his mother and grandmother, slave women operate almost totally as physical bodies, as sexual victims, "at the mercy," as he notes in *My Bondage and My Freedom* "of the fathers, sons or brothers of [their] master" (60). Though this is certainly true, slave women were just as often at the mercy of the wives, sisters, and mothers of these men," as Harriet Jacobs records in *Incidents in the Life of a Slave Girl*.[9] But in Douglass's account, the sexual villains are white men and the victims black women. Black men are largely impotent onlookers, condemned to watch the abuse. What Douglass watches and then narrates is astonishing—the whippings of slaves, one after another, in almost unbroken succession.

A scant four pages into the text, immediately following his account of his origins, Douglass begins to describe these whippings in graphic detail. He sees Mr. Plummer, the overseer, "cut and slash the women's heads" and "seem to take great pleasure" in it. He remembers being often awakened by the heart-rending shrieks of his aunt as she is beaten. He sees her "tie[d] up to a joist and whip[ped] upon her naked back till she was literally covered with blood. The louder she screamed, the harder he whipped; and where the blood ran fastest, there he whipped longest. He would whip her to make her scream, and whip her to make

8. Frances Foster, " 'In Respect to Females. . . .': Differences in the Portrayals of Women by Male and Female Narrators," *Black American Literature Forum*, 15 (Summer 1981), 67.
9. See "The Jealous Mistress," in *Incidents in the Life of a Slave Girl*. Even Douglass himself says as much at another point. He notes that the mistress "is ever disposed to find anything to please her; she is never more pleased than when she sees them under the lash" (23).

her hush; and not until overcome by fatigue, would he cease to swing the blood-clotted cowskin" (25) [14–15].

Though the whippings of women are not the only ones of which Douglass's *Narrative* gives account, they predominate by far in the text's economy as Douglass looks on. There was Mr. Severe, whom "I have seen . . . whip a woman, causing the blood to run half an hour at the time" (29) [17]. There was his master, who he had seen "tie up a *lame* young woman, and whip her with a heavy cowskin upon her naked shoulders, causing the warm red blood to drip. I have known him to tie her up early in the morning and whip her before breakfast; leave her, go to his store, return at dinner and whip her again, cutting in the places already made raw with his cruel lash" (68–69) [41]. There was Mr. Weeden, who kept the back of a slave woman "literally raw, made so by the lash of this merciless, religious wretch" (87) [53]. As the *Narrative* progresses, the beatings proliferate and the women, no longer identified by name, become absolutized as a bloody mass of naked backs.

What has been made of this recital of whippings? William L. Andrews is one of the few critics to comment on the function of whippings in the text. In a very suggestive reading, he argues that Douglass presents the fact of whipping in "deliberately stylized, plainly rhetorical, recognizably artificial ways." There is nothing masked about this presentation. On the contrary, "Douglass's choice of repetition" is his "chief rhetorical effect." It constitutes his "stylistic signature" and expresses his "performing self." In the whipping passages, Andrews adds, "Douglass calls attention to himself as an unabashed artificer, a maker of forms and efforts that recontextualize brute facts according to requirements of self. The freeman requires the freedom to demonstrate the potency of his own inventiveness and the sheer potentiality of language itself for rhetorical manipulation."[1]

However intriguing I find Andrews's reading, I fear that to explain the repetition of whippings solely in rhetorical terms and in the interest of Douglass's self-expression leads to some troubling elisions and rationalizations, perhaps the most troubling elision being the black woman's body. In other words, Douglass's "freedom"—narrative and physical alike—depends on narrating black women's bondage. He achieves his "stylistic signature" by objectifying black women. To be sure, delineating the sexual abuse of black women is a standard convention of the fugitive slave narrative, but the narration of that abuse seems to function beyond the mere requirements of form. A second look at the first recorded beating, his Aunt Hester's, forces out a different explanation.

---

1. Andrews, *To Tell a Free Story*, 134. Valerie Smith also offers an interesting reading of the whippings. They enable the reader to "visualize the blood that masters draw from their slaves . . . Passages such as [Douglass's Aunt Hester's beatings] provide vivid symbols of the process of dehumanization that slaves underwent as their lifeblood was literally sapped." *Self-Discovery and Authority*, 21–22.

His choice of words in this account—"spectacle," "exhibition"—is instructive, as is his telling admission that, in viewing the beating, he became both "witness and participant" (25) [15].

Critical commentary has focused almost completely on Douglass as witness to slavery's abuses, overlooking his role as participant, an omission that conceals his complex and troubling relationship to slave women, kin and nonkin alike. In calling for closer attention to the narration of whipping scenes, I do not mean to suggest that Douglass's autobiographies were alone among their contemporaries in their obsession with corporal punishment. As Richard Brodhead has observed, "Corporal punishment has been one of the most perennially vexed of questions in American cultural history," and it had its "historical center of gravity in America in the antebellum decades."[2] Both in antislavery literature and in the literature of the American Gothic, what Brodhead calls the "imagination of the lash" was pervasive. That much antislavery literature had strong sexual undercurrents has been well documented. As many critics have observed, much abolitionist literature went beyond an attack on slavery to condemn the South as a vast libidinal playground.

My aim here, then, is not to argue that Douglass's repeated depiction of whipping scenes is in any way unique to him, but rather to submit those scenes to closer scrutiny for their own sake. In other words, the preponderance of this pattern in antebellum literature should not preclude a detailed examination of its representation in a smaller textual sampling. Neither is my aim to psychoanalyze Douglass, nor to offer an "alternative," more "correct" reading, but rather to reveal that Douglass often has more than one voice, one motivation, and one response to his record of black women's abuse in his *Narrative*.

Freud notes in *Beyond the Pleasure Principle* that "repetition, the reexperiencing of something identical, is clearly in itself a source of pleasure."[3] If, as Douglass observes, the slave master derives pleasure from the repeated act of whipping, could Douglass, as observer, derive a vicarious pleasure from the repeated narration of the act? I would say yes. Douglass's repetition of the sexualized scene of whipping projects him into a voyeuristic relation to the violence against slave women, which he watches, and thus he enters into a symbolic complicity with the sexual crime he witnesses. In other words, the spectator becomes voyeur, reinforcing what many feminist film theorists have persuasively argued: sexualization "resides in the very act of looking."[4] Thus "the

---

2. Richard Brodhead, "Sparing the Rod: Discipline and Fiction in Antebellum America," *Representations* 21 (Winter 1988), 67. See also David Leverenz, *Manhood and the American Renaissance* for a discussion of beatings in Melville's *Moby Dick* and *White Jacket*, and in *Uncle Tom's Cabin*.
3. Sigmund Freud. *Beyond the Pleasure Principle*, Volume 18 of *Standard Edition of the Complete Psychological Works of Sigmund Freud* (London: The Hogarth Press, 1955), 36.
4. Jacqueline Rose. *Sexuality in the Field of Vision* (London: Verso, 1986), 112.

relationship between viewer and scene is always one of fracture, partial identification, pleasure and distrust."[5]

To be sure, Douglass sounds an urgently and warranted moral note in these passages, but he sounds an erotic one as well that is even more clear if the critical gaze moves from the first autobiography to the second. In a chapter titled "Gradual Initiation into the Mysteries of Slavery," Douglass describes awakening as a child to a slave woman being beaten. The way in which Douglass constructs the scene evokes the familiar male child's initiation into the mysteries of sexuality by peeking through the keyhole of his parents' bedroom:

> My sleeping place was the floor of a little, rough closet, which opened into the kitchen; and through the cracks of its unplaned boards, I could distinctly see and hear what was going on, without being seen by my master. Esther's wrists were firmly tied and the twisted rope was fastened to a strong staple in a heavy wooden joist above, near the fireplace. Here she stood, on a bench, her arms tightly drawn over her breast. Her back and shoulders were bare to the waist. Behind her stood old master, with cowskin in hand, preparing his barbarous work with all manner of harsh, coarse, and tantalizing epithets. The screams of his victim were most piercing. He was cruelly deliberate, and protracted the torture, as one who was delighted with the scene. Again and again he drew the hateful whip through his hand, adjusting it with a view of dealing the most pain-giving blow. Poor Esther had never yet been severely whipped, and her shoulders were plump and tender. Each blow vigorously laid on, brought screams as well as blood. (87–88)[6]

This passage in all its erotic overtones echoes throughout Douglass's autobiographies and goes well beyond pleasure to embrace its frequent symbiotic equivalent: power. It can be said both to imitate and articulate the pornographic scene, which starkly represents and reproduces the cultural and oppositional relation of the masculine to the feminine, the relation between seer and seen, agent and victim, dominant and dominated, powerful and powerless.[7]

Examining the narration of whipping scenes with regard to the sex of

5. Rose, *Sexuality*, 27. See also Laura Mulvey, "Visual Pleasure and Narrative Cinema," *Screen* 16 (Autumn 1975), and Teresa De Lauretis, *Alice Doesn't: Feminism, Semiotics, Cinema* (Bloomington: Indiana University Press, 1984).
6. Such passages run throughout *My Bondage and My Freedom*. Even in the series of appendices to the text, Douglass keeps his focus riveted on the violation of the slave woman's body. In "Letter to His Old Master" [Thomas Auld], for example, he writes: "When I saw the slave-driver whip a slave-woman, cut the blood out of her neck, and heard her piteous cries, I went away into the corner of the fence, wept and pondered over the mystery." He then asks Auld how he would feel if his daughter were seized and left "unprotected—a degraded victim to the brutal lust of fiendish overseers, who would pollute, blight, and blast the fair soul . . . destroy her virtue, and annihilate in her person all the grace that adorns the character of virtuous womanhood?" (427–28).
7. See Susanne Kappeler, *The Pornography of Representation* (Minneapolis: University of Minnesota, 1986), 104.

the slave reinforces this gendered division and illustrates its consequences. While the women are tied up—the classic stance of women
in pornography—and unable to resist, the men are "free," if you like, to
struggle. William Demby is a case in point. After Mr. Gore whips him,
Demby runs to the creek and refuses to obey the overseer's commands
to come out. Demby finally asserts the power over his own body, even
though it costs him his life.

But clearly the most celebrated whipping scene of all is Douglass's
two-hour-long fight with Covey, on which the 1845 *Narrative* pivots.
Positioned roughly midway through the text, it constitutes also the midway point between slavery and freedom. This explains in part why the
fight is dramatized and elaborated over several pages, an allotment
clearly disproportionate to other reported episodes. When the fight is
over, Douglass boasts that Covey "had drawn no blood from me, but I
had from him" and expresses satisfaction at "repell[ing] by force the
bloody arm of slavery." He concludes, "I had several fights, but was
never whipped" (81–83) [50–51].

The fight with Covey is the part of the *Narrative* most frequently
anthologized, and it is a rare critical text indeed that ignores this scene.
I agree with Donald Gibson that "most commentators on the conflict
have . . . interpreted it as though it were an arena boxing match." Gibson attributes such a view to what he terms the "public focus" of Douglass's narrative, "which requires that the slave defeat the slaveholder."[8] I
would add to Gibson's explanation that this defeat serves to incarnate a
critical/political view that equates resistance to power with physical
struggle, a view that fails to see that such struggle cannot function as the
beginning and end of our understanding of power relations.

The critical valorization of physical struggle and subsequent triumph
and control finds an interesting parallel in discussion of Douglass's narrative struggles, among the most provocative being that of Robert Stepto
in *From Behind the Veil*. In discussing the relation of Douglass's *Narrative* to the "authenticating" texts by William Garrison and Wendell Phillips, Stepto argues that these ancillary texts seem on the surface to be
"*at war* with Douglass's tale for authorial control of the narrative as a
whole."[9] While Stepto grants that there is a tension among all three
documents, Douglass's "tale *dominates* the narrative because it alone
authenticates the narrative" (Emphases added).[1]

In examining the issue of authorial control more generally, Stepto
argues: "When a narrator wrests this kind of preeminent authorial control from the ancillary voices in the narrative, we may say he controls

---

8. Donald Gibson, "Reconciling Public and Private in Frederick Douglass's *Narrative*," *American Literature*, 57 (December 1985), 562.
9. Robert Stepto, *From Behind the Veil: A Study of Afro-American Narrative* (Urbana: University of Illinois Press, 1979).
1. Stepto, *From Behind*, 17.

the presentation of his personal history, and that his tale is becoming autobiographical."[2] He continues, "Authorial control of a narrative need not always result from an author's defeat of competing voices or usurpation of archetypes or pregeneric myths, but is usually occasioned by such acts. What may distinguish one literary history or tradition from another is not the issue of whether such battles occur, but that of who is competing with whom and over what."[3]

This competition for authorial control in African-American letters, Stepto argues, does not conform to the Bloomian oedipal paradigm, for "the battle for authorial control has been more of a race ritual than a case of patricide."[4] Stepto is right to note that competition among African Americans is "rarely between artist and artist," but between "artist and authenticator (editor, publisher, guarantor, patron)."[5] Here, of course, Stepto could easily have inserted that these authenticators have generally been white males. Thus the battle for authorial control in Douglass's case was a battle between white and black males.

For Stepto, Douglass's ultimate control rests on his "extraordinary ability to pursue several types of writing with ease and with a degree of simultaneity."[6] But again, the explanation of Douglass's strength depends overmuch on a focus on style emptied of its contents. In other words, what is the "content" of Douglass's "syncretic phrasing," the "introspective analysis," the "participant observations" that make him a master stylist in Stepto's estimation? But, more important, does Douglass's "defeat" of competing white male voices enable him to find a voice distinct from theirs?

Since Douglass's authorial control is the logical outcome of his quest for freedom and literacy, one might approach that question from the angle of the thematics of literacy, of which much has been made by critics. Revealing perhaps more than he knew in the following passage, Douglass describes one of many scenes of stolen knowledge in the *Narrative*. Because his retelling of this episode is all the more suggestive in *My Bondage and My Freedom*, I've selected it instead. "When my mistress left me in charge of the house, I had a grand time; I got Master Tommy's copy books and a pen and ink, and, in the ample spaces between the lines, *I wrote other lines, as nearly like his as possible*" (172, emphasis added).[7]

This hand-to-hand combat between black and white men for physi-

2. Stepto, *From Behind*, 25.
3. Stepto, *From Behind*, 45.
4. Stepto, *From Behind*, 45.
5. Stepto, *From Behind*, 45.
6. Stepto, *From Behind*, 20.
7. Compare this passage with the same scene in the 1845 *Narrative*: "When left thus, I used to spend the time in writing in the spaces left in Master Thomas's copy-book, copying what he had written. I continued to do this until I could write a hand very similar to that of Master Thomas. Thus, after a long, tedious effort of years, I finally succeeded in learning how to write" (58) [35].

cal, then narrative, control over bodies and texts raises the question of who is on whose side? For, in its allegiance to the dialectics of dominance and subordination, Douglass's *Narrative* is, and not surprisingly so, a by-product of Master Tommy's copybook, especially of its gendered division of power relations. The representation of women being whipped, in form and function, is only one major instance of this point but the representation of women, in general, shows Master Tommy's imprint.

Abounding in this copybook are conventional ideas of male subjectivity that exclude women from language. The scenes of reading are again cases in point. Throughout the narrative Douglass employs what Lillie Jugurtha aptly terms "eye dialogue." That is, he presents personal exchanges that have the appearance of dialogue without being dialogue. In the following account, Douglass describes the scene in which Mrs. Auld is ordered to cease teaching Frederick to read:

> Mr. Auld found out what was going on, and at once forbade Mrs. Auld to instruct me further, telling her, among other things, that it was unlawful, as well as unsafe, to teach a slave to read. To use his own words . . . he said, "If you give a nigger an inch, he will take an ell. . . . Learning would spoil the best nigger in the world . . . if you teach that nigger (speaking of myself) how to read, there would be no keeping him. It would forever unfit him to be a slave. He would at once become unmanageable, and of no value to his master. As to himself, it would do him no good, but a great deal of harm. It would make him discontented and unhappy." (49) [29]

In glossing this passage, Jugurtha perceptively notices that "there is no second speaker presented here, no Lucretia Auld responding to her husband . . . One pictures, though one does not hear, a husband and a wife talking . . . Unobtrusively, perspectives are multiplied. Monologue functions as dialogue." [8] That Sophia Auld was regarded by Douglass early on as a substitute mother figure, links her erasure in the foregoing passage to the erasure of his biological mother in the first part of the 1845 *Narrative* and, by extension, to the erasure of the feminine. In this secular rewriting of the sacred text, Mrs. Auld is exiled from the scene of knowledge, of symbolic activity. As a woman she is not permitted "to teach or to have authority over men; she is to keep silent" (I Timothy 2:11–12). What critics have learned from and done with Douglass has often constituted a correspondingly mimetic process where the feminine is concerned. In other words, the literary and interpretive history of the *Narrative* has, with few exceptions, repeated with approval its salient assumptions and structural paradigms. This repetition has, in

8. Lillie Jugurtha, "Point of View in the Afro-American Slave Narratives by Douglass and Pennington," in John Sekora and Darwin Turner, eds., *The Art of Slave Narrative* (Western Illinois University, 1982), 113.

turn, created a potent and persistent critical language that positions and repositions Douglass on top, that puts him in a position of priority. This ordering has not only helped to establish the dominant paradigm of African-American criticism, but it has also done much to establish the dominant view of African-American literary history. In that view, Douglass is, to borrow from James Olney, "the founding father" who "produced a kind of Ur-text of slavery and freedom that, whether individual writers were conscious of imitating Douglass or not, would inform the Afro-American literary tradition from his time to the present."[9]

* * *

It is this choice of Douglass as "the first," as "representative man," as the part that stands for the whole, that reproduces the omission of women from view, except as afterthoughts different from "the same" (black men). And that omission is not merely an oversight, but given the discursive system that authorizes Douglass as the source and the origin, that omission is a necessity. But if, as [Edward] Said suggests, " 'beginning' is an eminently renewable subject,"[1] then we can begin again. We can begin to think outside the model that circumscribes an entire literary history into a genetic model and conscripts Douglass in the interest of masculine power and desire. In other words, we might start by putting an end to beginnings, even those that would put woman in the first place.

9. Olney, "The Founding Fathers—Frederick Douglass and Booker T. Washington" in Deborah E. McDowell and Arnold Rampersad, eds., *Slavery and the Literary Imagination* (Baltimore: Johns Hopkins, 1989), 81.
1. Edward Said, *Beginnings: Intention and Method* (New York: Columbia University Press, 1985), 38.

Frederick Douglass:
A Chronology

1818	Born a slave in Talbot County (Eastern Shore), Maryland.
1824	Taken by grandmother to Wye House, where their master, Aaron Anthony, is manager. Befriended by manager's daughter, Lucretia Auld, wife of Thomas Auld.
1826	Sent to Baltimore to live with Thomas Auld's brother, Hugh Auld, and his wife, Sophia.
1827	Returned to Talbot County for distribution of Anthony's estate. Awarded to Thomas Auld. Returned to Hugh Auld in Baltimore.
1833–34	Sent back to Thomas Auld. Rented to Edward Covey as fieldhand.
1835	Rented to William Freeland. Plans escape with other young slaves. Caught. Escapes hanging or sale south. Sent back to Baltimore, where he works as a caulker in a shipyard. Meets Anna Murray.
1838	Escapes slavery. Marries Anna Murray in New York City. They settle in New Bedford, Massachusetts.
1839	Rosetta Douglass born. Douglass hears William Lloyd Garrison speech.
1840	Lewis Henry Douglass born.
1841	Makes first great public antislavery speech, Nantucket, Massachusetts. Begins tours as an agent of the New England Anti-Slavery Society. Moves to Lynn, Massachusetts.
1842	Frederick Douglass, Jr. born.
1844	Charles Remond Douglass born.
1845	Publishes *Narrative of the Life of Frederick Douglass*.
1845–47	Travels in Ireland, Scotland, and England giving antislavery speeches.
1847	Moves to Rochester, New York. Publishes *North Star* (1847–51). Continues his speaking tours.
1849	Annie Douglass born.
1851	Publishes *Frederick Douglass' Paper* (1851–60).
1852	Gives "5th of July" speech.
1853	Publishes *The Heroic Slave*, a novella.

1855	Publishes *My Bondage and My Freedom.*
1859	Accused of being an accomplice to John Brown, goes to England, via Canada. Publishes *Douglass's Monthly* (1859–63).
1860	Annie Douglass dies. Douglass returns to Rochester.
1861	The Civil War begins. Douglass urges that the ending of slavery be the war's aim.
1863	Recruits for the African American 54th Massachusetts regiment.
1870	Publishes *New National Era* (1870–74).
1871	Secretary of commission sent to attempt to annex the Dominican Republic.
1872	Rochester house burned by arsonist. Moves to Washington, D.C.
1874	President of Freedman's Savings Bank, which fails.
1877	Marshall of District of Columbia.
1881	Recorder of Deeds, Washington, D.C. Publishes *Life and Times of Frederick Douglass.*
1882	Anna Murray Douglass dies.
1884	Marries Helen Pitts Douglass.
1889–91	United States Minister to Haiti.
1892	Publishes revised *Life and Times of Frederick Douglass.*
1893	Commissioner of the Republic of Haiti at the Chicago World's Fair.
1894	Gives last great speech, "Lessons of the Hour," opposing lynching.
1895	Dies in Washington, D.C. Buried in Rochester, New York.

Selected Bibliography

MAJOR WORKS BY FREDERICK DOUGLASS

Narrative of the Life of Frederick Douglass, an American Slave, Written by Himself. Boston: American Anti-Slavery Society, 1845.

My Bondage and My Freedom. New York: Miller, Orton, and Mulligan, 1855.

Life and Times of Frederick Douglass, Written by Himself. Hartford, CT: Park Publishing, 1881. Rev. 1882.

Life and Times of Frederick Douglass, Written by Himself: His early life as a slave, his escape from bondage, and his complete history to the present time. Boston: De Wolfe, Fiske, 1892.

Autobiographies. Ed. Henry Louis Gates, Jr. New York: Library of America, 1994.

Frederick Douglass on Women's Rights. Ed. Philip S. Foner. Westport, CT: Greenwood, 1976.

The Frederick Douglass Papers. Ed. John W. Blassingame et al. 5 vols. New Haven: Yale UP, 1979–.

Life and Writings of Frederick Douglass. Ed. Philip S. Foner. 5 vols. New York: International, 1950–75.

Oxford Frederick Douglass Reader. Ed. William L. Andrews. New York: Oxford UP, 1996.

• bullet indicates works included in or excerpted for this Norton Critical Edition

MAJOR BIOGRAPHIES

Holland, Frederic May. *Frederick Douglass, the Colored Orator.* New York: Funk & Wagnalls, 1891.

Huggins, Nathan Irvin. *Slave and Citizen: The Life of Frederick Douglass.* Boston: Little, Brown, 1980.

•McFeely, William S. *Frederick Douglass.* New York: W. W. Norton, 1991.

Preston, Dickson J. *Young Frederick Douglass: The Maryland Years.* Baltimore: Johns Hopkins UP, 1980.

Quarles, Benjamin. *Frederick Douglass.* Washington, D.C.: Associated Publishers, 1948. Reprint, New York, 1969.

GENERAL HISTORICAL AND LITERARY STUDIES

•Andrews, William L., ed. *Critical Essays on Frederick Douglass.* Boston: G. K. Hall, 1991.

•_____. *To Tell a Free Story: The First Century of Afro-American Autobiography, 1760–1865.* Urbana: U of Illinois P, 1986.

•Baker, Houston A., Jr. *Blues, Ideology, and Afro-American Literature.* Chicago: U of Chicago P, 1984.

_____. *The Journey Back.* Chicago: U of Chicago P, 1980.

Blassingame, John W. *The Slave Community.* 2nd ed. New York: Oxford UP, 1979.

_____, ed. *Slave Testimony.* Baton Rouge: Louisiana State UP, 1977.

Blight, David W. *Frederick Douglass' Civil War.* Baton Rouge: Louisiana State UP, 1989.

Butterfield, Stephen. *Black Autobiography in America.* Amherst: U of Massachusetts P, 1974.

Davis, Charles T., and Henry Louis Gates, Jr., eds. *The Slave's Narrative.* New York: Oxford UP, 1985.

Dudley, David L. *My Father's Shadow: Intergenerational Conflict in African American Men's Autobiography.* Philadelphia: U of Pennsylvania P, 1991.

•Fisher, Dexter, and Robert B. Stepto, eds. *Afro-American Literature: The Reconstruction of Instruction.* New York: Modern Language Association, 1979.

Foster, Frances Smith. *Witnessing Slavery.* 2nd ed. Madison: U of Wisconsin P, 1993.

Fredrickson, George M. *The Black Image in the White Mind.* New York: Harper & Row, 1971.

187

Gates, Henry Louis, Jr. *Figures in Black*. New York: Oxford UP, 1987.

Leverenz, David. *Manhood and the American Renaissance*. Ithaca, NY: Cornell UP, 1989.

McDowell, Deborah E., and Arnold Rampersad, eds. *Slavery and the Literary Imagination*. Baltimore: Johns Hopkins UP, 1989.

Martin, Waldo E. *The Mind of Frederick Douglass*. Chapel Hill: U of North Carolina P, 1982.

Meier, August. *Negro Thought in America, 1880–1915*. Ann Arbor: U of Michigan P, 1966.

Patterson, Orlando. *Slavery and Social Death*. Cambridge: Harvard UP, 1982.

Quarles, Benjamin. *Black Abolitionists*. New York: Oxford UP, 1969.

Ripley, C. Peter, et al., eds. *The Black Abolitionist Papers*, 5 vols., Chapel Hill: U of North Carolina P, 1985–1992.

———. "The Autobiographical Writings of Frederick Douglass," *Southern Studies* 24.1 (Spring 1985): 5–29.

Sekora, John, and Darwin T. Turner, eds. *The Art of Slave Narrative*. Macomb: Western Illinois University, 1982.

Smith, Valerie. *Self-Discovery and Authority in Afro-American Narrative*. Cambridge: Harvard UP, 1987.

Stepto, Robert B. *From Behind the Veil: A Study of Afro-American Narrative*. Urbana: U of Illinois P, 1979.

Sundquist, Eric J., ed. *Frederick Douglass: New Literary and Historical Essays*. Cambridge: Cambridge UP, 1990.

———. *To Wake the Nations: Race in the Making of American Literature*. Cambridge: Harvard UP, 1993.

Walker, Peter F. *Moral Choices: Memory, Desire, and Imagination in Nineteenth-Century American Abolition*. Baton Rouge: Louisiana State UP, 1978.